13x (¹¹/07) ¹²/07

Better Homes and Gardens®

One DISH Dinners

Better Homes and Gardens® Books
Des Moines, Iowa

Better Homes and Gardens® Books
An imprint of Meredith® Books

One Dish Dinners
Editor: Jennifer Dorland Darling
Associate Art Director: Mick Schnepf
Contributing Editors: Shelli McConnell, Joyce Trollope
Writer: Winifred Moranville
Recipe Developers: Amy Cotler, Jill Crum, Janet Pittman,
    Marcia Stanley
Copy Chief: Catherine Hamrick
Copy and Production Editor: Terri Fredrickson
Managers, Book Production: Pam Kvitne, Marjorie J. Schenkelberg
Contributing Copy Editor: Kim Catazanrite
Contributing Proofreaders: Gretchen Kauffman, Susan J. Kling,
    Elizabeth Duff Popplewell
Photographers: Pete Krumhardt, Kritsada Panichgul
Electronic Production Coordinator: Paula Forest
Editorial and Design Assistants: Judy Bailey, Mary Lee Gavin,
    Karen Schirm
Test Kitchen Director: Lynn Blanchard
Test Kitchen Product Supervisor: Marilyn Cornelius
Food Stylists: Dianna Nolin, Charles Worthington

Meredith® Books
Editor in Chief: James D. Blume
Design Director: Matt Strelecki
Managing Editor: Gregory H. Kayko

Director, Retail Sales and Marketing: Terry Unsworth
Director, Sales, Special Markets: Rita McMullen
Director, Sales, Premiums: Michael A. Peterson
Director, Sales, Retail: Tom Wierzbicki
Director, Sales, Home & Garden Centers: Ray Wolf
Director, Book Marketing: Brad Elmitt
Director, Operations: George A. Susral
Director, Production: Douglas M. Johnston

Vice President, General Manager: Jamie L. Martin

Better Homes and Gardens® Magazine
Editor in Chief: Jean LemMon
Executive Food Editor: Nancy Byal

Meredith Publishing Group
President, Publishing Group: Christopher M. Little
Vice President, Finance & Administration: Max Runciman

Meredith Corporation
Chairman and Chief Executive Officer: William T. Kerr

Chairman of the Executive Committee: E. T. Meredith III

All of us at Better Homes and Gardens® Books are dedicated to providing you with the information and ideas you need to create delicious foods. We welcome your comments and suggestions. Write to us at: Better Homes and Gardens Books, Cookbook Editorial Department, 1716 Locust St., Des Moines, IA 50309-3023.

If you would like to purchase any of our books, check wherever quality books are sold. Visit our website at bhg.com.

Our seal assures you that every recipe in *One Dish Dinners* has been tested in the Better Homes and Gardens® Test Kitchen. This means that each recipe is practical and reliable, and meets our high standards of taste appeal. We guarantee your satisfaction with this book for as long as you own it.

Pictured on front cover: Catalan Chicken Chowder, page 27

Contents

Introduction

What is it we love about one-dish meals? With most ingredients cooked or served in a single pan or dish, they're certainly convenient. We think their appeal goes beyond ease—heading into the realm of heartfelt warmth and satisfaction that only great home cooking brings.

This collection of more than 150 recipes revisits all the comfort and convenience you've come to expect in one-dish meals, yet takes the one-dish way of cooking a few steps further. Time-honored favorites such as chilies and chowders get stylish updates, while recipes from Pad Thai to Tuscan Lamb Chop Skillet introduce one-dish takes from other cultures. *One Dish Dinners* brings techniques such as braising, stir-frying, and roasting to the one-dish realm of cooking.

Whether you crave classics or new flavors and cooking techniques, rest assured that it's all here—the ease, the aromas, and the soul-satisfying results you rely on in one-dish meals.

❚ A recipe that bears this ♥ symbol has no more than 10 grams of fat per serving. A recipe labeled "crockery recipe" is prepared in an electric crockery cooker.

Wild
Rice
and
Cheese
Soup
Page 37

[*Soups and Stews*]

Spicy Shrimp Gazpacho
Page 30

[4]

Chili with
Double-Bean Toss
Page 12

Hamburger-Vegetable Soup

[Looking for a new way to serve always easy, always satisfying ground beef? Try this family favorite—it's quick, studded with colorful vegetables, and low fat, to boot.]

Prep: *20 minutes*   **Cook:** *15 minutes*   **Servings:** *6*

1	pound ground beef or ground pork
½	cup chopped onion
½	cup chopped green sweet pepper
4	cups beef broth
1	cup frozen whole kernel corn
1	7½-ounce can tomatoes, cut up
½	of a 9-ounce package frozen lima beans
½	cup chopped, peeled potato or ½ cup loose-pack frozen hash brown potatoes
1	medium carrot, cut into matchstick-size strips
1	tablespoon snipped fresh basil or 1 teaspoon dried basil, crushed
1	teaspoon Worcestershire sauce
1	bay leaf

[1] In a large saucepan cook beef, onion, and sweet pepper until meat is brown and onion is tender. Drain fat. Stir in broth, corn, undrained tomatoes, lima beans, potato, carrot, basil, Worcestershire sauce, bay leaf, and ⅛ teaspoon black pepper.

[2] Bring to boiling; reduce heat. Cover and simmer for 15 to 20 minutes or until vegetables are tender. Discard bay leaf. Ladle into bowls.

Nutrition Facts per serving: 243 cal., 10 g total fat (4 g sat. fat), 48 mg chol., 652 mg sodium, 19 g carbo., 3 g fiber, 20 g pro. Daily Values: 33% vit. A, 60% vit. C, 3% calcium, 18% iron

Good Bets for Broth

When you don't have time to make broth from scratch, choose from one of these:
❚ Canned broths: Some brands of canned chicken or beef broth can be used straight from the can. However, others are condensed and need diluting.
❚ Instant bouillon granules or cubes make an easy, instant broth: For 1 cup, dissolve 1 teaspoon of granules or one cube in 1 cup of hot water. These products can be purchased in beef, chicken, fish, or vegetable flavors.
❚ Remember that these substitutions are generally saltier than homemade broths. Hold off on adding extra salt until you've tasted dish at end of cooking. (Recipes were tested using canned broth; if using homemade, you may need more salt.)

Beef Borscht

[*Our take on this Polish and Russian specialty has all the right hallmarks—a beautiful, beet-red color, hearty, beefy flavor, a fresh spark of dill, and a dollop of sour cream. But a couple of convenience products, including coleslaw mix, add ease to the classic.*]

Prep: *20 minutes*   **Cook:** *1 hour 10 minutes*   **Servings:** *6*

2	tablespoons all-purpose flour
1½	pounds beef stew meat, cut into ¾-inch cubes
2	tablespoons cooking oil
½	cup chopped onion
1	14½-ounce can beef broth
1	cup water
1	teaspoon snipped fresh dillweed or ¼ teaspoon dried dillweed
¼	teaspoon pepper
1	14½-ounce can diced beets
1	14½-ounce can diced tomatoes
3	cups packaged shredded cabbage with carrot (coleslaw mix)
½	cup dairy sour cream

[1] Place flour in a plastic bag. Add meat cubes, a few at a time, shaking to coat. In a large saucepan or 4-quart Dutch oven heat oil. Brown meat, half at a time, in hot oil. Add onion with last half of meat. Drain fat. Return all meat to saucepan. Stir in broth, water, dried dillweed (if using), and pepper. Bring to boiling; reduce heat. Cover and simmer for 1 to 1½ hours or until the meat is tender.

[2] Stir in fresh dill (if using), undrained beets, undrained tomatoes, and coleslaw mix. Bring to boiling; reduce heat. Simmer, uncovered, about 10 minutes more or until cabbage is tender. Top individual servings with a dollop of sour cream.

Nutrition Facts per serving: 312 cal., 15 g total fat (6 g sat. fat), 91 mg chol., 621 mg sodium, 14 g carbo., 2 g fiber, 30 g pro. Daily Values: 35% vit. A, 53% vit. C, 7% calcium, 29% iron

To Make Ahead: Prepare mixture through Step 1, simmering until meat is tender. Transfer to a bowl. Cool quickly; cover and chill up to 24 hours. To serve, return to saucepan and bring to boiling, stirring occasionally. Proceed with Step 2.

Soups
and Stews

Oxtail Ragout

[Our forebears may truly have used the tail of an ox in their stews, but the oxtail you'll find at the supermarket these days is usually a tail of beef or veal. This bony, flavorful cut requires long, slow simmering. It's worth it—you'll love the richness oxtail brings to this hearty stew.]

Prep: *30 minutes*   **Cook:** *1½ hours*   **Servings:** *5 or 6*

- 2   tablespoons cooking oil
- 1   pound oxtails, cut into 1½- to 2-inch pieces (optional)
- 1   pound boneless beef short ribs (if omitting oxtails, use an additional 4 ounces boneless beef short ribs)
- 2   14½-ounce cans beef broth (about 3½ cups)
- ½   cup dry red wine or beef broth
- ½   cup coarsely chopped shallots
- 4   cloves garlic, minced
- 2   bay leaves
- ½   teaspoon salt
- ¼   to ½ teaspoon coarsely ground black pepper
- 1   pound carrots, peeled and cut into ¾-inch pieces
- 1   pound rutabagas or turnips, peeled and cut into ¾-inch cubes
- 1   cup coarsely chopped onion
- ⅓   cup all-purpose flour
- ⅓   cup snipped fresh parsley

[1] In a 4- to 6-quart Dutch oven heat cooking oil. Brown oxtails and short ribs on all sides in hot oil. Drain fat. To avoid spattering, carefully add beef broth, wine, shallots, garlic, bay leaves, salt, and coarsely ground black pepper to meat in pan. Bring to boiling; reduce heat. Cover and simmer about 1 hour or until meat is nearly tender.

[2] Add carrots, rutabagas, and onion to meat mixture in pan. Return to boiling; reduce heat. Cover and simmer for 30 to 45 minutes more or until meat and vegetables are tender. Discard bay leaves. Remove meat; allow to cool slightly.

[3] Meanwhile, in a small mixing bowl stir ⅓ cup cold water into the flour until smooth (or shake together in a screw-top jar). Stir into pan. Cook and stir until thickened and bubbly. Cook and stir for 1 minute more. Cut meat into bite-size pieces, discarding any bones. Return meat to pan; heat through. Stir in snipped parsley. If desired, season to taste with additional salt and pepper and serve meat and vegetables over hot cooked couscous.

Nutrition Facts per serving: 441 cal., 27 g total fat (11 g sat. fat), 53 mg chol., 881 mg sodium, 28 g carbo., 6 g fiber, 18 g pro. **Daily Values:** 227% vit. A, 48% vit. C, 8% calcium, 24% iron

Basil Beef Stew

[*It's amazing how much time a soup mix can shave off your dinnertime preparation. Amazing, too, is the windfall of fresh flavor a sprinkling of snipped basil brings to a stew. Convenience from the soup mix and freshness from the fresh herb? Talk about the best of both worlds!*]

Prep: *20 minutes*   **Cook:** *1½ hours*   **Servings:** *6 to 8*

1	2-pound boneless beef chuck roast
¼	cup all-purpose flour
½	teaspoon seasoned salt
2	tablespoons margarine or butter
1	pound tiny new potatoes, quartered
2	cups whole fresh mushrooms, halved
1½	cups packaged, peeled baby carrots
1	2.4-ounce envelope tomato-basil soup mix
2	cups water
1	large tomato, chopped
2	tablespoons snipped fresh basil

[1] Trim fat from beef. Cut beef into 1½-inch pieces. Place flour and seasoned salt in a plastic bag. Add beef pieces, a few at a time, shaking to coat. In a 4-quart Dutch oven melt margarine over medium-high heat. Brown beef, half at a time, in hot margarine. Drain fat. Return all of the meat to the Dutch oven.

[2] Add potatoes, mushrooms, and carrots. Sprinkle with soup mix; stir in water. Bring to boiling; reduce heat. Cover and simmer for 1½ hours or until meat and vegetables are tender. Stir in tomato and basil; heat through.

Nutrition Facts per serving: 444 cal., 16 g total fat (5 g sat. fat), 110 mg chol., 716 mg sodium, 33 g carbo., 3 g fiber, 40 g pro. Daily Values: 94% vit. A, 31% vit. C, 3% calcium, 43% iron

To Make Ahead: Prepare stew, simmering until meat, potatoes, and carrots are tender. Transfer to a bowl. Cool quickly; cover and chill up to 24 hours. To serve, return to Dutch oven and bring to boiling, stirring occasionally. Stir in fresh tomato and basil; heat through.

Indo-Texan Bowls of Red

[*At the risk of messing with Texas, we made a few changes to their famous "bowls of red." With the complex, spicy appeal of curry powder, cumin, and coriander and the sweet richness of coconut milk, the down-home Lone Star stew takes on an Indonesian flair.*]

Prep: *20 minutes*   **Cook:** *1½ hours*   **Servings:** *6*

2	pounds coarsely ground beef
4	cloves garlic, minced
1	tablespoon hot Madras curry powder, salt-free curry seasoning blend, or curry powder
2	teaspoons ground coriander
1	teaspoon ground cumin
1	teaspoon finely shredded lemon peel
2	cups chopped red sweet pepper
1	15-ounce can tomato puree
2	10-ounce cans chopped tomatoes and green chili peppers
1	10½-ounce can condensed beef broth
1	cup canned unsweetened coconut milk
¼	cup catsup
	Hot cooked rice

[1] In a 4-quart Dutch oven cook ground beef and garlic until meat is brown. Drain fat. Stir in curry powder, coriander, cumin, and lemon peel. Stir in sweet pepper, tomato puree, undrained tomatoes with peppers, broth, coconut milk, and catsup. Bring to boiling; reduce heat. Simmer, uncovered, for 1½ hours or until desired consistency.

[2] To serve, ladle into bowls over hot cooked rice. If desired, garnish with snipped fresh basil and serve with chopped peanuts, raisins, and/or chutney.

Nutrition Facts per serving: 511 cal., 23 g total fat (12 g sat. fat), 95 mg chol., 923 mg sodium, 42 g carbo., 3 g fiber, 34 g pro. Daily Values: 42% vit. A, 140% vit. C, 6% calcium, 46% iron

To Make Ahead: Simmer mixture until desired consistency through Step 1. Transfer to a bowl. Cool quickly (see tip, page 19); cover and chill up to 24 hours. To serve, return to Dutch oven and bring to boiling, stirring occasionally. Serve over rice as above.

Chili with Double-Bean Toss

[*In some parts, adding beans to chili is heresy, while in others, it's essential. This recipe will appease both camps—it has beans, all right, but they're served as a refreshing side-dish salad, if you like.*]

Prep: *25 minutes*   **Cook:** *10 hours*   **Servings:** *6*

1	pound boneless beef top round steak
1	tablespoon cooking oil
2	14½-ounce cans diced tomatoes
1	14½-ounce can beef broth
1	cup chopped onion
1	or 2 fresh jalapeño or serrano peppers, finely chopped (see tip, page 21)
2	cloves garlic, minced
4	teaspoons chili powder
1	tablespoon brown sugar
1½	teaspoons dried oregano, crushed
½	teaspoon ground cumin
¼	teaspoon black pepper
1	recipe Double-Bean Toss (optional)

[1] Trim fat from meat. Cut meat into ¾-inch chunks. In a large skillet heat oil. Brown beef, half at a time, in hot oil. Drain fat.

[2] In a 3½- or 4-quart electric crockery cooker combine undrained tomatoes, broth, onion, jalapeño peppers, garlic, chili powder, brown sugar, oregano, cumin, and black pepper. Stir in browned beef pieces.

[3] Cover and cook on low-heat setting for 10 to 12 hours or on high-heat setting for 5 to 6 hours. Serve chili in bowls. If desired, serve with Double-Bean Toss on the side and top with a dollop of sour cream; garnish with fresh cilantro or parsley and tortilla chips.

Double-Bean Toss: In a bowl combine one 15-ounce can pinto beans and one 15-ounce can black beans, rinsed and drained. Add ½ teaspoon finely shredded lime peel, 1 tablespoon lime juice, 1 tablespoon salad oil, and 1 clove garlic, minced. Toss to mix.

Nutrition Facts per serving (without beans): 200 cal., 8 g total fat (2 g sat. fat), 45 mg chol., 511 mg sodium, 13 g carbo., 2 g fiber, 18 g pro. Daily Values: 10% vit. A, 36% vit. C, 8% calcium, 16% iron

Lamb and Fruit Stew

[*Remember this recipe in the chilly fall and winter months when you're craving something hearty but missing the sweetness of summer's fruits.*]

Prep: *30 minutes* **Cook:** *7½ hours* **Servings:** *6 to 8*

2	pounds boneless leg of lamb or beef bottom round roast
1	to 2 teaspoons crushed red pepper
¾	teaspoon ground turmeric
¾	teaspoon ground ginger
¾	teaspoon ground cinnamon
½	teaspoon salt
2	tablespoons olive oil or cooking oil
2	cups chopped onions
3	cloves garlic, minced
1	14½-ounce can beef broth
1	tablespoon cornstarch
2	tablespoons cold water
1	cup pitted dates
1	cup dried apricots
	Hot cooked couscous or rice
¼	cup slivered almonds, toasted

[1] Trim fat from meat. Cut meat into 1- to 1½-inch pieces. In a shallow bowl combine red pepper, turmeric, ginger, cinnamon, and salt. Coat meat with seasoning mixture. In a large skillet heat oil over medium-high heat. Brown meat, a third at a time, in hot oil.

[2] Transfer meat to a 3½- or 4-quart electric crockery cooker. Add onions and garlic; stir to combine. Pour beef broth over all. Cover and cook on low-heat setting for 7 to 9 hours or on high-heat setting for 3½ to 4½ hours or until meat is tender.

[3] Skim fat from the surface of the juices in the crockery cooker. In a small mixing bowl stir together cornstarch and water; stir into crockery cooker. Add dates and apricots; stir to combine. If using low-heat setting, turn to high-heat setting. Cover and cook 30 minutes more or until mixture is bubbly and slightly thickened. To serve, spoon stew over hot cooked couscous or rice. Top individual servings with toasted almonds.

Nutrition Facts per serving: 550 cal., 14 g total fat (3 g sat. fat), 76 mg chol., 475 mg sodium, 75 g carbo., 12 g fiber, 34 g pro. Daily Values: 18% vit. A, 7% vit. C, 6% calcium, 29% iron

Cassoulet-Style Lamb Stew

[*Rather than white beans—the legume traditionally used in this French stew—this recipe calls on black-eyed peas for a little stateside Southern comfort.*]

Prep: *50 minutes* **Stand:** *1 hour* **Cook:** *1¾ hours* **Servings:** *12*

- 1 pound dry navy beans
- 1 tablespoon olive oil or cooking oil
- 1 meaty lamb shank (1 to 1½ pounds)
- 2 cups chopped celery (include leaves)
- 2 medium unpeeled potatoes, coarsely chopped
- ¾ cup coarsely chopped carrot
- ¾ cup coarsely chopped parsnip
- 3 cloves garlic, minced
- 3 cups sliced fresh mushrooms
- 1¼ cups dry black-eyed peas, rinsed and drained
- ½ cup dry red wine or beef broth
- 1 28-ounce can diced tomatoes
- 2 tablespoons snipped fresh thyme
- 1 tablespoon snipped fresh rosemary

[1] Rinse beans. In a saucepan combine beans and 6 cups water. Bring to boiling; reduce heat. Simmer, uncovered, for 2 minutes. Remove from heat. Cover and let stand for 1 hour. Drain and rinse the soaked beans.

[2] In an 8- to 10-quart Dutch oven or kettle heat oil. Brown lamb in hot oil. Add celery, potatoes, carrot, parsnip, and garlic. Cook over medium-high heat for 5 minutes, stirring frequently. Add 7 cups water, mushrooms, black-eyed peas, wine, 2 teaspoons salt, ½ teaspoon pepper, and soaked beans. Bring to boiling; reduce heat. Cover and simmer about 1½ hours or until beans and black-eyed peas are tender. Remove shank; let cool.

[3] Add undrained tomatoes, thyme, and snipped rosemary to beans. Remove meat from shank; chop meat and add to stew. Cover and simmer for 15 minutes more. To serve, ladle stew into bowls. If desired, garnish stew with fresh rosemary sprigs.

Nutrition Facts per serving: 287 cal., 4 g total fat (1 g sat. fat), 14 mg chol., 553 mg sodium, 46 g carbo., 5 g fiber, 18 g pro. Daily Values: 24% vit. A, 29% vit. C, 10% calcium, 36% iron

[15]

To Make Ahead: Prepare stew as directed. Let cool 30 minutes. Place in freezer containers; freeze up to 3 months. To serve, place frozen stew in a saucepan. Heat, covered, over medium-low heat about 45 minutes or until heated through; stir occasionally and break apart.

Soups
and Stews

Mexican Pork and Hominy Soup

[*Many Americans tend to associate Mexican food with fiery flavors. Truth is, much Mexican food isn't hot, just flavorful, as this classic soup demonstrates. The recipe is much like the country's famed posole— a hominy and pork soup often served around Christmastime.*]

Prep: *20 minutes*　**Cook:** *1 hour 20 minutes*　**Servings:** *6*

12	ounces lean boneless pork
1	tablespoon cooking oil
1	cup chopped onion
2	cloves garlic, minced
3	cups chicken broth
1	14½-ounce can tomatoes, cut up
2	teaspoons dried oregano, crushed
¼	teaspoon ground cumin
1	14½-ounce can golden hominy, drained, or one 10-ounce package frozen whole kernel corn, thawed
1	cup sliced carrots
½	cup sliced celery
	Shredded Mexican cheese or Monterey Jack cheese with jalapeño peppers

[1] Trim fat from pork. Cut pork into ½-inch pieces. In a large saucepan heat oil. Brown pork, half at a time, in hot oil over medium-high heat. Remove pork from saucepan; set aside. Add onion and garlic to drippings in pan. Cook over medium heat until tender. Drain fat. Return all pork to saucepan.

[2] Stir in broth, undrained tomatoes, oregano, cumin, and ¼ teaspoon black pepper. Bring to boiling; reduce heat. Cover and simmer for 1 hour. Stir in hominy, carrots, and celery. Return to boiling; reduce heat. Cover and simmer for 20 to 30 minutes more or until vegetables are tender. Garnish with shredded cheese.

Nutrition Facts per serving: 205 cal., 10 g total fat (3 g sat. fat), 32 mg chol., 680 mg sodium, 15 g carbo., 2 g fiber, 14 g pro. Daily Values: 59% vit. A, 21% vit. C, 8% calcium, 12% iron

Say Cheese — Mexican Style

Move over Monterey Jack! Now you can choose from a wide array of Mexican cheeses in supermarkets and Hispanic specialty stores. For shredding, anejo enchilado is a pungent, salty hard cheese. For melting, asadero has a buttery flavor and excellent melting qualities. For crumbling, queso fresco is a mild-flavored soft white cheese.

Golden Harvest Soup

[*Three great autumn flavors—apple, parsnips, and butternut squash—bring a mellow sweetness to this seasonal soup. Served with freshly baked bread, it's a partnership that's hard to beat.*]

Prep: *20 minutes* **Cook:** *55 minutes* **Servings:** *4*

12	ounces lean boneless pork
1	tablespoon cooking oil
2	cloves garlic, minced
1	stalk celery, sliced
2	teaspoons curry powder
2	14½-ounce cans reduced-sodium chicken broth
3	cups cubed, peeled butternut squash
1½	cups sliced parsnips
1	large green cooking apple, cored and cut into ¾-inch pieces

[1] Trim fat from pork. Cut pork into ¾-inch pieces. In a 4-quart Dutch oven heat oil. Brown pork in hot oil. Stir in garlic, celery, and curry powder. Cook 1 minute longer.

[2] Stir in broth. Bring to boiling; reduce heat. Cover and simmer about 45 minutes or until meat is almost tender. Stir in squash, parsnips, and apple. Return to boiling; reduce heat. Cover and simmer for 10 minutes more or until squash is tender.

Nutrition Facts per serving: 262 cal., 10 g total fat (2 g sat. fat), 38 mg chol., 632 mg sodium, 29 g carbo., 6 g fiber, 16 g pro. Daily Values: 54% vit. A, 37% vit. C, 5% calcium, 11% iron

Salad Serve-Alongs

Pairing a hearty, steaming bowl of soup or stew with a refreshing, crisp, light salad seems like a match made in heaven. Enhance the meal even more by moving beyond the usual head lettuce, tomato, and shredded carrot combination. Here are just a few ideas:

▌ Toss Bibb lettuce, oranges, avocado, and walnuts with an orange vinaigrette.
▌ Toss strawberries, toasted almonds, spinach, crumbled bacon, and hard-cooked eggs; then drizzle with a western or French dressing.
▌ Toss romaine lettuce with a fruit-flavored vinaigrette (such as a raspberry); then arrange grapefruit sections, red onion slices, and feta cheese over the top.

Italian Pasta and Bean Soup with Sausage

[*White kidney beans (also called cannellini beans) bring a Tuscan touch to this soup. And, perhaps there is a market in your town that sells a brand of homemade Italian sausage loved by the locals—search it out so you can bring your own region's touch to this recipe.*]

Start to Finish: *30 minutes*   **Servings:** *4*

- 8   ounces uncooked Italian sausage
- 1   cup chopped onion
- 1   cup chopped celery
- 1   14½-ounce can chicken broth
- 1   14½-ounce can diced tomatoes with basil, oregano, and garlic
- 1¾   cups water
- ½   cup dried elbow macaroni
- 1   15-ounce can white kidney (cannellini) beans, rinsed and drained
- 2   tablespoons snipped fresh Italian parsley

[1] Remove casing from sausage, if present. In a large saucepan cook sausage, onion, and celery until sausage is no longer pink and vegetables are tender. Drain fat. Add broth, undrained tomatoes, and water. Bring to boiling. Stir in macaroni. Return to boiling; reduce heat. Simmer, uncovered, for 15 minutes or until pasta is tender. Stir in beans and parsley; heat through. If desired, sprinkle with grated Parmesan cheese.

Nutrition Facts per serving: 306 cal., 12 g total fat (4 g sat. fat), 33 mg chol., 1,418 mg sodium, 35 g carbo., 7 g fiber, 20 g pro. Daily Values: 8% vit. A, 35% vit. C, 7% calcium, 19% iron

Freeze Your Assets

When freezing leftover soups and stews, keep these tips in mind:

▮ To freeze leftovers, first cool the hot food by placing it in a bowl set over another bowl filled with ice water. This lets the food cool more quickly, which is important.

▮ Transfer the food to freezer-safe containers. Use small, shallow containers to allow food to freeze more quickly, which slows bacteria growth.

▮ Soups and stews expand when they freeze, so leave about ½ inch of space below rim.

▮ Thaw frozen foods in the refrigerator or microwave—never at room temperature. You can also slowly reheat frozen food without thawing by placing it in an appropriate-size saucepan. Cook the food, covered, until it is thawed, stirring occasionally to break it up. Then heat to boiling, stirring frequently.

▮ Cornstarch or flour-thickened soups do not freeze well, as the starch breaks down during freezing, altering the soup's consistency. Cheese soups also do not freeze well.

[19]

Spicy Pork and Potato Stew

[*Poblano peppers are long, deep-green peppers with an irregular bell-pepper shape and a mild to medium-hot flavor. The jalapeño, on the other hand, is a smaller pepper that adds plenty of heat to the stew.*]

Prep: *30 minutes* **Cook:** *8 hours* **Servings:** *6*

1	pound boneless pork shoulder roast
1	tablespoon cooking oil
1	pound tiny new potatoes, quartered
1	cup chopped onion
2	fresh poblano peppers, seeded and cut into 1-inch pieces (see tip, page 21)
1	fresh jalapeño pepper, seeded and chopped (see tip, page 21)
4	cloves garlic, minced
2	inches stick cinnamon
3	cups chicken broth
1	14½-ounce can diced tomatoes
1	tablespoon chili powder
1	teaspoon dried oregano, crushed
¼	teaspoon black pepper
¼	cup snipped fresh cilantro or parsley

[1] Trim fat from pork. Cut pork into 1-inch cubes. In a large skillet heat oil. Brown pork, half at a time, in hot oil. Drain fat.

[2] In a 3½- or 4-quart electric crockery cooker place potatoes, onion, poblano peppers, jalapeño pepper, garlic, and stick cinnamon. Add meat. In a bowl combine broth, undrained tomatoes, chili powder, oregano, and black pepper; pour over all.

[3] Cover and cook on low-heat setting for 8 to 10 hours or on high-heat setting for 4 to 5 hours. Discard stick cinnamon. Stir in cilantro or parsley. If desired, serve stew over hot cooked basmati rice or long grain rice.

Nutrition Facts per serving: 285 cal., 11 g total fat (3 g sat. fat), 50 mg chol., 753 mg sodium, 28 g carbo., 3 g fiber, 19 g pro. Daily Values: 12% vit. A, 202% vit. C, 5% calcium, 21% iron

To Tote: After the food is completely cooked, wrap the crockery cooker in heavy foil, several layers of newspaper, or a heavy towel. Then place the cooker in an insulated container so it doesn't tip over. The food should stay hot for up to 2 hours (do not hold for longer than 2 hours). If there is electricity at your party site, plug in the cooker. The food will stay warm on the low-heat setting. Stir in the snipped cilantro or parsley before serving.

Creamy Chicken-Vegetable Soup

[*Some creamy soups start with a white sauce-like base. As easy as that is, we've made this recipe even easier by eliminating that step and using a refrigerated light Alfredo sauce instead.*]

Start to Finish: *30 minutes*   **Servings:** *4*

- 3 cups chicken broth
- 2 medium carrots, thinly sliced
- 2 stalks celery, thinly sliced
- 1 cup chopped cooked chicken
- 1 small zucchini, thinly sliced (about 1 cup)
- ½ cup uncooked instant rice
- 1 10-ounce container refrigerated light Alfredo sauce
- ¼ cup chopped roasted red sweet peppers or one 4-ounce jar diced pimientos, drained
- 1 tablespoon snipped fresh thyme

[1] In a Dutch oven combine broth, carrots, and celery. Bring to boiling; reduce heat. Cover and simmer for 10 minutes.

[2] Stir in chicken, zucchini, and rice. Remove from heat. Cover and let stand about 5 minutes or until rice is tender. Stir in sauce, red peppers, and thyme; heat through.

Nutrition Facts per serving: 349 cal., 14 g total fat (7 g sat. fat), 65 mg chol., 1,286 mg sodium, 34 g carbo., 2 g fiber, 22 g pro. Daily Values: 99% vit. A, 49% vit. C, 16% calcium, 12% iron

Too Hot to Handle?

Because fresh chili peppers, such as jalapeños, contain volatile oils that can burn your skin and eyes, avoid direct contact with them as much as possible. When working with chili peppers, wear plastic or rubber gloves. No gloves? Work with plastic bags over your hands. But, if your bare hands do touch the chili peppers, wash your hands thoroughly with soap and water.

Turkey and Mushroom Soup

[*If you can, seek out the less-common varieties of mushrooms, such as the meaty shiitake or the earthy porcini. They'll add an exotic richness to the soup. Accompany the soup with crisp breadsticks.*]

Start to Finish: *35 minutes*   **Servings:** *4*

2   cups sliced fresh mushrooms (such as crimini, shiitake, porcini, or button)
1   stalk celery, thinly sliced
1   medium carrot, thinly sliced
1   small onion, chopped
1   tablespoon margarine or butter
1   tablespoon instant chicken bouillon granules
½   cup dried orzo pasta (rosamarina)
1½ cups chopped cooked turkey
2   tablespoons snipped fresh parsley
1   teaspoon fresh thyme

[1] In a large saucepan cook mushrooms, celery, carrot, and onion in hot margarine until crisp-tender. Add 4½ cups water, bouillon granules, and ⅛ teaspoon pepper.

[2] Bring to boiling; stir in orzo. Return to boiling; reduce heat. Simmer, uncovered, 5 to 8 minutes or until orzo is tender but still firm. Stir in turkey, parsley, and thyme; heat.

Nutrition Facts per serving: 199 cal., 6 g total fat (2 g sat. fat), 40 mg chol., 767 mg sodium, 17 g carbo., 2 g fiber, 19 g pro. Daily Values: 63% vit. A, 10% vit. C, 4% calcium, 17% iron

Favorite Fungi

Here are just a few mushroom varieties that have become easier to find in the supermarkets the last few years:

▌ Shiitakes possess a rich, meaty flavor, though only the caps are used.
▌ Portobellos yield a deep mushroom flavor, have a large-cap, and are velvety-brown.
▌ Crimini are cousins to the button mushroom, with a similar, though stronger, flavor.
▌ Chanterelles have a large, flowerlike cap, a golden to yellow-orange color, and a buttery flavor that's best shown off in simple recipes.
▌ Morels have an intense flavor and aroma, and look like an irregularly shaped sponge.
▌ Enoki look a little like bean sprouts, with long, slender stems and tiny caps. They have a delicate flavor and are good in salads.

Turkey and Black Bean Chili

[*Think you've "bean there, done that" with chili? Try this variation. With black beans instead of red, and turkey instead of beef, it's a whole new stew.*]

Start to Finish: *45 minutes* **Servings:** *6*

1	pound turkey breast tenderloins or skinless, boneless chicken breast halves or thighs
2	tablespoons cooking oil
1	cup chopped green sweet pepper
1	cup chopped onion
2	cloves garlic, minced
2	28-ounce cans tomatoes, cut up
2	15-ounce cans black beans or Great Northern beans, drained
1	12-ounce can beer
2	tablespoons red wine vinegar
1	tablespoon chili powder
1	teaspoon dried oregano, crushed
1	teaspoon ground cumin
½	teaspoon salt
¼	teaspoon black pepper
¼	teaspoon bottled hot pepper sauce
1	bay leaf
1	cup shredded Monterey Jack or cheddar cheese (4 ounces)

[1] Cut turkey into bite-size pieces. In a 4-quart Dutch oven heat 1 tablespoon of the oil. Cook half of the turkey in hot oil over medium heat until no longer pink; remove from pan. Repeat with remaining oil and turkey; remove turkey. Add green pepper, onion, and garlic to pan. Cook about 5 minutes or until vegetables are just tender; stir occasionally. Drain fat.

[2] Return turkey to pan. Add undrained tomatoes, beans, beer, vinegar, chili powder, oregano, cumin, salt, black pepper, hot pepper sauce, and bay leaf. Bring to boiling; reduce heat. Cover and simmer for 20 minutes or until turkey is tender, stirring occasionally. Discard bay leaf. Sprinkle cheese over each serving.

Nutrition Facts per serving: 358 cal., 12 g total fat (4 g sat. fat), 63 mg chol., 887 mg sodium, 32 g carbo., 10 g fiber, 34 g pro. Daily Values: 19% vit. A, 67% vit. C, 26% calcium, 21% iron

Chicken Chowder

[*Chowders chock-full of potatoes are great cold-weather fare, but sometimes you just don't feel like peeling the spuds. Not a problem in this recipe—instant mashed potatoes get the job done.*]

Prep: *10 minutes*　　**Cook:** *15 minutes*　　**Servings:** *4*

- 12　ounces skinless, boneless chicken breast halves or thighs
- 3　slices bacon, chopped
- ⅓　cup chopped onion
- ¼　cup chopped red sweet pepper
- 1　14¾- or 15-ounce can cream-style corn
- 1　14½-ounce can reduced-sodium chicken broth
- 1　cup milk
- ¾　cup packaged instant mashed potatoes
- ¼　teaspoon dried thyme, crushed

[1] Cut chicken into ½-inch pieces; set aside. In a Dutch oven cook bacon over medium heat until crisp. Remove bacon from Dutch oven with a slotted spoon, reserving drippings in pan; set bacon aside. Cook chicken, onion, and sweet pepper in bacon drippings over medium heat about 3 minutes or until onion is crisp-tender. Stir in corn, broth, and milk. Stir in instant potatoes, thyme, and ⅛ teaspoon coarsely ground black pepper. Bring to boiling; reduce heat. Cover and simmer for 8 minutes or until chicken is tender and no longer pink and soup is thickened; stir occasionally. Sprinkle with bacon pieces.

Nutrition Facts per serving: 270 cal., 7 g total fat (2 g sat. fat), 53 mg chol., 743 mg sodium, 31 g carbo., 2 g fiber, 23 g pro. Daily Values: 9% vit. A, 41% vit. C, 7% calcium, 8% iron

Shortcuts for Soups and Stews

Make soup prep time even shorter—or at least break it up into stages—with these tips:

▌Cut or chop all of the vegetables the night before and store, covered, in the refrigerator until you're ready to prepare the rest of the soup.

▌Instead of soaking beans, use canned beans. A 15-ounce can of beans contains about 1¾ cups drained beans. For a recipe calling for 1 cup dried beans, you'll need approximately 3½ cups of canned beans (about two 15-ounce cans). Drain and rinse beans, and reduce or omit salt from the recipe. If the recipe involves long simmering times, add the canned beans toward the end of cooking time and heat through; that way the beans will keep some of their firmness.

Soups
   and Stews

Catalan Chicken Chowder

[This soup brims with some of the same hallmark ingredients of the Spanish specialty Paella—saffron-scented rice, onions, artichoke hearts, and peas.]

Prep: *10 minutes* **Cook:** *20 minutes* **Servings:** *4*

- 1 5-ounce package saffron-flavored yellow rice mix
- 2 teaspoons olive oil
- 8 ounces skinless, boneless chicken breast halves, cut into bite-size pieces
- ½ cup chopped onion
- 1 clove garlic, minced
- 1 14½-ounce can diced tomatoes
- 1 14½-ounce can reduced-sodium chicken broth
- ½ of a 14-ounce can artichoke hearts, drained and quartered (about ¾ cup)
- ½ cup loose-pack frozen baby sweet peas
- ½ of a 7-ounce jar roasted red sweet peppers, drained and cut into strips
- 2 tablespoons toasted sliced almonds

[1] Prepare rice mix according to package directions; set aside and keep warm. Meanwhile, in a large saucepan heat oil. Cook chicken, onion, and garlic in hot oil over medium-high heat about 5 minutes or until chicken is no longer pink.

[2] Add undrained tomatoes, broth, and artichoke hearts to chicken mixture. Bring to boiling; reduce heat. Simmer, uncovered, for 10 minutes, stirring occasionally. Add peas and red peppers. Cook for 3 to 4 minutes more or until heated through.

[3] To serve, ladle chowder into bowls. Spoon a mound of cooked rice into the center of each serving. Sprinkle with almonds.

Nutrition Facts per serving: 321 cal., 10 g total fat (2 g sat. fat), 30 mg chol., 1,099 mg sodium, 42 g carbo., 4 g fiber, 19 g pro. Daily Values: 20% vit. A, 133% vit. C, 5% calcium, 23% iron

Hot from the Pot

Don't let a cold bowl of chili or soup let you down! Keep soups and stews warm longer by serving them in warmed bowls. Just before ladling, rinse bowls under hot tap water; dry. Or, if the vessels are ovenproof, let them sit briefly in the oven at a low temperature.

Turkey and Wild Rice Chowder

[*Chances are, you have most of these ingredients in your kitchen already. Now just make a point to add turkey sausage links to your list of on-hand items, and you can make this one-dish warmer at a few minutes' notice (25 minutes to be exact).*]

Start to Finish: *25 minutes*   **Servings:** *4*

6	ounces cooked smoked turkey sausage links
2	cups milk
½	cup chopped onion
½	cup chopped red or green sweet pepper
½	cup frozen whole kernel corn
2	teaspoons instant chicken bouillon granules
2	teaspoons snipped fresh marjoram or ½ teaspoon dried marjoram, crushed
¼	teaspoon black pepper
2	tablespoons all-purpose flour
1½	cups cooked wild or brown rice (see tip below)

[1] Cut turkey sausage links in half lengthwise; cut into ½-inch slices. In a large saucepan combine sausage, 1¾ cups of the milk, 1½ cups water, onion, sweet pepper, corn, bouillon granules, dried marjoram (if using), and black pepper. Bring to boiling.

[2] Meanwhile, combine flour and remaining ¼ cup milk. Stir into turkey mixture. Cook and stir until thickened and bubbly. Cook and stir for 1 minute more. Stir in cooked rice and fresh marjoram (if using); heat through.

Nutrition Facts per serving: 236 cal., 7 g total fat (3 g sat. fat), 40 mg chol., 742 mg sodium, 30 g carbo., 2 g fiber, 15 g pro. Daily Values: 8% vit. A, 16% vit. C, 15% calcium, 9% iron

Need Some Cooked Wild Rice?
Cook a batch of wild rice to have on hand for future use. To cook, rinse 1 cup wild rice. Bring 2 cups water to boiling in a medium saucepan. Stir in rice and return to boiling. Cover and simmer about 40 minutes or until most of the water is absorbed. Drain, if necessary. Makes about 2⅔ cups cooked rice. If freezing, divide cooked rice into recipe-size portions and place in freezer bags. Seal, label, and freeze up to 6 months. Or, tightly cover and store in the refrigerator for several days.

Fish and Vegetable Chowder

[*We borrowed the idea of a Manhattan-style clam chowder (that's the tomato-based one), but substituted fish for the clams. Enjoy it with a slice of crusty, country-style bread.*]

Prep: *15 minutes*   **Cook:** *25 minutes*   **Servings:** *4*

12	ounces fresh or frozen skinless cod or sea bass
4	slices bacon, cut into 1-inch pieces
½	cup chopped onion
2	cups chopped peeled potatoes
1	14½-ounce can chicken broth
1	14½-ounce can diced tomatoes
½	cup chopped carrot
½	cup sliced celery
2	teaspoons dried Italian seasoning, crushed
⅛	to ¼ teaspoon ground red pepper

[1] Thaw fish, if frozen. Cut into 1-inch pieces. Cover and refrigerate until needed. In a large saucepan cook bacon over medium heat until crisp. Drain fat, reserving 1 tablespoon drippings in pan with bacon. Cook onion in drippings until tender. Stir in potatoes, broth, undrained tomatoes, carrot, celery, Italian seasoning, and ground red pepper. Bring to boiling; reduce heat. Cover and simmer for 15 to 20 minutes or until potatoes are tender.

[2] Gently stir in fish. Return to boiling; reduce heat. Simmer the chowder, uncovered, for 3 to 5 minutes more or until fish flakes easily when tested with a fork. If desired, stir in 2 tablespoons dry sherry.

Nutrition Facts per serving: 214 cal., 5 g total fat (1 g sat. fat), 38 mg chol., 743 mg sodium, 23 g carbo., 3 g fiber, 20 g pro. Daily Values: 47% vit. A, 43% vit. C, 5% calcium, 13% iron

Spicy Shrimp Gazpacho

[*You may have had gazpacho before, but sweet shrimp and fragrant peaches or nectarines give this version of summer's favorite soup a definite edge!*]

Prep: *20 minutes* **Chill:** *2 to 24 hours* **Servings:** *4 to 6*

2	**cups chopped, peeled tomatoes**
2	**cups tomato juice**
1	**cup beef broth or vegetable broth**
2	**medium peaches or nectarines, peeled and chopped (1½ cups)**
½	**cup chopped, seeded cucumber**
¼	**cup sliced green onions**
¼	**cup snipped fresh cilantro**
2	**medium fresh jalapeño peppers, seeded and finely chopped (see tip, page 21)**
2	**tablespoons lime juice**
2	**tablespoons tequila (optional)**
1	**clove garlic, minced**
1	**teaspoon sugar**
	Several dashes bottled hot pepper sauce
1	**8-ounce package frozen, peeled, cooked shrimp, thawed**

[1] In a large mixing bowl stir together the tomatoes, tomato juice, broth, peaches, cucumber, green onions, cilantro, jalapeño peppers, lime juice, tequila (if desired), garlic, sugar, and bottled hot pepper sauce. Cover and chill mixture for 2 to 24 hours.

[2] Just before serving, stir in shrimp. If desired, garnish with a cilantro sprig and a few additional cooked shrimp threaded onto a bamboo skewer.

Nutrition Facts per serving: 153 cal., 1 g total fat (0 g sat. fat), 111 mg chol., 761 mg sodium, 23 g carbo., 4 g fiber, 15 g pro. Daily Values: 24% vit. A, 98% vit. C, 4% calcium, 22% iron

Caribbean Clam Chowder

[*With clams, onion, celery, tomatoes, and thyme, this version has its roots in the time-honored Eastern Seaboard tradition. But we've also added sweet potatoes, chili peppers, and lime juice for extra interest.*]

Start to Finish: *35 minutes*   **Servings:** *4*

½ pint shucked clams or one 6½-ounce can minced clams
2 cups peeled and cubed sweet potatoes (1 to 2 medium)
½ cup chopped onion
1 stalk celery, chopped
¼ cup chopped red sweet pepper
2 cloves garlic, minced
1½ teaspoons snipped fresh thyme or ½ teaspoon dried thyme, crushed
1 10-ounce can chopped tomatoes and green chili peppers
1 tablespoon lime juice

[1] Drain clams, reserving juice. Add enough water to clam juice to make 2½ cups liquid. If using fresh clams, chop clams; set aside.

[2] In a large saucepan bring the clam liquid to boiling. Stir in sweet potatoes, onion, celery, sweet pepper, garlic, and dried thyme (if using). Return to boiling; reduce heat. Cover and simmer about 10 minutes or until sweet potatoes are tender.

[3] Mash mixture slightly with a potato masher. Stir in clams, undrained tomatoes, lime juice, and fresh thyme (if using). If desired, stir in 1 tablespoon dark rum. Return to boiling; reduce heat. Cook for 1 to 2 minutes more.

Nutrition Facts per serving: 128 cal., 1 g total fat (0 g sat. fat), 19 mg chol., 337 mg sodium, 22 g carbo., 3 g fiber, 9 g pro.
Daily Values: 141% vit. A, 66% vit. C, 6% calcium, 57% iron

Split Pea Soup with Cilantro Salsa

[*What's cilantro salsa doing in a split pea soup? Spiking it with wonderfully fresh flavors, that's what! Be sure to stir the salsa mixture into the soup just before serving.*]

Prep: *15 minutes*   **Cook:** *1 hour*   Servings: *6*

1	tablespoon cooking oil
1	cup chopped onion
1	cup sliced carrots
3	cloves garlic, minced
1	pound dry split peas, rinsed and drained
2	14½-ounce cans chicken broth
3½	cups water
3	medium tomatoes, chopped (1½ cups)
¼	cup chopped fresh cilantro
¼	cup sliced green onions

[1] In a 4-quart Dutch oven heat oil. Cook onion, carrots, and garlic in hot oil over medium heat about 5 minutes or until onion is tender.

[2] Add peas, broth, and water. Bring mixture to boiling; reduce heat. Cover and simmer for 45 minutes or until peas are very tender. Place about half (about 4 cups) of the pea mixture, half at a time, into a blender container or food processor bowl. Cover and blend or process until smooth. Return all pea mixture to Dutch oven; heat through.

[3] Meanwhile, for cilantro salsa, in a small bowl combine tomatoes, cilantro, and green onions. Just before serving, stir tomato mixture into hot soup.

Nutrition Facts per serving: 304 cal., 4 g total fat (1 g sat. fat), 1 mg chol., 627 mg sodium, 49 g carbo., 5 g fiber, 20 g pro. Daily Values: 58% vit. A, 20% vit. C, 6% calcium, 26% iron

To Make Ahead: Prepare pea soup through Step 2, except do not heat through. Transfer to a bowl. Cool quickly; cover and chill up to 24 hours. To serve, return to Dutch oven and bring to boiling over low heat, stirring frequently. Just before serving, prepare cilantro salsa and stir into hot soup.

Three-Pepper Navy Bean Soup

[*Green spinach, roasted red peppers, and white beans add a trio of eye-catching colors, while chipotle peppers lend their characteristic smoky flavor to the mix. Look for chipotle peppers in adobo sauce in the Mexican foods aisle of the supermarket.*]

Prep: *10 minutes* **Stand:** *1 hour* **Cook:** *1 hour 35 minutes* **Servings:** *6*

1	pound dry navy beans
4	cups chicken broth or vegetable broth
½	cup chopped onion
1	or 2 canned chipotle peppers in adobo sauce, chopped, or 1 fresh jalapeño pepper, seeded and finely chopped (see tip, page 21)
½	teaspoon coarsely ground black pepper
1	clove garlic, minced
1	teaspoon dried oregano, crushed
½	teaspoon salt
2	tomatoes, seeded and cut up
2	cups torn fresh spinach
½	of a 7-ounce jar roasted red sweet peppers, drained and chopped (about ½ cup)

[1] Rinse beans. In a 4-quart Dutch oven combine beans and 6 cups water. Bring to boiling; reduce heat. Simmer, uncovered, for 2 minutes. Remove from heat; cover and let stand 1 hour. (Or, place beans in 6 cups water in a Dutch oven. Cover and let soak in a cool place for 6 to 8 hours or overnight.) Drain and rinse beans.

[2] Return beans to Dutch oven. Add broth, 3 cups fresh water, onion, chipotle pepper, black pepper, garlic, oregano, and salt. Bring to boiling; reduce heat. Cover and simmer for 1½ hours or until beans are tender, stirring occasionally. Stir in tomatoes, spinach, and roasted red peppers. Simmer 5 minutes longer to heat through.

Nutrition Facts per serving: 304 cal., 2 g total fat (1 g sat. fat), 0 mg chol., 766 mg sodium, 52 g carbo., 20 g fiber, 21 g pro. Daily Values: 19% vit. A, 79% vit. C, 13% calcium, 27% iron

To Make Ahead: Prepare bean soup through simmering until beans are tender. Transfer to a bowl. Cool quickly; cover and chill up to 24 hours. To serve, return to Dutch oven and bring to boiling over low heat, stirring occasionally. Stir in tomatoes, spinach, and roasted red peppers. Simmer 5 minutes longer to heat through.

Butternut and Barley Vegetarian Soup

♥

[*Barley and winter squash make the soup hearty; fresh mushrooms make it meaty. This tasty soup is enough to make vegetarians of us all!*]

Prep: *20 minutes* **Cook**: *20 minutes* **Servings**: *4*

4	cups sliced fresh mushrooms
1½	cups chopped onion
3	cloves garlic, minced
2	tablespoons cooking oil
4	cups vegetable broth or reduced-sodium chicken broth
1	cup cubed, peeled butternut or buttercup squash
¾	cup chopped red sweet pepper
½	cup quick-cooking barley
2	tablespoons dry sherry
2	teaspoons snipped fresh dillweed or ½ teaspoon dried dillweed
¼	teaspoon lemon-pepper seasoning

[1] In a large saucepan or 4-quart Dutch oven cook mushrooms, onion, and garlic in hot oil until vegetables are tender and most of the liquid has evaporated.

[2] Add broth, squash, red pepper, barley, sherry, dillweed, and lemon-pepper seasoning. Bring to boiling; reduce heat. Cover and simmer for 20 to 25 minutes or until vegetables and barley are tender. If desired, garnish individual servings of soup with a dollop of yogurt or dairy sour cream.

Nutrition Facts per serving: 216 cal., 9 g total fat (1 g sat. fat), 0 mg chol., 1,002 mg sodium, 35 g carbo., 4 g fiber, 5 g pro. Daily Values: 36% vit. A, 69% vit. C, 2% calcium, 15% iron

[35]

Soups
and Stews

Wild Rice and Cheese Soup

[*Sometimes referred to as "the caviar of grains," wild rice brings a nutty flavor and slightly crunchy texture to recipes. And with smoked Gouda cheese in the mix, the flavors become especially opulent.*]

Start to Finish: *20 minutes*   **Servings:** *4*

- 1 tablespoon margarine or butter
- 2 tablespoons finely chopped onion
- 1 tablespoon all-purpose flour
- 1/4 teaspoon ground white pepper
- 2/3 cup half-and-half or light cream
- 1 1/4 cups reduced-sodium chicken broth
- 1/2 cup brown ale or amber beer
- 1 medium cooking apple, cored and chopped (1 cup)
- 1/2 cup cooked wild rice (see tip, page 28)
- 2 cups shredded smoked Gouda or smoked cheddar cheese (8 ounces)

[1] In a medium saucepan melt margarine. Cook and stir onion in hot margarine over medium-high heat until tender. Stir in flour and white pepper; cook and stir for 1 minute. Stir in half-and-half; cook and stir until thickened and bubbly.

[2] Stir in broth, beer, 3/4 cup of the apple, and cooked rice. Bring to boiling; reduce heat. Simmer, uncovered, for 10 minutes. Slowly add the cheese, whisking until cheese is melted. Top individual servings with remaining chopped apple.

Nutrition Facts per serving: 311 cal., 21 g total fat (13 g sat. fat), 60 mg chol., 1,104 mg sodium, 16 g carbo., 1 g fiber, 13 g pro. Daily Values: 52% vit. A, 4% vit. C, 41% calcium, 3% iron

Warm Chicken
Salad with
Oranges and
Almonds
Page 62

[38]

Pork Tenderloin
Sandwiches
Page 47

[Sandwiches and Salads]

Sizzling Vegetable Sandwiches Page 57

Roast Beef and Red Pepper Sandwiches

[*Two great features of this colorful, varied sandwich are that it keeps well when wrapped and chilled, and it's easy to tote. Think of it on picnic-perfect days—or on those less-than-perfect days when everyone is eating at different times.*]

Start to Finish: *25 minutes*   **Servings:** *12 (½ sandwich per serving)*

⅓	cup light mayonnaise dressing or mayonnaise
⅓	cup Dijon-style mustard
2	to 4 tablespoons prepared horseradish
6	6- to 7-inch Italian bread shells (Boboli) or Italian flatbreads (focaccia)
12	ounces thinly sliced cooked roast beef
1	12-ounce jar roasted red sweet peppers, drained and cut into ¼-inch-wide strips
6	ounces thinly sliced Monterey Jack cheese
2	cups fresh watercress, tough stems removed
2	cups fresh spinach

[1] In a small bowl combine mayonnaise dressing, Dijon-style mustard, and horseradish. Using a serrated knife, slice bread shells in half horizontally.

[2] For each sandwich, spread one side of bread shell with mayonnaise mixture. Top each with roast beef, roasted red peppers, Monterey Jack cheese, watercress, spinach, and remaining half of bread. To serve, slice each sandwich in half.

Nutrition Facts per serving: 303 cal., 14 g total fat (4 g sat. fat), 41 mg chol., 656 mg sodium, 27 g carbo., 2 g fiber, 20 g pro. Daily Values: 18% vit. A, 65% vit. C, 15% calcium, 17% iron

To Make Ahead: Prepare sandwiches. Cut each sandwich in half and wrap in plastic wrap. Chill in the refrigerator for up to 24 hours.

To Tote: Pack wrapped sandwiches with an ice pack in an insulated cooler.

Focaccia Facts

A little like a lightly topped pizza without the sauce, focaccia is a much-loved Italian flatbread from the coastal region of Liguria. Olive oil is a key ingredient, used both in the dough as well as being generously brushed on top before baking. Focaccia is often topped with ingredients such as minced garlic, onions, fresh herbs, tomatoes, olives, or a sprinkling of cheese. Generally you'll find the best focaccia at artisanal or Italian bakeries; however, your grocery store may make its own version.

Citrus Corned Beef Sandwiches

[*Keep some corned beef on hand—when the sealed vacuum-packed product is refrigerated, it has a shelf life of several weeks. That way, you can pop the meat in the crockery cooker any morning before work. On the way home, pick up some fresh rolls and cheese, and you have an instant homemade supper.*]

Prep: *30 minutes* **Cook:** *8 hours* **Servings:** *8*

- 1   2- to 3-pound corned beef brisket with spice packet
- 1   cup water
- ¼   cup Dijon-style mustard
- ⅓   cup orange juice
- 4   teaspoons all-purpose flour
- 8   kaiser rolls, split
- 6   ounces sliced Muenster cheese

[1] Trim fat from meat. Rub brisket with spices from spice packet. If necessary, cut the brisket to fit into a 3½-, 4-, or 5-quart electric crockery cooker. Place brisket in cooker. Combine water and Dijon-style mustard; pour over brisket. Cover and cook on low-heat setting for 8 to 10 hours or on high-heat setting for 4 to 5 hours. Remove meat; cover to keep warm. Skim fat from juices. Reserve juices; discard whole spices.

[2] In a small saucepan stir together orange juice, flour, and, if desired, ¼ teaspoon finely shredded orange peel. Gradually stir ¼ cup of the reserved cooking juices into the mixture in the saucepan. Cook and stir until mixture is thickened and bubbly. Cook and stir for 1 minute more. Remove from heat.

[3] To serve, thinly slice meat across the grain. Arrange rolls, cut side up, on the unheated rack of a broiler pan. Broil 4 to 5 inches from heat for 1 to 2 minutes or until toasted. Remove roll tops from broiler pan. Place sliced meat on bottom halves of rolls. Drizzle about 1 tablespoon of cooking juices over meat. Top with Muenster cheese. Broil 1 to 2 minutes more or until cheese melts. If desired, top with lettuce leaves and orange slices. Add roll tops.

Nutrition Facts per serving: 464 cal., 24 g total fat (9 g sat. fat), 99 mg chol., 1,539 mg sodium, 33 g carbo., 0 g fiber, 26 g pro. Daily Values: 7% vit. A, 30% vit. C, 17% calcium, 23% iron

Crockery Cookers 101

For our recipes, use a crockery cooker known as a "continuous slow cooker." Such cookers have heating coils that wrap around the sides of the cooker, allowing for continuous slow cooking. Note that intermittent cookers (those with heating elements or coils located below the food container) will not work for the recipes in this book.

[41]

Steak with Italian Green Sauce

[*Tuck steak, red onion, red sweet pepper, and yellow summer squash into a pita, then drizzle with an Italian-style sauce of parsley leaves, lemon juice, and capers for a pocketful of color and freshness.*]

Start to Finish: *35 minutes*   **Servings:** *6 (½ sandwich per serving)*   **Oven:** *300°*

3	large pita bread rounds, halved crosswise
3	tablespoons olive oil
½	cup packed fresh parsley leaves
1	tablespoon lemon juice
1	tablespoon capers, drained
1	clove garlic, minced
½	teaspoon Dijon-style mustard
1	tablespoon olive oil
2	medium red sweet peppers, cut into strips
2	medium yellow summer squash, sliced
12	ounces boneless sirloin steak, trimmed of fat, if necessary, and cut into thin strips
4	thin slices red onion, separated into rings

[1] Wrap the pita bread rounds in foil. Bake in a 300° oven about 10 minutes or until heated through.

[2] Meanwhile, in a blender container combine the 3 tablespoons olive oil, the parsley, lemon juice, capers, half of the garlic, and the Dijon-style mustard. Cover and blend until smooth, scraping sides of container as necessary. Add water, 1 teaspoon at a time, if necessary, to make sauce pourable. Season to taste with salt and pepper; set aside.

[3] Pour the 1 tablespoon olive oil into a wok or very large skillet. (Add more oil as necessary during cooking.) Preheat over medium-high heat. Cook and stir remaining garlic, red sweet pepper, and squash in hot oil for 1 to 2 minutes or until vegetables are crisp-tender. Remove from wok. Add the beef to hot wok. Cook and stir for 2 to 3 minutes or to desired doneness. Return vegetables to wok and heat through.

[4] To serve, fill each pita half with beef and vegetable mixture; top with onion rings. Pass the green sauce.

Nutrition Facts per serving: 285 cal., 15 g total fat (3 g sat. fat), 38 mg chol., 251 mg sodium, 22 g carbo., 1 g fiber, 16 g pro. Daily Values: 22% vit. A, 87% vit. C, 4% calcium, 18% iron

Sandwiches and Salads

[43]

Pulled Pork with Root Beer Barbecue Sauce

[*Root beer in barbecue sauce? Why not—it adds a sweet, caramely appeal. You'll find root beer concentrate in the spice section of supermarkets.*]

Prep: *15 minutes*   **Cook:** *8 hours*   **Servings:** *8 to 10*

1	2½- to 3-pound pork sirloin roast
1	tablespoon cooking oil
2	medium onions, cut into thin wedges
1	cup root beer (not diet root beer)
2	tablespoons minced garlic
2	12-ounce cans or bottles root beer (3 cups) (not diet root beer)
1	cup bottled chili sauce
8	to 10 hamburger buns, split and toasted (see tip, page 54)

[1] Trim fat from meat. If necessary, cut roast to fit into crockery cooker. Sprinkle meat with ½ teaspoon salt and ½ teaspoon pepper. In a large skillet heat oil over medium-high heat. Brown roast on all sides in hot oil. Drain fat. Transfer meat to a 3½-, 4-, or 5-quart electric crockery cooker. Add onions, the 1 cup root beer, and garlic. Cover and cook on low-heat setting for 8 to 10 hours or on high-heat setting for 4 to 5 hours.

[2] Meanwhile, for sauce, in a medium saucepan combine the 2 cans or bottles of root beer and the bottled chili sauce. Bring to boiling; reduce heat. Boil gently, uncovered, about 30 minutes or until mixture is reduced to 2 cups, stirring occasionally. If desired, add ¼ teaspoon root beer concentrate and several dashes bottled hot pepper sauce.

[3] Transfer roast to a cutting board or serving platter. Using a slotted spoon, remove onions from juices and place on serving platter. Discard juices. Using two forks, pull meat apart into shreds. To serve, if desired, line bottom halves of buns with lettuce leaves and sliced tomatoes. Add meat and onions; spoon on sauce. Add bun tops.

Nutrition Facts per serving: 356 cal., 10 g total fat (3 g sat. fat), 59 mg chol., 786 mg sodium, 44 g carbo., 1 g fiber, 22 g pro. Daily Values: 4% vit. A, 9% vit. C, 4% calcium, 13% iron

To Tote: After the meat is completely cooked, remove it from the crockery cooker and quickly shred as directed. Discard any liquid in cooker. Return meat and onions to the hot cooker. Stir in the heated sauce; cover. Wrap the crockery cooker in heavy foil, several layers of newspaper, or a heavy towel. Then place the cooker in an insulated container. The food should stay hot for up to 2 hours (do not hold for longer than 2 hours). If there is electricity at your party site, plug in the cooker. The food will stay warm for hours on the low-heat setting.

Hearty Stromboli

[Traditionally a warm pepperoni-and-cheese sandwich wrapped in pizza dough, this Philadelphia classic shows up all over the country in a variety of versions. Refrigerated pizza dough simplifies our recipe, while olives, pepper, and spinach add additional flavors and textures.]

Prep: *20 minutes* **Bake:** *25 minutes* **Stand:** *10 minutes* **Servings:** *4 to 6* **Oven:** *375°*

- 1 10-ounce package refrigerated pizza dough
- 4 ounces thinly sliced ham
- 1 cup shredded mozzarella cheese (4 ounces)
- 4 ounces thinly sliced Genoa salami
- ¼ cup kalamata olives, pitted and chopped
- ⅓ cup chopped yellow, red, or green sweet pepper
- 1 beaten egg

[1] Lightly brush a baking sheet with 2 teaspoons olive oil; sprinkle with 1 tablespoon cornmeal. Set aside. On a lightly floured surface, carefully stretch or roll the pizza dough into a 13×10-inch rectangle. Layer evenly, one at a time, the ham, half of the mozzarella cheese, 1 cup torn spinach (if desired), salami, remaining mozzarella cheese, olives, and sweet pepper, to about ½-inch from edges. Roll up, starting from a long side. Seal the seam and ends by pinching the dough with your fingers.

[2] Transfer loaf to prepared baking sheet. Brush with beaten egg. Using a sharp knife, cut slits in top for steam to escape. Bake in a 375° about 25 minutes or until golden brown. Let stand 10 minutes. To serve, slice loaf into serving-size pieces.

Nutrition Facts per serving: 471 cal., 23 g total fat (8 g sat. fat), 107 mg chol., 1613 mg sodium, 38 g carbo., 1 g fiber, 27 g pro. Daily Values: 7% vit. A, 35% vit. C, 16% calcium, 17% iron

Sandwich Serve-Alongs

Some sandwiches are so full of variety, they hardly need a side dish. Still, if you're looking for something beyond a pickle spear and potato chips to accompany your creation, consider these swift sides:

▌Spear chunks of in-season fresh fruits onto wooden skewers for fun, colorful kabobs.
▌You can't go wrong with soups—especially in winter. Keep your favorite canned varieties on hand.
▌Cut-up raw vegetables add color and crunch. You could serve them with ranch dressing for dipping.
▌Stir together a little antipasto-style salad with canned artichoke hearts, pepperoncini, black olives, and fresh cherry tomatoes. Toss with your favorite bottled vinaigrette.

Sandwiches
and Salads

Pork Tenderloin Sandwiches

[*With fresh-tasting Jicama Coleslaw topping the ever-popular pork tenderloin, this hearty sandwich is the sort of twist-on-the-classic that you'd expect to find at contemporary brew pubs across the country.*]

Prep: *35 minutes (sandwiches), 20 minutes (coleslaw)* **Chill:** *2 hours (coleslaw)* **Servings:** *4*

- 12   ounces pork tenderloin
- 3   tablespoons all-purpose flour
- ¼   teaspoon onion powder or garlic powder
- ¼   teaspoon ground red pepper
- ¼   teaspoon black pepper
- 2   tablespoons cooking oil
- 4   slices Muenster cheese
- 4   kaiser rolls, sourdough rolls, or large buns, split and toasted (see tip, page 54)
- 1   recipe Jicama Coleslaw

[1] Cut pork crosswise into four pieces. Place one pork piece between two pieces of clear plastic wrap. Working from the center, pound lightly with the flat side of a mallet to ¼-inch thickness. Remove plastic wrap. Repeat with remaining pork pieces.

[2] In a shallow dish combine flour, onion powder, ground red pepper, and black pepper. Dip meat into the flour mixture to coat. In a very large skillet heat oil. Cook pork in hot oil over medium heat for 6 to 8 minutes or until no pink remains and juices run clear, turning once. (If all slices won't fit in skillet, fry in two batches, adding additional oil if necessary.)

[3] To serve, place the Muenster cheese slices and pork on bottom halves of rolls. If desired, top with red onion slices, about ¼ cup of the Jicama Coleslaw, and the roll tops. Serve additional Jicama Coleslaw as a side dish. If desired, pass mustard, catsup, green onions, and/or dill pickle slices.

Jicama Coleslaw: In a screw-top jar combine 3 tablespoons vinegar, 3 tablespoons salad oil, 1 tablespoon honey, ¼ teaspoon salt, ⅛ to ¼ teaspoon black pepper, and several dashes bottled hot pepper sauce (if desired). Cover and shake well. In a salad bowl combine 4 cups of 2-inch-long matchlike strips peeled jicama, 1 cup shredded red or green cabbage, 1 cup shredded carrots, and ¼ cup thinly sliced green onions. Pour dressing over vegetable mixture, tossing to coat. Cover and chill for 2 to 24 hours.

Nutrition Facts per serving: 500 cal., 22 g total fat (8 g sat. fat), 77 mg chol., 559 mg sodium, 40 g carbo., 2 g fiber, 34 g pro. Daily Values: 31% vit. A, 15% vit. C, 27% calcium, 20% iron

Grilled Chicken Mole Sandwiches

[*Mole (pronounced MO-lay) means mixture. Traditionally this Mexican-Indian sauce base includes ground roasted pumpkin seeds, onions, herbs, and two or more types of chilies. Our version is a little simpler. If your supermarket doesn't have all the ingredients, locate an Hispanic grocery store in your area.*

Prep: *25 minutes* **Chill:** *30 minutes* **Grill:** *12 minutes* **Servings:** *4*

3	dried New Mexico peppers or dried pasilla peppers (see tip, page 21)
¼	cup chopped onion
3	cloves garlic, chopped
1	tablespoon cooking oil
1½	ounces Mexican-style sweet chocolate or semisweet chocolate, chopped (about 3 tablespoons)
4	large skinless, boneless chicken breast halves
1	small avocado, halved, seeded, peeled, and mashed
2	tablespoons light mayonnaise dressing
2	bolitos, bollilos, or other Mexican rolls or hard rolls, approximately 6 inches in diameter, split
	Baby romaine or other green lettuce leaves, and tomato slices
½	of a medium papaya, peeled, seeded, and sliced

[1] For mole, remove stems and seeds from dried peppers. Coarsely chop peppers; set aside. In a large skillet cook onion and garlic in hot oil over medium-high heat for 4 to 5 minutes or until onions are brown. Add dried peppers and ½ cup water; reduce heat and stir in chocolate. Cook and stir over medium heat for 3 to 5 minutes or until thickened and bubbly. Cool slightly. Transfer pepper mixture to a food processor bowl or blender container. Cover and process or blend until a smooth paste. Set aside to cool. Reserve 1 to 2 tablespoons mole.

[2] If desired, season chicken with salt. Using a sharp knife, carefully butterfly-cut each chicken breast by cutting a slit horizontally two-thirds of the way through. Open each breast piece and spread inside of each with mole; fold closed. Rub outside of each breast with reserved mole. Grill chicken breasts on rack of an uncovered grill directly over medium coals 12 to 15 minutes or until tender and no longer pink, turning once halfway through. Cover; chill.

[3] In a small bowl stir together avocado, light mayonnaise dressing, ¼ teaspoon ground red pepper (if desired), and ⅛ teaspoon salt. To serve, slice the chicken into ¼- to ½-inch slices. Spread avocado mixture onto split rolls; layer with chicken slices, romaine, and tomato slices. Garnish with papaya slices. Serve sandwiches open-faced.

Nutrition Facts per serving: 524 cal., 24 g total fat (6 g sat. fat), 59 mg chol., 448 mg sodium, 52 g carbo., 7 g fiber, 28 g pro. Daily Values: 8% vit. A, 120% vit. C, 7% calcium, 25% iron

Sandwiches and Salads

To Make Ahead: Prepare chicken through Step 2. Cover and chill in the refrigerator for up to 24 hours. To serve, proceed with Step 3.

Chicken and Pear Monte Cristo

[*Like any Monte Cristo deserving of its opulent name, this batter-dipped, golden brown sandwich oozes with melted cheese. But in our version, fresh pears add a particularly regal touch. A light salad with a cucumber dressing would provide a terrific contrast.*]

Prep: *20 minutes* **Bake:** *25 minutes* **Servings:** *8 (2 triangles per serving)* **Oven:** *350°*

- 4   to 6 teaspoons prepared horseradish
- 8   thick slices firm-textured white bread
- 8   thin slices mozzarella cheese
- 8   thin slices fully cooked chicken or turkey breast (12 ounces)
- 1   to 2 medium pears, cored, peeled, and thinly sliced
- 2   beaten eggs
- ⅔   cup half-and-half, light cream, or whipping cream

[1] Spread 1 to 1½ teaspoons horseradish on one side of half of the bread slices. Top each with a slice of cheese, a slice of chicken, and several pear slices. Add another slice of cheese and a slice of chicken. Top with a slice of bread.

[2] Meanwhile, in a shallow dish combine eggs and half-and-half. Dip both sides of sandwiches in egg mixture, allowing each side of sandwiches to stand 10 seconds until egg mixture is absorbed. Place sandwiches in a greased 15×10×1½-inch baking pan. Bake in a 350° oven for 15 minutes. Carefully turn sandwiches over; bake about 10 minutes more or until bread is golden and cheese is just melted. To serve, slice each sandwich into four triangles.

Nutrition Facts per serving: 321 cal., 16 g total fat (8 g sat. fat), 116 mg chol., 428 mg sodium, 19 g carbo., 1 g fiber, 26 g pro. Daily Values: 13% vit. A, 2% vit. C, 27% calcium, 9% iron

Perfect Pears

Juicy, ripe pears are great not only for snacking out of hand, but they add a honey-sweet flavor and, if left unpeeled, a lovely color to recipes. While often thought of as a fall and winter fruit, numerous varieties and extended growing seasons mean pears of all sizes and colors can be plucked practically year-round from supermarket shelves. Some tips:

❙ Look for pears that are free from bruises and cuts. Select fairly firm pears if you plan to bake them.

❙ To ripen pears, place them in a paper bag at room temperature for 2 to 3 days. Or, store them in a fruit bowl in a cool, dark place. You'll know they're ripe when the stem end yields to pressure when touched.

❙ Ripe pears can be kept in the refrigerator for several days.

Sandwiches
and Salads

Thai Chicken Wraps

[*Thanks to quick-cooking chicken, convenient broccoli slaw mix, and an easy peanut sauce, 25 minutes is all it takes to wrap up a dinner bursting with the intriguing flavors of the Pacific Rim.*]

Start to Finish: *25 minutes*   **Servings:** *6*   **Oven:** *350°*

- 6   8- to 10-inch green, red, and/or plain flour tortillas
- ½   teaspoon garlic salt
- ¼   to ½ teaspoon pepper
- 12   ounces skinless, boneless chicken breast strips for stir-frying
- 1   tablespoon cooking oil
- 4   cups packaged shredded broccoli (broccoli slaw mix)
- 1   medium red onion, cut into thin wedges
- 1   teaspoon grated fresh ginger
- 1   recipe Peanut Sauce

[1] Wrap tortillas in foil. Bake in a 350° oven about 10 minutes or until heated and softened. Meanwhile, in a medium mixing bowl combine garlic salt and pepper. Add chicken, tossing to coat evenly.

[2] In a large skillet heat oil. Cook and stir seasoned chicken in hot oil over medium-high heat for 2 to 3 minutes or until no longer pink. Remove chicken from skillet; keep warm. Add broccoli, onion, and ginger to skillet. Cook and stir for 2 to 3 minutes or until vegetables are crisp-tender. Remove from heat.

[3] To assemble, spread each tortilla with about 1 tablespoon Peanut Sauce. Top with chicken strips and vegetable mixture. Roll up each tortilla, securing with a wooden toothpick. Serve immediately with remaining Peanut Sauce.

Peanut Sauce: In a small saucepan combine ¼ cup sugar, ¼ cup creamy peanut butter, 3 tablespoons soy sauce, 3 tablespoons water, 2 tablespoons cooking oil, and 1 teaspoon bottled minced garlic. Heat until sugar is dissolved, stirring frequently.

Nutrition Facts per serving: 330 cal., 16 g total fat (3 g sat. fat), 30 mg chol., 911 mg sodium, 30 g carbo., 3 g fiber, 17 g pro. Daily Values: 3% vit. A, 39% vit. C, 4% calcium, 11% iron

Turkey and Chutney Sandwiches

[*Chutney, an East Indian relish often made of mangoes, tamarinds, raisins, and spices, is traditionally served alongside curries or meats. It also makes a great sandwich spread when combined with mayonnaise. Serve this sandwich now or later—it keeps well up to 24 hours.*]

Start to Finish: *25 minutes* **Servings:** *12 (½ sandwich per serving)*

3	medium carrots
½	cup chutney, snipped
⅓	cup light mayonnaise dressing or mayonnaise
6	6- or 7-inch Italian bread shells (Boboli) or Italian flatbreads (focaccia)
12	ounces thinly sliced cooked turkey
6	ounces thinly sliced smoked Gouda cheese
6	large romaine leaves
6	fresh tarragon sprigs

[1] Peel carrots. Using a vegetable peeler, carefully cut carrots into long, thin ribbons. Place in cold water to crisp; set aside.

[2] In a small bowl stir together the chutney and light mayonnaise dressing. Using a serrated knife, slice bread shells or flatbreads in half horizontally.

[3] For each sandwich, spread a cut side of bread shell with mayonnaise mixture. Top with the turkey, Gouda cheese, a romaine leaf, carrot ribbons, a fresh tarragon sprig, and the remaining half of the bread. To serve, slice each sandwich in half.

Nutrition Facts per serving: 283 cal., 10 g total fat (3 g sat. fat), 29 mg chol., 818 mg sodium, 34 g carbo., 2 g fiber, 16 g pro. Daily Values: 55% vit. A, 5% vit. C, 14% calcium, 11% iron

To Make Ahead: Prepare sandwiches. Cut each sandwich in half and wrap in plastic wrap. Chill in the refrigerator for up to 24 hours.

To Tote: Pack wrapped sandwiches with an ice pack in an insulated cooler.

Sandwiches
and Salads

Fish Fillet Muffuletta

[Battered fish fillets have always been easy dinner fare, but this recipe gives them Big-Easy flair by adding olives and capers—much-loved ingredients in the traditional New Orleans muffuletta. Be sure to assemble the sandwiches just before serving to keep the fish captivatingly crisp.]

Start to Finish: *25 minutes*   **Servings:** *4*

- 4   frozen battered or breaded fish fillets
- 3   tablespoons mayonnaise or salad dressing
- 1   teaspoon finely shredded lime peel
- 2   teaspoons lime juice
- 1   cup packaged shredded cabbage with carrots (coleslaw mix)
- 4   individual French-style or club rolls (3½ to 4 inches long), split horizontally
- ½   cup salsa
- ½   cup sliced pitted kalamata olives

[1] Cook fish according to package directions. Meanwhile, in a small mixing bowl stir together mayonnaise, lime peel, and lime juice. Add the cabbage and, if desired, 2 tablespoons drained capers. Stir until well combined; set aside.

[2] Hollow out inside of top halves of rolls, leaving a ½-inch-thick shell. Spoon cabbage mixture onto bottom halves. Top with fish and salsa. Sprinkle with olives. Add roll tops.

Nutrition Facts per serving: 447 cal., 25 g total fat (4 g sat. fat), 26 mg chol., 937 mg sodium, 45 g carbo., 1 g fiber, 14 g pro. Daily Values: 5% vit. A, 35% vit. C, 6% calcium, 16% iron

Take It Away!

Next time you're looking for a good choice for outdoor dining, remember that some of the salads and cold sandwiches in this chapter make great picnic or tailgate fare. When toting, remember safe-picnicking rule number one: Keep hot foods hot and cold foods cold! Here's how to accomplish the latter:

▌Start by refrigerating your salad or sandwich overnight so it's thoroughly chilled.
▌Transport cold food in an insulated cooler that has been cleaned. Chill the cooler by filling it with ice for at least 30 minutes prior to packing.
▌Wait until just before you leave home to pack the cooler. Then tuck ice around foods.
▌On summer outings, keep the cooler with you in the car, not in the trunk.
▌Once at your picnic site, set the tightly closed cooler in a shady area. Add ice often.
▌Serve the cold sandwiches and salads within 2 hours of packing.
▌For mixed green salads, pack the dressing separately and toss before serving. Same goes for garnishes, such as croutons.

Grilled Fish Sandwiches

[*Name your pleasure! Choose from lemon-pepper, Cajun, or Jamaican jerk seasonings to rub onto the fish. Present it on focaccia for worldly appeal, or keep it simple with hamburger buns, and garnish as you like.*]

Prep: *15 minutes*　**Grill:** *8 minutes*　**Servings:** *4*

- 4　fresh or frozen fish fillets (about 4 ounces each)
- 1　tablespoon lemon or lime juice
- 1　teaspoon lemon-pepper seasoning, Jamaican jerk seasoning, or Cajun seasoning
- ½　cup mayonnaise or salad dressing
- 4　teaspoons Dijon-style mustard
- 1　to 3 teaspoons honey
- 4　slices Italian flatbread (focaccia) or 4 hamburger buns or kaiser rolls, split and toasted (see tip, below)
- Watercress or lettuce leaves (optional)
- Roasted red sweet pepper strips or tomato slices (optional)

[1] Thaw fish, if frozen. Brush fish fillets with lemon. Rub desired seasoning evenly onto all sides of fish. Place the seasoned fish fillets in a well-greased wire grill basket. Grill in the wire basket on an uncovered grill directly over medium coals for 4 to 6 minutes for each ½-inch thickness of fish or just until fish begins to flake easily with a fork.

[2] Meanwhile, for spread, in a small mixing bowl stir together mayonnaise, Dijon-style mustard, and honey to taste.

[3] To serve, spread cut sides of focaccia with spread. Top bottom halves of focaccia slices with watercress (if desired), the fish, additional spread, roasted red pepper strips or tomato slices (if desired), and top halves of focaccia slices.

Nutrition Facts per serving: 311 cal., 14 g total fat (2 g sat. fat), 51 mg chol., 676 mg sodium, 24 g carbo., 1 g fiber, 22 g pro. Daily Values: 2% vit. A, 4% vit. C, 3% calcium, 10% iron

Sandwiches and Salads

Toasting Tips
Toasting sandwich buns adds a little crunch to the meal. The easiest way to toast rolls and hoagies is in a toaster oven; however, you can also use your broiler. Simply place, cut side up, on the unheated rack of a broiler pan and broil 4 to 5 inches from heat for 1 to 2 minutes, or until golden brown.

Cucumber and Apricot Sandwiches

[*Cool as a you-know-what, this crunchy, fruit-studded cream-cheese sandwich will taste refreshing in summer. Try it with a cup of gazpacho.*]

Start to Finish: *15 minutes* **Servings:** *4*

- 1 **large cucumber**
- ½ **of an 8-ounce package reduced-fat cream cheese (Neufchâtel)**
- 2 **tablespoons snipped fresh basil**
- 8 **slices firm-textured whole wheat bread**
- 2 **large apricots or 1 nectarine, pitted and thinly sliced**
- ½ **cup arugula leaves or cilantro sprigs**

[1] Peel cucumber. Cut cucumber in half lengthwise and scoop out seeds. Thinly slice cucumber; set aside. In a small bowl stir together the cream cheese, basil, and, if desired, ⅛ teaspoon salt.

[2] Spread about 1 tablespoon cheese mixture on one side of each bread slice. Top four bread slices with cucumber, apricot, and arugula. Top with remaining bread slices, cream cheese side down. To serve, cut each sandwich in half diagonally.

Nutrition Facts per serving: 234 cal., 9 g total fat (5 g sat. fat), 21 mg chol., 413 mg sodium, 32 g carbo., 5 g fiber, 9 g pro. **Daily Values:** 16% vit. A, 12% vit. C, 8% calcium, 13% iron

To Make Ahead: Prepare sandwiches. Cut each sandwich in half and wrap in plastic wrap. Chill in the refrigerator for up to 2 hours.

To Tote: Pack wrapped sandwiches with an ice pack in an insulated cooler.

Sandwiches
and Salads

Sizzling Vegetable Sandwiches

[Don't hold the mayo! Instead make your own version—flavored with cumin, garlic, and lime—to bring spark to this colorful sandwich. The dressing tastes great with beef, pork, or chicken, too.]

Prep: *20 minutes* **Grill:** *12 minutes* **Servings:** *4*

1	small eggplant, cut crosswise into ½-inch slices
1	medium zucchini, cut lengthwise into ¼-inch slices
1	medium yellow summer squash, cut lengthwise into ¼-inch slices
1	medium red sweet pepper, seeded and cut into ¼-inch strips
1	small onion, cut into ½-inch slices
⅓	cup olive oil
4	poppy seed kaiser rolls, split
¼	cup Cumin Mayo or Easy Cumin Mayo

[1] Brush the vegetables with some of the olive oil. Place onion slices on a long metal skewer. Grill onion on the rack of an uncovered grill directly over medium coals for 5 minutes. Add remaining vegetables and grill for 12 to 15 minutes more or until vegetables are tender, turning once.* (If some vegetables cook more quickly than others, remove and keep warm.) Brush split sides of rolls with remaining olive oil. Grill rolls, split sides down, about 1 minute or until toasted.

[2] To serve, layer the vegetables atop the bottom halves of rolls. Spread roll tops with 1 tablespoon Cumin Mayo. Add roll tops.

Note: To broil, place half of the vegetables on the rack of a broiler pan. Broil 3 to 4 inches from heat for 12 to 15 minutes or until vegetables are tender, turning once. Remove vegetables; keep warm. Repeat with remaining vegetables. To toast rolls under broiler, see tip on page 54.

Cumin Mayo: In a blender container or food processor bowl, combine ¼ cup refrigerated or frozen egg product, thawed; 2 tablespoons lime juice; 1 clove garlic, cut up; 1 teaspoon cumin seed, crushed; and ¼ teaspoon salt. Cover and blend or process a few seconds until combined. With the blender or processor running, gradually add ¾ cup salad oil in a thin, steady stream. When necessary, stop machine and scrape down sides of the container. Store in the refrigerator for up to 2 weeks.

Easy Cumin Mayo: In a small mixing bowl combine 1 cup light mayonnaise dressing; 2 tablespoons lime juice; 1 clove garlic, minced; and 1 teaspoon cumin seed, crushed.

[57]

Nutrition Facts per serving: 405 cal., 25 g total fat (3 g sat. fat), 0 mg chol., 347 mg sodium, 40 g carbo., 3 g fiber, 8 g pro. Daily Values: 16% vit. A, 60% vit. C, 6% calcium, 17% iron

Flank Steak Salad with Cantaloupe

[*Marinate the flank steak in the morning. Then after work you can relax outdoors as you sizzle it up for this colorful salad. What a great way to unwind on a glorious summer night!*]

Prep: *20 minutes* **Marinate:** *12 hours* **Grill:** *12 minutes* **Servings:** *6*

- 1   8-ounce bottle Italian salad dressing
- 2   teaspoons finely shredded lemon peel
- 1   pound beef flank steak
-     Lemon-pepper seasoning
- 8   ounces fresh haricots vert or other young, tender green beans, trimmed
- 5   cups torn leaf lettuce
- 3   cups watercress or arugula
- 1   medium cantaloupe, cut into wedges

[1] Combine dressing and lemon peel. Sprinkle both sides of steak with lemon-pepper seasoning. Place steak in a plastic bag set in a glass dish; pour ¾ cup of the dressing mixture over meat. Seal bag; marinate in the refrigerator 12 to 24 hours, turning occasionally. Remove steak from bag; discard excess marinade. Grill steak on rack of an uncovered grill directly over medium-hot coals 12 to 14 minutes or until desired doneness, turning once.

[2] Meanwhile, in a saucepan add beans to boiling water. Cover; simmer about 2 minutes or until crisp-tender. Drain; rinse in cold water and set aside. In a large mixing bowl toss beans with lettuce and watercress. Arrange salad mixture on a serving platter. Thinly slice flank steak across grain. Arrange steak slices on top of greens. Serve with cantaloupe wedges. If desired, garnish with cherry tomatoes. Drizzle salad with remaining dressing.

Nutrition Facts per serving: 248 cal., 15 g total fat (4 g sat. fat), 35 mg chol., 245 mg sodium, 12 g carbo., 1 g fiber, 16 g pro. Daily Values: 37% vit. A, 76% vit. C, 4% calcium, 14% iron

Sandwiches and Salads

Lettuce Spice Up Your Salads!

Tired of mild-mannered salads featuring the usual head lettuce? Turn to the rich array of lettuces and greens on the market today. Mix and match a few in each of the following categories for salads that are bursting with a wide variety of flavors and textures:

▌Strongly Flavored Greens: dandelion (bitter); arugula (bitter, peppery, mustardlike); watercress (clean, yet peppery); radicchio (bitter and peppery), spinach (slightly bitter); Belgian endive (bitter); sorrel (sour); frisee (bitter)

▌Sweet: Boston and Bibb (butterhead) lettuce

▌Mild: green tip, red tip, romaine

Spicy Steak and Ranch Salad

[*Cajun-spiced steak is quickly pan-broiled and served over a bed of greens, carrots, and radishes, then topped with crunchy and convenient French-fried onions. Talk about a fresh take on steak and onions!*]

Start to Finish: *25 minutes*   **Servings:** *4*

½	cup French-fried onions
1	tablespoon Cajun seasoning
1	tablespoon lime juice
1	clove garlic, minced
1	pound boneless beef top sirloin steak, cut 1 inch thick
1	10-ounce package European-style salad greens
2	carrots, cut into thin bite-size strips or peeled into thin strips
½	cup thinly sliced radishes
½	cup bottled fat-free ranch salad dressing

[1] In a large nonstick skillet cook French-fried onions over medium-high heat about 2 minutes or until brown, stirring occasionally. Set aside.

[2] Meanwhile, in a small bowl combine Cajun seasoning, lime juice, and garlic. Rub mixture over both sides of steak. In the same skillet cook steak over medium heat to desired doneness, turning once. (Allow 6 to 8 minutes for medium-rare or 9 to 12 minutes for medium.) Remove skillet from heat; let stand for 10 minutes. Cut steak into thin bite-size slices. If desired, season with salt.

[3] On a large serving platter toss together the salad greens, carrots, and radishes. Arrange the steak strips over salad greens. Drizzle the dressing over salad. Sprinkle with the French-fried onions.

Nutrition Facts per serving: 310 cal., 13 g total fat (4 g sat. fat), 76 mg chol., 557 mg sodium, 16 g carbo., 3 g fiber, 28 g pro. Daily Values: 126% vit. A, 40% vit. C, 5% calcium, 28% iron

Greek Lamb Salad with Yogurt Dressing

[*Take a tip from Mediterranean cooking—you don't need a lot of red meat to add a lot of flavor to recipes. Here a small amount of lamb brings its robust appeal to other hearty ingredients, including garbanzo beans and spinach, for a salad that's satisfying and healthful.*]

Start to Finish: *30 minutes*   **Servings:** *4*

2	teaspoons snipped fresh rosemary or ½ teaspoon dried rosemary, crushed
1	clove garlic, minced
8	ounces boneless lamb leg sirloin chops, cut ½ inch thick
8	cups torn fresh spinach or torn mixed salad greens
1	15-ounce can garbanzo beans, rinsed and drained
¼	cup chopped, seeded cucumber
½	cup plain low-fat yogurt
¼	cup chopped green onions
⅛	to ¼ teaspoon salt
⅛	teaspoon pepper
1	clove garlic, minced
¼	cup dried tart red cherries or golden raisins

[1] In a small bowl combine the rosemary and 1 clove garlic. Rub mixture evenly over both sides of lamb chops. Place chops on the unheated rack of a broiler pan. Broil 4 to 5 inches from the heat for 12 to 15 minutes, turning once halfway through.* Cut lamb chops into thin bite-size slices.

[2] Meanwhile, on a serving platter toss together spinach, garbanzo beans, and cucumber. Arrange lamb slices over spinach mixture.

[3] For dressing, in a small bowl combine yogurt, green onions, salt, pepper, and 1 clove garlic. Drizzle dressing over salad. Sprinkle with cherries.

*Note: To grill, place chops on the rack of an uncovered grill directly over medium coals to desired doneness, turning once halfway through. (Allow 10 to 14 minutes for medium-rare or 14 to 16 minutes for medium.)

Nutrition Facts per serving: 243 cal., 6 g total fat (2 g sat. fat), 36 mg chol., 569 mg sodium, 29 g carbo., 8 g fiber, 20 g pro. Daily Values: 80% vit. A, 63% vit. C, 17% calcium, 42% iron

Sandwiches and Salads

Thai Cobb Salad

[*Next time you grill out, sizzle up some extra meat with this salad in mind. With its refreshing mix of cubed avocado, peanuts, and a spicy ginger-soy dressing, the recipe will transform leftovers into an entirely different dinner experience.*]

Start to Finish: *25 minutes*   **Servings:** *4*

½	cup bottled fat-free Italian salad dressing
1	tablespoon soy sauce
1	to 1½ teaspoons grated fresh ginger
¼	to ½ teaspoon crushed red pepper
8	cups torn mixed salad greens*
1½	cups coarsely chopped cooked pork, beef, or chicken (8 ounces)
1	avocado, halved, seeded, peeled, and cut into ½-inch pieces
1	cup coarsely shredded carrots
¼	cup fresh cilantro leaves
¼	cup thinly sliced green onions

[1] For dressing, in a large bowl combine Italian salad dressing, soy sauce, ginger, and crushed red pepper. Add salad greens, tossing lightly to coat.

[2] Arrange salad greens on a serving platter. Top greens with meat, avocado, carrots, cilantro, green onions, and, if desired, ¼ cup honey-roasted peanuts.

*Note: To carry through with the Asian flavors, include Chinese cabbage as part of the torn mixed salad greens.

Nutrition Facts per serving: 255 cal., 15 g total fat (4 g sat. fat), 52 mg chol., 743 mg sodium, 11 g carbo., 4 g fiber, 19 g pro. Daily Values: 86% vit. A, 19% vit. C, 3% calcium, 13% iron

Proceed Gingerly!

Loved for its hot flavor and sprightly aroma, fresh ginger is also surprisingly easy to keep on hand. For long-term storage, immerse slices of peeled ginger in dry sherry or wine and refrigerate up to 3 months. And it lasts almost indefinitely when frozen. To freeze, place an unpeeled piece of ginger in a freezer bag. You can grate or slice ginger while it's frozen. To grate ginger, hold a piece of unpeeled ginger at a 45-degree angle and rub it across a fine grating surface. Young ginger that has a pale, thin skin needs no peeling; however, peel the tough skin of older ginger before grating.

[61]

Warm Chicken Salad with Oranges and Almonds

[*With its enticing colors and irresistible mix of fruity-sweet flavor and vinegar tang, this salad is perfect special-luncheon fare. For added crunch, serve topped with croutons.*]

Start to Finish: *20 minutes*   **Servings:** *4*

- 2 medium oranges
- 6 cups torn romaine
- 1 medium red sweet pepper, cut into bite-size strips
- ½ of a small red onion, halved and thinly sliced
- ⅓ cup slivered or sliced almonds, toasted
- 1 pound skinless, boneless chicken breast strips for stir-frying or 1 pound skinless, boneless chicken breast halves, cut into thin bite-size strips
- 1 tablespoon olive oil
- ⅓ cup orange juice
- 1 tablespoon red wine vinegar
- 1 tablespoon olive oil
- 1 teaspoon Dijon-style mustard
- Coarsely ground black pepper

[1] Peel oranges. Cut into ¼-inch slices; quarter each orange slice. In a large salad bowl toss together orange slices, romaine, sweet pepper, onion, and almonds. Set aside.

[2] Season chicken with salt and black pepper. In a large skillet heat oil. Cook and stir chicken in hot oil for 4 to 5 minutes or until no longer pink. Remove skillet from heat. Toss chicken with mixture in salad bowl. Divide salad among four dinner plates.

[3] Stir orange juice and vinegar into the hot skillet, scraping up any brown bits in the skillet. Whisk in 1 tablespoon olive oil and Dijon-style mustard. Serve salad with warm dressing. Season to taste with coarsely ground black pepper.

Nutrition Facts per serving: 310 cal., 16 g total fat (2 g sat. fat), 59 mg chol., 161 mg sodium, 17 g carbo., 5 g fiber, 26 g pro. Daily Values: 45% vit. A, 169% vit. C, 8% calcium, 15% iron

Tuscan Chicken and Rice Salad

[*You can take this hearty, easy-to-tote salad anywhere—to the game, beach, or park—as long as you keep food safety in mind—see note below for toting instructions.*]

Prep: *35 minutes* **Chill:** *4 hours* **Servings:** *6*

1	cup long grain rice
2	cups water
1	2¼-ounce can sliced ripe olives, drained
½	cup roasted red sweet peppers, drained and chopped
½	cup cooked or canned garbanzo beans, drained
¼	cup thinly sliced green onions
1	6- or 6½-ounce jar marinated artichoke hearts
12	ounces skinless, boneless chicken breasts
2	teaspoons chili powder
½	teaspoon dried rosemary, crushed
½	cup crumbled feta cheese with basil and tomato or plain crumbled feta cheese (2 ounces)

[1] In a medium saucepan combine rice and water. Bring to boiling; reduce heat. Cover and simmer about 15 minutes or until water is absorbed. Place rice in a colander; rinse with cold water. Set aside to drain.

[2] In a large salad bowl combine olives, roasted sweet peppers, garbanzo beans, and green onions. Drain artichokes, reserving marinade. Chop artichokes; add to salad mixture along with cooked rice.

[3] Cut chicken into bite-size strips. Sprinkle with chili powder and rosemary. In a large nonstick skillet cook chicken in 1 tablespoon of the reserved artichoke marinade over medium heat for 3 to 4 minutes or until no pink remains.

[4] Add cooked chicken to rice mixture along with remaining marinade. Add feta cheese, tossing gently to combine. Cover and chill for 4 to 24 hours.

Nutrition Facts per serving: 264 cal., 8 g total fat (2 g sat. fat), 38 mg chol., 376 mg sodium, 33 g carbo., 2 g fiber, 16 g pro. Daily Values: 13% vit. A, 71% vit. C, 7% calcium, 19% iron

To Tote: Transfer chilled salad to a bowl with a lid. Pack on ice in an insulated cooler.

Peanut-Crusted Chicken Salad

[*With their jazzy coating of basil, red pepper, and peanuts, the quickly fried chicken breasts crown a bed of fresh greens tossed with tomatoes, oranges, mozzarella cheese, and balsamic vinaigrette. The result? Fried chicken like you've never had it before!*]

Prep: *35 minutes* **Cook:** *10 minutes* **Servings:** 6

- ½   cup finely chopped peanuts
- 3   tablespoons fine dry bread crumbs
- 1   tablespoon snipped fresh basil
- ¼   to ½ teaspoon crushed red pepper
- 4   medium skinless, boneless chicken breast halves
- 1   slightly beaten egg white or 2 tablespoons milk
- 2   tablespoons cooking oil
- 8   cups torn mixed greens
- 3   medium oranges, peeled and sectioned
- 3   medium tomatoes, cored and cut into wedges
- 8   ounces fresh mozzarella cheese, cut into ¼-inch-thick slices and quartered
- 1   recipe Balsamic Vinaigrette

[1] In a shallow dish stir together the peanuts, bread crumbs, basil, and crushed red pepper. Set aside.

[2] Brush both sides of each piece of chicken with egg white or milk. Dip in peanut mixture, pressing firmly to coat. In a large skillet heat oil. Cook the chicken in hot oil over medium-low heat for 10 to 12 minutes or until no longer pink, turning once. Cool slightly. Cut chicken into ½-inch slices.

[3] Meanwhile, in a very large bowl combine mixed greens, oranges, tomatoes, and mozzarella cheese. Shake Balsamic Vinaigrette. Drizzle vinaigrette over all, tossing to coat. Spoon salad onto a serving platter. Top with sliced chicken.

Balsamic Vinaigrette: In a screw-top jar combine 3 tablespoons olive oil or salad oil, 3 tablespoons balsamic vinegar, 1 tablespoon snipped fresh basil, ¼ teaspoon salt, ¼ teaspoon crushed red pepper, and ¼ teaspoon freshly ground black pepper. Cover and shake well.

Nutrition Facts per serving: 420 cal., 27 g total fat (8 g sat. fat), 73 mg chol., 429 mg sodium, 15 g carbo., 4 g fiber, 30 g pro. Daily Values: 17% vit. A, 53% vit. C, 25% calcium, 10% iron

Curried Chicken and Pasta Salad

[*Chicken salad takes an adventurous turn when you add the worldly flavors of papaya and curry. Choose a fresh papaya—free from bruises and soft spots—that is at least half yellow and feels somewhat soft when pressed. If it feels firm, ripen at room temperature 3 to 5 days until yellow to yellow-orange.*]

Start to Finish: *40 minutes*   **Servings:** *4*

1	cup dried gemelli or rotini pasta
1	small pineapple
1	small papaya
5	cups shredded romaine
1½	cups cubed cooked chicken
½	cup light mayonnaise dressing or salad dressing
1	tablespoon honey
1	tablespoon rice vinegar or white vinegar
1	teaspoon curry powder
1	teaspoon toasted sesame oil
1	to 2 fresh jalapeño peppers, seeded and chopped (see tip, page 21)
2	tablespoons cashew halves and pieces, toasted (optional)

[1] Cook pasta according to package directions. Drain pasta. Rinse with cold water; drain again. Meanwhile, to prepare pineapple, remove crown. Wash and peel pineapple; remove eyes and core. Slice pineapple; cut slices in half. To prepare papaya, peel, halve, and scoop out seeds. Slice papaya.

[2] In a large salad bowl combine cooked pasta, pineapple, papaya, romaine, and chicken. Toss lightly to mix. Divide salad among four plates.

[3] For dressing, in a small mixing bowl stir together mayonnaise dressing, honey, rice vinegar, curry powder, sesame oil, and jalapeño peppers. Drizzle dressing over salads. If desired, sprinkle with cashew halves and pieces.

Nutrition Facts per serving: 411 cal., 18 g total fat (4 g sat. fat), 51 mg chol., 305 mg sodium, 42 g carbo., 3 g fiber, 21 g pro. Daily Values: 26% vit. A, 103% vit. C, 4% calcium, 20% iron

[67]

Seafood Salad with Green Goddess Dressing

[*With fennel, seafood, and herblike salad greens known as mesclun, this recipe makes a wonderfully fresh and elegant one-dish meal. And, if you omit the seafood, it makes a terrific side-dish salad, too.*]

Start to Finish: *25 minutes*   **Servings:** *4*

4	cups mesclun or torn mixed salad greens
1	medium fennel bulb, cut into very thin wedges (1½ cups)
½	cup sliced celery
6	ounces fresh or frozen peeled, cooked shrimp
6	ounces cooked lobster meat, cut into bite-size pieces
¾	cup packed fresh parsley sprigs
⅓	cup mayonnaise or salad dressing
3	tablespoons dairy sour cream
3	tablespoons plain low-fat yogurt
2	tablespoons sliced green onion
1	tablespoon vinegar
1	tablespoon snipped fresh basil or 1 teaspoon dried basil, crushed
2	teaspoons anchovy paste or 1 large anchovy filet, cut up
1	clove garlic, halved
1	teaspoon snipped fresh tarragon or ¼ teaspoon dried tarragon, crushed

[1] In a large salad bowl toss together salad greens, fennel, and celery. Top with shrimp and lobster; set aside.

[2] For dressing, in a food processor bowl or blender container combine parsley, mayonnaise, sour cream, yogurt, green onion, vinegar, basil, anchovy paste, garlic, and tarragon. Cover and process or blend until nearly smooth. Drizzle ¼ cup of the dressing over salad, tossing gently. Pass remaining salad dressing.

Nutrition Facts per serving: 276 cal., 19 g total fat (4 g sat. fat), 127 mg chol., 440 mg sodium, 8 g carbo., 10 g fiber, 21 g pro. Daily Values: 25% vit. A, 55% vit. C, 12% calcium, 20% iron

To Tote: Transfer salad mixture to a bowl with a lid. Pour dressing into a separate container. Pack the salad and dressing on ice in an insulated cooler. Just before serving, drizzle the salad with the dressing.

Scallop Stir-Fry Salad

[*So many flavors and textures—all brought together in so little time! That's the essence of this quick-toss salad meal. If your market doesn't offer bay scallops, you can substitute the larger sea scallops. Cut them in half crosswise before cooking.*]

Start to Finish: *30 minutes* **Servings:** *4*

 2   tablespoons orange juice
 2   tablespoons reduced-sodium soy sauce
 1   tablespoon rice wine vinegar or white wine vinegar
 1   teaspoon sugar
 1   teaspoon toasted sesame oil
12   ounces bay scallops
 1   cup fresh snow pea pods, strings and tips removed
 2   tablespoons cooking oil
 1   medium red sweet pepper, coarsely chopped
½   cup sliced green onions
 1   8-ounce jar baby corn, rinsed and drained
 2   cups shredded Chinese cabbage
 2   cups shredded fresh spinach or romaine

[1] In a small bowl stir together orange juice, soy sauce, wine vinegar, sugar, and sesame oil; set aside. Rinse scallops; pat dry. Halve pea pods lengthwise. Pour 1 tablespoon of the cooking oil into a wok or large skillet. Preheat over medium-high heat. Cook and stir scallops in hot oil for 3 to 4 minutes or until scallops are opaque. Remove scallops from wok.

[2] Add remaining cooking oil to wok. Cook and stir pea pods, sweet pepper, and green onions for 2 to 3 minutes or until crisp-tender. Add cooked scallops, corn, and orange juice mixture to wok. Cook and stir about 1 minute or until heated through. Remove from heat.

[3] In a large salad bowl combine the cabbage and spinach. Top with scallop mixture, tossing lightly to combine.

Nutrition Facts per serving: 171 cal., 9 g total fat (1 g sat. fat), 26 mg chol., 421 mg sodium, 10 g carbo., 3 g fiber, 15 g pro. Daily Values: 40% vit. A, 113% vit. C, 10% calcium, 21% iron

Mexican Fiesta Salad

[*Often salads require last-minute preparation. Not this one. Though you can serve it immediately, it will also keep for 24 hours. Why not stir it up this morning and enjoy it for a fuss-free supper tonight?*]

Start to Finish: *30 minutes* **Servings:** *4*

2	cups dried penne or rotini pasta
½	cup frozen whole kernel corn
½	cup light dairy sour cream
⅓	cup mild or medium chunky salsa
1	tablespoon snipped fresh cilantro
1	tablespoon lime juice
1	15-ounce can black beans, rinsed and drained
1	cup chopped Roma tomatoes
1	cup chopped zucchini
½	cup shredded sharp cheddar cheese (2 ounces)

[1] Cook pasta according to package directions, adding the corn the last 5 minutes of cooking. Drain pasta and corn. Rinse with cold water; drain again.

[2] Meanwhile, for dressing, in a small bowl stir together sour cream, salsa, cilantro, and lime juice. Set dressing aside.

[3] In a large salad bowl combine pasta mixture, black beans, Roma tomatoes, zucchini, and cheddar cheese. Pour dressing over pasta mixture, tossing lightly to coat.

Nutrition Facts per serving: 373 cal., 9 g total fat (4 g sat. fat), 19 mg chol., 470 mg sodium, 61 g carbo., 7 g fiber, 20 g pro. Daily Values: 15% vit. A, 36% vit. C, 15% calcium, 23% iron

To Make Ahead: Prepare salad, except do not add tomatoes. Cover and chill for up to 24 hours. After chilling, if necessary, stir in enough milk to make desired consistency. Stir in tomatoes just before serving.

To Tote: Transfer salad to a bowl with a lid. Pack on ice in an insulated cooler.

Middle Eastern Bulgur and Spinach Salad

[*Go with the grain! Bulgur, a Middle-Eastern staple, offers comfort and heartiness in this satisfying vegetarian combination of fruits, vegetables, and legumes.*]

Start to Finish: *30 minutes*   **Servings:** *4*

- 1   **cup bulgur**
- 1   **cup boiling water**
- ½   **cup plain yogurt**
- ¼   **cup bottled red wine vinaigrette salad dressing**
- 2   **tablespoons snipped fresh parsley**
- ½   **teaspoon ground cumin**
- 6   **cups torn fresh spinach**
- 1   **15-ounce can garbanzo beans, rinsed and drained**
- 1   **cup coarsely chopped apple**
- ½   **of a medium red onion, thinly sliced and separated into rings**

[1] In a medium bowl combine bulgur and boiling water. Let stand about 10 minutes or until bulgur has absorbed all the water. Cool 15 minutes more.

[2] Meanwhile, for dressing, in a small bowl stir together yogurt, vinaigrette salad dressing, parsley, and cumin.

[3] In a large salad bowl combine bulgur, spinach, garbanzo beans, apple, red onion, and if desired, 3 tablespoons raisins. Pour dressing over salad, tossing lightly to coat.

Nutrition Facts per serving: 340 cal., 11 g total fat (2 g sat. fat), 2 mg chol., 673 mg sodium, 53 g carbo., 16 g fiber, 13 g pro. Daily Values: 58% vit. A, 55% vit. C, 16% calcium, 40% iron

The Magic Bean

Beans are not only hearty, filling, and virtually fat-free, they're also a good way to add fiber—especially soluble fiber—to the diet. What's so important about fiber? For starters, soluble fiber can help lower blood cholesterol. Fiber also aids in digestion, and a diet low in fat and high in fiber may help reduce the risk of some types of cancer. Need more reasons to fill your pantry with the humble bean? They're also high in protein, complex carbohydrates, and iron—not to mention an inexpensive and satisfying substitute for (or way to stretch) meat.

Layered Polenta
Casserole
Page 117

[*Meat*]

Rotini–Kielbasa Skillet
Page 121

[72]

Braised Lamb
Shanks
Page 112

Hamburger Pie

[*Enjoy the bold Italian flavors of sausage and tomato sauce bubbling under a savory mashed potato crust. Use homemade mashed potatoes or timesaving refrigerated mashed potatoes for the savory topping.*]

Prep: *25 minutes* **Bake:** *30 minutes* **Stand:** *5 minutes* **Servings:** *6* **Oven:** *375°*

¾ cup shredded pizza cheese or Italian-blend cheeses (3 ounces)
2 cups mashed potatoes* or refrigerated mashed potatoes
4 ounces sweet Italian sausage
8 ounces lean ground beef
½ cup chopped onion
2 cups sliced zucchini or yellow summer squash
1 14½-ounce can chunky pasta-style tomatoes
½ of a 6-ounce can (⅓ cup) tomato paste
¼ teaspoon pepper

[1] Stir ½ cup of the cheese into the potatoes; set aside. Remove casings from sausage, if present. In a large skillet cook sausage, ground beef, and onion until meat is no longer pink and onion is tender. Drain fat. Stir in squash, undrained tomatoes, tomato paste, and pepper. Bring to boiling. Transfer mixture to a 2-quart casserole.

[2] Spoon mashed potato mixture into a large pastry bag fitted with a large round tip. Starting at one end, fill in the center of the casserole with rows of the mashed potato mixture until the meat mixture is covered. (Or, spoon mashed potato mixture in mounds on top of hot mixture.) Sprinkle with remaining cheese. If desired, sprinkle with paprika.

[3] Bake in a 375° oven for 30 minutes or until mashed potato top is golden brown. Let stand 5 minutes before serving. If desired, sprinkle with fresh flat-leaf parsley.

__Note:__ To make mashed potatoes, wash and peel 1 pound of potatoes. Cut into quarters or cubes. Cover and cook in a small amount of boiling salted water for 20 to 25 minutes or until tender. Mash the potatoes until lumps are gone. If desired, add a little milk.

Nutrition Facts per serving: 254 cal., 12 g total fat (3 g sat. fat), 39 mg chol., 644 mg sodium, 21 g carbo., 3 g fiber, 16 g pro. Daily Values: 8% vit. A, 47% vit. C, 2% calcium, 11% iron

To Make Ahead: After bringing meat filling mixture to a boil, divide evenly among six 10-ounce individual casserole dishes. Top with potatoes. Cover with plastic wrap; chill up to 48 hours. To bake, remove plastic wrap. Place casseroles in a 15×10×1-inch baking pan. Cover with foil. Bake, covered, in a 375° oven for 35 minutes. Remove foil. Bake, uncovered, 5 minutes more. Let stand 5 minutes before serving.

Meat

Italian Beef and Spinach Pie

[To add a little spark to dinner, serve a romaine lettuce salad tossed with colorful citrus fruits alongside this hearty lasagna-flavored meat pie.]

Prep: *50 minutes*   **Bake:** *1 hour*   **Stand:** *10 minutes*   **Servings:** *8*   **Oven:** *450°/350°*

1	unbaked 9-inch pastry shell
8	ounces lean ground beef
4	ounces mild ground Italian turkey sausage
¾	cup chopped red and/or yellow sweet pepper
½	cup sliced fresh mushrooms
1	clove garlic, minced
1	cup water
½	cup tomato paste
1½	teaspoons dried Italian seasoning, crushed
½	teaspoon salt
1	10-ounce package frozen chopped spinach, thawed and well drained
⅔	cup light ricotta cheese
¾	cup shredded mozzarella cheese (4 ounces)
1	cup chopped tomato

[1] Line pastry shell with a double thickness of foil. Bake in a 450° oven for 8 minutes. Remove foil. Bake 4 to 5 minutes more or until set and dry; set aside.

[2] In a medium skillet cook beef, sausage, sweet pepper, mushrooms, and garlic until meat is brown and vegetables are tender; drain fat. Stir in water, tomato paste, Italian seasoning, and salt. Bring to boiling; reduce heat. Cover and simmer for 10 minutes.

[3] Meanwhile, in a medium bowl stir together spinach, ricotta cheese, and ¼ cup of the mozzarella cheese. Spoon the spinach filling into baked pastry shell. Top with meat mixture. Cover edge of pastry with foil to prevent overbrowning.

[4] Bake in a 350° oven for 45 minutes. Remove foil. Top with tomato and remaining ½ cup mozzarella cheese. Bake 2 minutes more or until heated through and cheese is just melted. Let stand 10 minutes before serving. If desired, garnish with fresh oregano sprigs.

Nutrition Facts per serving: 290 cal., 16 g total fat (5 g sat. fat), 33 mg chol., 417 mg sodium, 22 g carbo., 2 g fiber, 16 g pro. Daily Values: 34% vit. A, 51% vit. C, 12% calcium, 19% iron

Meat

Southwestern Stuffed Pizza

[If the crust is your favorite part of the pizza, then a stuffed pizza is definitely for you—it has a top and bottom crust. Thanks to a hot roll mix, the crust here is made fresh, yet simple.]

Prep: *40 minutes* **Bake:** *30 minutes* **Servings:** *8* **Oven:** *375°*

1½	pounds ground beef
1	12-ounce jar (1½ cups) salsa
1	8-ounce can whole kernel corn, drained
1½	cups shredded cheddar cheese (6 ounces)
½	cup sliced pitted ripe olives
2	to 3 tablespoons snipped fresh cilantro
¾	teaspoon ground cumin
¼	teaspoon pepper
1	16-ounce package hot roll mix
¼	cup cornmeal
½	teaspoon ground cumin
1	beaten egg

[1] For filling, in a very large skillet cook ground beef until brown. Drain fat. Stir in salsa, corn, cheese, olives, cilantro, the ¾ teaspoon cumin, and pepper. Set aside.

[2] Prepare hot roll mix according to package directions, except stir the cornmeal and the ½ teaspoon cumin into the flour mixture and increase hot tap water to 1¼ cups. Turn dough out onto a lightly floured surface. Knead about 5 minutes or until smooth and elastic. Divide dough in half. Cover and let rest 5 minutes.

[3] Meanwhile, grease an 11- to 13-inch pizza pan. If desired, sprinkle with additional cornmeal. On a lightly floured surface, roll each half of dough into a circle 1 inch larger than the pizza pan. Transfer one crust to pan. Spread meat mixture over dough. Cut several slits in remaining crust or prick with the tines of a fork. Place top crust on meat mixture. With moist fingers, pinch top and bottom edges together to seal. Brush with beaten egg. If desired, sprinkle with grated Parmesan cheese or additional cornmeal.

[4] Bake in a 375° oven for 30 to 35 minutes or until pastry is deep golden and the meat and vegetable filling is bubbly.

Nutrition Facts per serving: 551 cal., 23 g total fat (9 g sat. fat), 114 mg chol., 789 mg sodium, 54 g carbo., 2 g fiber, 32 g pro. Daily Values: 11% vit. A, 10% vit. C, 18% calcium, 23% iron

Beef and Bean Burritos

[*Traditional burritos aren't exactly low-fat fare. So we've replaced some of the meat with black or pinto beans and used reduced-fat cheese to help keep the fat in check. Packed with savory spices and served on a bed of spinach and lettuce, the burrito becomes a satisfying and healthful dinner.*]

Prep: *25 minutes*   **Bake:** *20 minutes*   **Servings:** *8*   **Oven:** *350°*

8	8-inch flour tortillas
8	ounces lean ground beef
1	cup chopped onion
2	cloves garlic, minced
1	15-ounce can black beans or pinto beans, rinsed and drained
½	cup salsa
2	teaspoons chili powder
	Several dashes bottled hot pepper sauce
1	cup shredded reduced-fat cheddar cheese (4 ounces)
1½	cups shredded fresh spinach
1½	cups shredded lettuce

[1] Stack tortillas; wrap in foil. Heat in a 350° oven for 10 minutes to soften. Meanwhile, for filling, in a large skillet cook beef, onion, and garlic until meat is brown and onion is tender. Drain fat. Stir in beans, salsa, chili powder, and hot pepper sauce. Heat through.

[2] Spoon about ⅓ cup filling onto each tortilla and top with 1 tablespoon cheese. Fold bottom edge up and over filling, just until covered. Fold in opposite sides. Roll up, tucking in sides. Secure with wooden toothpicks. Arrange tortillas, seam side down, on a foil-lined baking sheet; cover with foil. Bake in a 350° oven about 10 minutes or until heated.

[3] Serve burritos on a mixture of spinach and lettuce. Sprinkle with remaining cheese. If desired, serve with additional salsa and dairy sour cream.

Nutrition Facts per serving: 238 cal., 9 g total fat (4 g sat. fat), 25 mg chol., 417 mg sodium, 25 g carbo., 4 g fiber, 15 g pro. **Daily Values:** 9% vit. A, 8% vit. C, 17% calcium, 15% iron

Moo Shu-Style Beef and Cabbage Wraps

[*The secret to our moo-shu-made-easy is sweet, tongue-tingling hoisin sauce. This condiment is made with fermented soybeans, molasses, vinegar, mustard, sesame seed, garlic, and chilies, allowing you to bring all these wonderful flavors to the dish with just one pour. Find it next to soy sauce at the supermarket.*]

Start to Finish: *20 minutes*　**Servings:** *4*　**Oven:** *350°*

8	8-inch flour tortillas
12	ounces lean ground beef
½	cup chopped red or green onion
2	cups packaged shredded cabbage with carrot (coleslaw mix)
1	cup fresh cut or frozen whole kernel corn
¼	cup hoisin sauce
1	teaspoon toasted sesame oil

[1] Stack tortillas; wrap in foil. Heat in a 350° oven for 10 minutes to soften. Meanwhile, for filling, in a large skillet cook beef and onion until meat is brown. Drain fat. Stir in cabbage and corn. Cover and cook about 4 minutes or until vegetables are tender, stirring once. Stir in hoisin sauce and sesame oil. Cook and stir until heated through.

[2] Spoon ½ cup filling onto each tortilla just below center. Fold bottom edge up and over filling. Fold in opposite sides just until they meet. Roll up from bottom. If desired, serve with additional hoisin sauce.

Nutrition Facts per serving: 431 cal., 14 g total fat (5 g sat. fat), 54 mg chol., 604 mg sodium, 52 g carbo., 4 g fiber, 21 g pro. Daily Values: 20% vit. A, 37% vit. C, 7% calcium, 25% iron

Herbed Beef Pinwheels

[These pinwheels are a take on "brasciole," a vegetable-stuffed meat roll much loved in Italy. Here we've transformed this continental classic into an American one-dish meal by roasting the potatoes and onions right alongside the meat.]

Prep: *25 minutes*   **Bake:** *1¼ hours*   **Servings:** *4*   **Oven:** *350°*

1	1- to 1¼-pound beef flank steak
2	tablespoons olive oil or cooking oil
2	medium leeks, sliced (⅔ cup total)
2	cloves garlic, minced
3	tablespoons snipped fresh basil
¼	teaspoon salt
⅛	teaspoon pepper
2	Yukon gold potatoes, cut into eighths
1	large onion, cut into thin wedges
1	14½-ounce can diced tomatoes with basil, oregano, and garlic

[1] Score meat by making shallow diagonal cuts at 1-inch intervals in a diamond pattern on both sides. Place between two pieces of plastic wrap. Working from center to edges, use flat side of meat mallet to pound steak into a 12×8-inch rectangle. Remove wrap; set aside.

[2] In a large skillet heat 1 tablespoon of the oil over medium-high heat. Add leeks and garlic. Cook 3 to 5 minutes or until leek is tender. Stir in basil, salt, and pepper. Remove from heat. Spread leek mixture evenly on one side of steak. Starting at a short end, tightly roll up meat into a spiral. Tie string around steak in four evenly spaced places. In same large skillet heat remaining oil over medium-high heat. Brown meat on all sides in the hot oil. Transfer meat to a 2-quart rectangular baking dish.

[3] Arrange potatoes and onion wedges around meat in dish. Pour undrained tomatoes over beef and vegetables. Bake, uncovered, in a 350° oven for 1¼ to 1½ hours or until beef is tender. Transfer meat to a cutting board. Cut into serving-size pieces. Remove string. Serve with vegetables.

Nutrition Facts per serving: 355 cal., 15 g total fat (4 g sat. fat), 53 mg chol., 722 mg sodium, 30 g carbo., 4 g fiber, 25 g pro. Daily Values: 7% vit. A, 49% vit. C, 6% calcium, 27% iron

To Make Ahead: Score and pound meat. Prepare leek filling and spread on meat. Roll up and tie, but do not brown meat before refrigerating. Wrap tightly and place in refrigerator for up to 24 hours. To cook, brown meat roll in hot oil in a large skillet; transfer meat to baking dish with vegetables and bake as directed above.

Steak and Pepper Fajitas

[*Drive right past the long line at a drive-through and head home to a fresher, more colorful Mexican dish that's ready in 20 minutes. It's a fun-to-eat way to sneak a little veggie action into a kid's diet.*]

Prep: *10 minutes* **Cook:** *10 minutes* **Servings:** *8*

- 12 ounces beef flank steak or boneless beef sirloin steak
- 8 8-inch plain or flavored flour tortillas
- 1 tablespoon cooking oil
- 2 cloves garlic, minced
- 1 large onion, cut into thin wedges
- 1 small red sweet pepper, cut into bite-size strips
- 1 small green or yellow sweet pepper, cut into bite-size strips
- 1 cup packaged shredded cabbage with carrot (coleslaw mix)
- ⅓ cup bottled stir-fry sauce

[1] Slice steak across grain into thin bite-size strips; set aside. Stack tortillas; wrap in foil. Heat in a 350° oven for 10 minutes to soften; or, heat according to package directions.

[2] Meanwhile, in a large skillet heat oil over medium-high heat. Add beef and garlic. Cook and stir for 2 minutes. Add onion and sweet peppers; cook and stir for 4 to 5 minutes more or until vegetables are crisp-tender. Stir in cabbage and stir-fry sauce; heat through.

[3] To serve, using tongs or a slotted spoon fill warm tortillas with the beef-vegetable mixture. Roll up tortillas.

Nutrition Facts per serving: 197 cal., 7 g total fat (2 g sat. fat), 17 mg chol., 499 mg sodium, 21 g carbo., 2 g fiber, 12 g pro. Daily Values: 19% vit. A, 50% vit. C, 5% calcium, 10% iron

Steak and Winter Squash Skillet

[Smoky bacon, sweet winter squash, beef, herbs, and robust tomatoes—it's amazing what just seven ingredients (and only 15 minutes of preparation time) can do to bring such a variety of flavors to a dish.]

Prep: *15 minutes*   **Cook:** *1¼ hours*   **Servings:** *4*

- 1 **pound boneless beef round steak**
- 3 **slices bacon**
- ½ **teaspoon seasoned salt**
- 1 **14½-ounce can diced tomatoes with green peppers and onion**
- 1 **medium onion, halved and sliced**
- 1 **teaspoon dried marjoram, crushed**
- 1 **medium butternut squash (about 1½ pounds), peeled, halved, seeded, and cut into 1½-inch pieces**

[1] Trim fat from beef. Cut beef into four serving-size pieces; set aside. In a large skillet cook bacon until crisp. Remove bacon, reserving 2 tablespoons drippings in skillet; drain bacon on paper towels, crumble, and set aside in the refrigerator.

[2] Sprinkle beef with seasoned salt. Brown beef on both sides in reserved drippings over medium heat. Add undrained tomatoes, onion, and marjoram to skillet. Bring to boiling; reduce heat. Cover and simmer for 20 minutes. Add squash to skillet. Cover and simmer for 55 minutes more or until beef and squash are tender. To serve, sprinkle bacon over top.

Nutrition Facts per serving: 337 cal., 14 g total fat (5 g sat. fat), 82 mg chol., 684 mg sodium, 22 g carbo., 4 g fiber, 31 g pro. Daily Values: 90% vit. A, 46% vit. C, 6% calcium, 24% iron

Mixed Bags

The prepackaged salad revolution is underway, taking over produce aisles. The selection of pretrimmed lettuce packages—once limited to head lettuce and carrot, coleslaw, or Caesar salad mixtures—has truly blossomed into a salad-lover's paradise, with all sorts of exotic names and blends of gourmet greens. Most can be simply tossed with your favorite dressings, but consider these uses, too:

❚ Southern Shortcut: Stir a little mayonnaise and milk into a coleslaw mix and spoon it on a sandwich for added color and crunch.

❚ Niçoise in No Time: Toss mesclun—that South-of-France-inspired melange of baby greens—with pitted black olives, tuna, tomatoes, red onions, and a good garlicky vinaigrette for a quick main-dish salad.

❚ Greek Treat: Toss a romaine blend with tomatoes, feta, red onions, and pitted kalamata olives with a lemon-sparked olive oil dressing.

[83]

Orange-Beef Stir-Fry

[This version of the classic Szechwan recipe is a bit less pungent than you might find at a Chinese restaurant. We've also added spinach and water chestnuts for extra color and crunch.]

Prep: *30 minutes* **Cook:** *6 minutes* **Servings:** *4*

12	ounces beef top round steak
1	teaspoon finely shredded orange peel
½	cup orange juice
1	tablespoon cornstarch
1	tablespoon soy sauce
1	teaspoon sugar
1	teaspoon instant beef bouillon granules
2	tablespoons cooking oil
4	green onions, bias-sliced into 1-inch pieces
1	clove garlic, minced
5	cups coarsely shredded fresh spinach (5 to 6 ounces)
½	of an 8-ounce can sliced water chestnuts, drained
3	cups hot cooked rice

[1] Trim fat from beef. Partially freeze beef. Thinly slice across the grain into bite-size strips. Set aside. For sauce, in a small bowl stir together orange peel, orange juice, cornstarch, soy sauce, sugar, and bouillon granules. Set aside.

[2] In a wok or large skillet heat 1 tablespoon of the oil over medium-high heat. Add green onions and garlic; cook and stir in hot oil for 1 minute. Remove onion mixture from wok using a slotted spoon. Add remaining 1 tablespoon oil to wok or skillet. Add beef to hot wok. (Add more oil as necessary during cooking.) Cook and stir for 2 to 3 minutes or to desired doneness. Push beef from center of wok.

[3] Stir sauce. Add sauce to center of wok. Cook and stir until thickened and bubbly. Return green onion mixture to wok. Add spinach and water chestnuts. Stir all ingredients together to coat with sauce. Cover and cook for 1 minute more or until heated through. Serve immediately over hot cooked rice. If desired, garnish with slivered orange-peel strips and additional green onions.

Nutrition Facts per serving: 366 cal., 9 g total fat (2 g sat. fat), 37 mg chol., 527 mg sodium, 45 g carbo., 3 g fiber, 25 g pro. Daily Values: 25% vit. A, 38% vit. C, 8% calcium, 26% iron

Linguine with Steak and Spicy Garlic Sauce

[*This recipe updates the classic pepper steak by calling on red pepper or tomato pasta for a clever, contemporary touch. And with six cloves of garlic in the fresh and simple sauce, you know it's going to be good. When buying garlic, choose plump heads and store in a cool, dry place.*]

Start to Finish: *25 minutes*   **Servings:** *4*

1	9-ounce package refrigerated tomato or red pepper linguine or fettuccine
1	small yellow summer squash or zucchini, halved lengthwise and sliced
1	medium green sweet pepper, cut into bite-size strips
½	teaspoon coarsely ground black pepper
8	ounces beef top loin steak, cut ¾ inch thick
1	tablespoon olive oil or cooking oil
½	cup chicken broth
¼	cup dry white wine
6	cloves garlic, minced

[1] Cook pasta according to package directions, adding summer squash and sweet pepper the last 2 minutes of cooking; drain. Return pasta and vegetables to saucepan.

[2] Meanwhile, rub black pepper onto both sides of steak. In a large skillet heat oil. Cook steak in hot oil over medium heat to desired doneness, turning once. (Allow 10 to 12 minutes for medium doneness.) Remove meat from skillet.

[3] For sauce, stir broth, wine, and garlic into skillet. Bring to boiling; reduce heat. Simmer, uncovered, for 2 minutes. Remove skillet from heat. Cut steak into thin bite-size strips. Pour sauce over pasta mixture; add steak slices. Toss gently to combine. Transfer pasta-meat mixture onto a warm serving platter.

Nutrition Facts per serving: 247 cal., 13 g total fat (4 g sat. fat), 49 mg chol., 238 mg sodium, 13 g carbo., 1 g fiber, 18 g pro. Daily Values: 5% vit. A, 36% vit. C, 6% calcium, 16% iron

South-of-the-Border Steak and Beans

[Queso fresco (pronounced KAY-so FRESK-o) means "fresh cheese." This semisalty Mexican cheese, found in Hispanic specialty food stores, makes a terrific topper for this chili-spiced mixture.]

Prep: *25 minutes*   **Cook:** *7½ hours*   **Servings:** *6*

1½	pounds beef flank steak
1	10-ounce can chopped tomatoes and green chili peppers
½	cup chopped onion
2	cloves garlic, minced
1	tablespoon snipped fresh oregano or 1 teaspoon dried oregano, crushed
1	teaspoon chili powder
1	teaspoon ground cumin
¼	teaspoon salt
¼	teaspoon black pepper
2	small green, red, and/or yellow sweet peppers, cut into strips
1	15-ounce can pinto beans, rinsed and drained
3	cups hot cooked rice

[1] Trim fat from meat. Place meat in a 3½- or 4-quart electric crockery cooker. In a bowl stir together undrained tomatoes, onion, garlic, dried oregano (if using), chili powder, cumin, salt, and black pepper. Pour over meat.

[2] Cover and cook on low-heat setting for 7 to 9 hours or on high-heat setting for 3½ to 4½ hours.

[3] If using low-heat setting, turn to high-heat setting. Add sweet pepper strips and pinto beans. Cover and cook for 30 minutes more. Remove meat; cool slightly. Shred or thinly slice meat across the grain. Stir fresh oregano (if using) into bean mixture.

[4] To serve, spoon rice into soup bowls. Arrange meat on top of rice. Spoon bean mixture over meat. If desired, sprinkle with crumbled queso fresco or feta cheese and additional snipped fresh oregano.

Nutrition Facts per serving: 345 cal., 9 g total fat (4 g sat. fat), 53 mg chol., 642 mg sodium, 37 g carbo., 4 g fiber, 28 g pro. Daily Values: 4% vit. A, 30% vit. C, 5% calcium, 33% iron

[87]

Beef-Vegetable Ragout

[*This recipe fits the bill for casual get-togethers, and it's prepared in only 30 minutes. Spoon the mixture over pasta and serve with crusty bread or corn bread and wedges of melon. Such a hearty and impressive main course calls for a simple finish—a refreshing sorbet and sugar cookies would be just perfect.*]

Start to Finish: *30 minutes*　**Servings:** *4*

12	ounces beef tenderloin
1	tablespoon olive oil or cooking oil
1½	cups sliced fresh shiitake or button mushrooms (4 ounces)
½	cup chopped onion
2	cloves garlic, minced
3	tablespoons all-purpose flour
½	teaspoon salt
¼	teaspoon pepper
1	14½-ounce can beef broth
¼	cup port wine or dry sherry
2	cups sugar snap peas or one 10-ounce package frozen sugar snap peas, thawed
1	cup cherry tomatoes, halved

[1] Cut beef into ¾-inch pieces. In a large nonstick skillet heat oil. Cook and stir meat in hot oil for 2 to 3 minutes or until meat is of desired doneness. Remove meat; set aside. In the same skillet cook mushrooms, onion, and garlic until tender.

[2] Stir in flour, salt, and pepper. Add broth and wine. Cook and stir until thickened and bubbly. Stir in sugar snap peas; cook and stir for 2 to 3 minutes more or until peas are tender. Stir in meat and tomatoes; heat through. If desired, serve the meat and vegetable mixture over hot cooked bow-tie pasta or wide noodles.

Nutrition Facts per serving: 252 cal., 9 g total fat (3 g sat. fat), 48 mg chol., 647 mg sodium, 17 g carbo., 3 g fiber, 21 g pro. Daily Values: 4% vit. A, 74% vit. C, 4% calcium, 32% iron

Don't Confuse the Peas, Please!

Sugar snap peas (also called sugar peas), those wonderfully sweet peas encased in an edible pod, should not be confused with snow peas. While both have edible pods, the peas inside the snow pea are tiny, and the pod is almost translucent. The peas inside the sugar snap pea are larger. Each legume yields different flavors and textures.

Asian Beef and Noodle Bowl

[*To speed up this already-speedy recipe, make a short stop at the grocery store and head to the salad bar aisle for prewashed spinach and shredded carrots.*]

Start to Finish: *30 minutes*   **Servings:** *4*

2	3-ounce packages ramen noodles
12	ounces beef flank steak or beef top round steak
2	teaspoons chili oil or 2 teaspoons cooking oil plus ⅛ to ¼ teaspoon ground red pepper
1	teaspoon grated fresh ginger
2	cloves garlic, minced
1	cup beef broth
1	tablespoon soy sauce
2	cups torn fresh spinach
1	cup shredded carrots
¼	cup snipped fresh mint or cilantro

[1] In a large saucepan bring 4 cups of water to boiling. If desired, break up noodles; drop noodles into the boiling water. (Do not use the flavor packets.) Return to boiling; boil for 2 to 3 minutes or just until noodles are tender but firm, stirring occasionally. Drain noodles.

[2] Cut beef into bite-size strips. In a wok or large skillet heat oil over medium-high heat. Cook and stir beef, ginger, and garlic in hot oil for 2 to 3 minutes or to desired doneness. Push beef from center of wok. Add broth and soy sauce. Bring to boiling; reduce heat. Stir meat into broth mixture. Cook and stir 1 to 2 minutes more or until heated through.

[3] Add noodles, spinach, carrots, and mint to mixture in wok; toss to combine. Ladle mixture into soup bowls. If desired, sprinkle with chopped peanuts.

Nutrition Facts per serving: 211 cal., 10 g total fat (3 g sat. fat), 47 mg chol., 690 mg sodium, 11 g carbo., 2 g fiber, 20 g pro. Daily Values: 101% vit. A, 23% vit. C, 4% calcium, 26% iron

A Little Dab Will Do!
Much loved in Chinese cookery, chili oil adds a good amount of heat with just a small dose. Made by steeping spicy chilies in vegetable oil, this fiery concoction can be found wherever Asian foods are sold. Store it in the refrigerator.

Creamy Mustard-Mushroom Beef

[*Reminiscent of the French braised meat dish called "pot-au-feu" (literally, pot on the fire), this recipe is a wonderful cross between a home-style Sunday roast and a continental classic. The elegance comes from the sauce—the pan juices meld with sour cream for a rich and creamy finish.*]

Prep: *10 minutes*   **Cook:** *1¾ hours*   **Servings:** *6 to 8*

1	2- to 2½-pound boneless beef round rump roast
2	tablespoons cooking oil
¾	cup beef broth
½	teaspoon dried thyme, crushed
¼	teaspoon dried marjoram, crushed
¼	teaspoon pepper
4	cups halved fresh mushrooms
12	ounces packaged, peeled baby carrots
2	cups frozen small whole onions
1	8-ounce carton dairy sour cream
¼	cup Dijon-style mustard
¼	cup all-purpose flour
3	to 4 cups hot cooked noodles

[1] Trim fat from meat. In a 4- to 6-quart Dutch oven heat oil. Brown meat on all sides in hot oil. Drain fat. Combine broth, thyme, marjoram, and pepper. Carefully pour over meat. Bring to boiling; reduce heat. Cover and simmer for 1¼ hours.

[2] Add mushrooms, carrots, and onions to meat. Return to boiling; reduce heat. Cover and simmer for 30 to 40 minutes or until vegetables are tender. Transfer meat and vegetables to a serving platter. Cover with foil to keep warm.

[3] For sauce, skim fat from pan juices; measure juices. If necessary, add enough water to equal 1⅓ cups. Return to Dutch oven. Stir together sour cream, mustard, and flour. Stir into juices in Dutch oven. Cook and stir over medium heat until thickened and bubbly. Cook and stir 1 minute more. Serve sauce with meat, vegetables, and noodles.

Nutrition Facts per serving: 455 cal., 18 g total fat (7 g sat. fat), 115 mg chol., 465 mg sodium, 38 g carbo., 5 g fiber, 36 g pro. Daily Values: 137% vit. A, 9% vit. C, 7% calcium, 35% iron

Greek Beef

[*Greek cooking often flavors meat with a hint of aromatic spices and fruity sweetness. Here cinnamon and currants add those hallmark Hellenic touches. To keep the Greek theme going, serve with warm pita bread and a green salad garnished with onions, kalamata olives, tomatoes, and feta cheese.*]

Prep: *15 minutes* **Cook:** *2 hours 10 minutes* **Servings:** *6 to 8*

1	2- to 2½-pound boneless beef chuck pot roast
2	tablespoons cooking oil
½	cup beef broth
3	cloves garlic, minced
¼	teaspoon ground cinnamon
¼	teaspoon cracked black pepper
8	carrots, peeled and bias cut into 2-inch pieces
2	large onions, cut into wedges
¼	cup dried currants
1	14½-ounce can diced tomatoes
2	tablespoons tomato paste
3	to 4 cups hot cooked fettuccine

[1] Trim fat from meat. In a 4- to 6-quart Dutch oven heat oil. Brown meat on all sides in hot oil. Drain fat. Combine broth, garlic, cinnamon, and pepper. Carefully pour over meat. Bring to boiling; reduce heat. Cover and simmer for 1¼ hours.

[2] Add carrots, onions, and currants to meat. Return to boiling; reduce heat. Cover and simmer for 50 to 60 minutes or until meat and vegetables are tender. Transfer meat and vegetables to a serving platter; reserve cooking liquid in pan. Cover with foil to keep warm.

[3] For sauce, stir undrained tomatoes and tomato paste into mixture in pan. Bring to boiling; reduce heat. Simmer, uncovered, about 5 minutes or until slightly thickened. Pour some of the sauce over meat and vegetables. Serve with noodles. Pass remaining sauce.

Nutrition Facts per serving: 586 cal., 30 g total fat (11 g sat. fat), 129 mg chol., 308 mg sodium, 43 g carbo., 5 g fiber, 35 g pro. Daily Values: 197% vit. A, 31% vit. C, 9% calcium, 32% iron

Herbed Tenderloin Steaks and Vegetables

[*It's easy to think of one-dish meals as winter fare, but the cook-it-all-together concept works equally well with summertime barbecues, as this garden-fresh vegetable and steak recipe demonstrates. For a simple side, stir purchased roasted garlic into deli mashed potatoes.*]

Prep: *15 minutes*   **Grill:** *8 minutes*   **Servings:** *4*

- 2   cloves garlic
- ¼   cup loosely packed fresh basil leaves
- 2   tablespoons fresh thyme leaves
- 1   tablespoon fresh rosemary
- 1   tablespoon fresh mint leaves
- 2   tablespoons olive oil
- ½   teaspoon salt
- ½   teaspoon pepper
- 4   beef tenderloin steaks, cut 1 inch thick (about 1 pound total)
- 2   large yellow tomatoes, halved crosswise
- 1   pound asparagus spears, trimmed

[1] With food processor or blender running, add garlic through feed tube or lid. Process or blend until garlic is finely chopped. Add basil, thyme, rosemary, and mint. Cover and process or blend until herbs are chopped. With food processor or blender running, add oil in a thin, steady stream. (When necessary, stop food processor or blender and use a rubber scraper to scrape the sides of bowl or container.) Stir in salt and pepper.

[2] Spread some of the herb mixture evenly over both sides of the steaks and over cut sides of tomatoes; set aside. Fold an 18×12-inch piece of heavy foil in half to make a double thickness of foil that measures 9×12 inches. Place asparagus in the center of the foil. Add remaining herb mixture, turning asparagus to coat evenly.

[3] Grill steaks and asparagus (on foil) on the rack of an uncovered grill directly over medium heat for 5 minutes. Turn steaks and asparagus spears; add tomatoes to grill. Grill until steaks are desired doneness. (Allow 3 to 7 minutes more for medium-rare and 7 to 10 minutes for medium doneness.) Grill vegetables until asparagus is crisp-tender and tomatoes are hot (do not turn).

Nutrition Facts per serving: 245 cal., 14 g total fat (4 g sat. fat), 65 mg chol., 322 mg sodium, 6 g carbo., 2 g fiber, 24 g pro. Daily Values: 8% vit. A, 47% vit. C, 3% calcium, 3% iron

Curried Beef and Carrots

[*Can't wait to get to the table after a long day at work? Choose couscous for the side dish—it cooks much more quickly than rice, and it complements the flavors of this dish well.*]

Prep: *15 minutes* **Cook:** *8 hours* **Servings:** *6*

5	medium carrots, cut into 2-inch pieces
1	pound boiling onions, peeled, or 2 cups chopped onion
1	1½- to 2-pound boneless beef chuck pot roast
½	cup apple juice or water
⅓	cup chutney
2	tablespoons quick-cooking tapioca
2	teaspoons curry powder
½	teaspoon ground coriander
½	teaspoon dried mint, crushed
3	cups hot cooked couscous or rice

[1] Place carrots and onions in a 3½- or 4-quart electric crockery cooker. If necessary, cut roast to fit into the cooker. Place meat on top of the vegetables. In a small bowl combine apple juice, chutney, tapioca, curry powder, coriander, and mint. Pour over meat.

[2] Cover and cook on low-heat setting for 8 to 10 hours or on high-heat setting for 4 to 5 hours. Transfer meat and vegetables to a platter. Skim fat from juices. Serve meat, vegetables, and juices with couscous or rice.

Nutrition Facts per serving: 588 cal., 27 g total fat (11 g sat. fat), 113 mg chol., 119 mg sodium, 48 g carbo., 7 g fiber, 36 g pro. Daily Values: 151% vit. A, 23% vit. C, 5% calcium, 32% iron

[95]

Meat

Garden Pot Roast

[Adapt this recipe to whatever vegetables look their freshest at the market. It's based on a popular Rumanian dish that celebrates spring by pairing fresh vegetables with meat.]

Prep: *30 minutes* **Cook:** *2½ hours* **Servings:** *6 plus leftover meat*

- 1 **3-pound beef bottom round roast**
- ½ **to 1 teaspoon cracked black pepper**
- ¼ **teaspoon salt**
- 1 **tablespoon cooking oil**
- 1 **cup beef broth**
- 2 **tablespoons tomato paste**
- ½ **cup coarsely chopped onion**
- 2 **cloves garlic, minced**
- ½ **teaspoon dried marjoram, crushed**
- ½ **teaspoon dried thyme, crushed**
- ⅓ **cup golden raisins**
- 3 **cups vegetables (such as whole green beans, or peeled and cut-up winter squash, parsnips, celery, broccoli, and/or cauliflower)**
- 1 **cup sugar snap peas**
- 1 **tablespoon cornstarch**

[1] Trim fat from meat. Sprinkle with cracked pepper and salt. In a 4- to 6-quart Dutch oven heat oil. Brown meat on all sides in hot oil about 5 minutes. Drain fat. Combine broth and tomato paste. Carefully pour over meat. Add onion, garlic, marjoram, and thyme. Bring to boiling; reduce heat. Cover and simmer for 2 hours or until meat is tender.

[2] Add raisins and (if using) green beans, squash, or parsnips. Return to boiling; reduce heat. Cover and simmer for 10 to 15 minutes more or until vegetables are just tender. Stir in sugar snap peas and (if using) celery, broccoli, or cauliflower. Cook 3 to 4 minutes more or until vegetables are crisp-tender. Transfer meat and vegetables to a serving platter; reserve cooking liquid in pan. Cover platter with foil to keep warm.

[3] For gravy, strain juices into a glass measuring cup. Skim fat from juices; return 1¼ cups juices to Dutch oven (discard remaining juices). In a small bowl stir cornstarch into 2 tablespoons cold water until smooth (or shake together in a screw-top jar). Stir into juices in Dutch oven. Cook and stir until thickened and bubbly. Cook and stir 2 minutes more. Slice meat. Spoon some of the gravy over meat and vegetables. Pass remaining gravy.

Nutrition Facts per serving: 303 cal., 10 g total fat (3 g sat. fat), 82 mg chol., 277 mg sodium, 23 g carbo., 4 g fiber, 30 g pro. Daily Values: 20% vit. A, 30% vit. C, 5% calcium, 29% iron

Italian Pot Roast

[*Fennel brings delicate, licorice-like undertones to the luscious roast. Choose fennel bulbs that are smooth and firm, without cracks and brown spots. The stalks should be crisp, and the leaves should be bright green and fresh-looking.*]

Prep: *25 minutes*   **Roast:** *2 hours 20 minutes*   **Stand:** *15 minutes*   **Servings:** *6 to 8*   **Oven:** *325°*

2	tablespoons fennel seed, crushed
2	tablespoons dried parsley, crushed
4	teaspoons dried Italian seasoning, crushed
1½	teaspoons garlic salt
1	teaspoon pepper
1	3- to 4-pound boneless pork shoulder roast
1	tablespoon cooking oil
5	carrots, quartered
6	small potatoes, peeled
1	large fennel bulb, trimmed and cut into wedges
¼	cup instant-type flour

[1] Combine fennel seed, parsley, Italian seasoning, garlic salt, and pepper; set aside. Untie pork roast and unroll. Trim fat from meat. Rub meat with seasoning mixture. Retie roast with heavy kitchen string. In an oven-going 4- to 6-quart Dutch oven heat oil. Brown pork slowly on all sides. Drain fat.

[2] Carefully pour ¾ cup water over meat. Cover and roast in a 325° oven for 1½ hours. Arrange carrots, potatoes, and fennel around roast in Dutch oven. Cover and roast 50 to 60 minutes more or until vegetables and meat are tender, adding water if necessary. Transfer meat to a serving platter and cover with foil to keep warm; let stand 15 minutes. Remove strings and carve meat. Using a slotted spoon, transfer vegetables to a serving bowl; cover and keep warm.

[3] For gravy, strain juices, if desired, into a glass measuring cup. Skim fat from juices; measure juices. If necessary, add enough water to equal 1½ cups. Return to Dutch oven. Cook over medium-high heat until bubbly. Combine ½ cup cold water and flour, stirring until smooth. Gradually add to the hot pan juices, whisking until smooth and bubbly. Cook and stir 1 minute more. Serve with roast.

Nutrition Facts per serving: 552 cal., 26 g total fat (8 g sat. fat), 149 mg chol., 686 mg sodium, 35 g carbo., 4 g fiber, 43 g pro. Daily Values: 143% vit. A, 21% vit. C, 7% calcium, 30% iron

Peppery Pot Roast

[*Three kinds of pepper—black pepper, red pepper, and hot red pepper sauce—make for one of the most eye-opening pot roasts around! The sweet, earthy flavors of the parsnips, carrots, and potatoes add a nice contrast. Be sure to try the leftover roast on hearty rye bread for a lunchtime sandwich, too.*]

Prep: *20 minutes*   **Cook:** *2 hours*   **Servings:** *8 to 10*

1	2½- to 3-pound boneless beef chuck pot roast
½	teaspoon ground black pepper
¼	teaspoon ground red pepper
2	tablespoons cooking oil
¾	cup vegetable juice
¼	teaspoon bottled hot pepper sauce
4	cloves garlic, minced
1	teaspoon instant beef bouillon granules
½	teaspoon dry mustard
3	medium potatoes, peeled and cut into eighths (1 pound)
3	medium carrots, halved crosswise and halved lengthwise
2	medium parsnips, peeled, halved crosswise, and halved lengthwise
4	stalks celery, bias-sliced into 1-inch pieces (2 cups)
1	medium onion, cut into wedges
¼	cup all-purpose flour

[1] Trim fat from meat. Rub black pepper and red pepper over surface of meat. In a 4-quart Dutch oven heat oil. Brown meat on all sides in hot oil. Drain fat.

[2] Stir together vegetable juice, hot pepper sauce, garlic, bouillon granules, and mustard. Pour over meat. Bring to boiling; reduce heat. Cover and simmer for 1¼ hours.

[3] Add potatoes, carrots, parsnips, celery, and onion to meat mixture. Cover and simmer for 45 to 60 minutes more or until meat and vegetables are tender. Remove meat and vegetables from pan, reserving juices.

[4] For gravy, skim fat from pan juices; measure juices. If necessary, add enough water to juices to equal 1½ cups. Return to Dutch oven. Combine flour and ½ cup cold water. Stir into juices in pan. Cook and stir until thickened and bubbly. Cook and stir 1 minute more. If desired, season to taste with salt. Slice meat. Serve gravy with meat and vegetables.

Nutrition Facts per serving: 434 cal., 25 g total fat (9 g sat. fat), 92 mg chol., 277 mg sodium, 21 g carbo., 3 g fiber, 29 g pro. Daily Values: 50% vit. A, 32% vit. C, 4% calcium, 23% iron

Roasted Beef with Horseradish Potatoes

[*Horseradish and thyme make a great pair, flavoring both the roast and the vegetables. The roast is finished with a simple sauce made by deglazing the pan (that's the simple process of adding liquid to a pan to help loosen the flavorful brown bits left by the meat).*]

Prep: *20 minutes*   **Roast:** *1¾ hours*   **Stand:** *15 minutes*   **Servings:** *8 to 10*   **Oven:** *350°*

1	2½- to 3-pound boneless beef rib eye roast
⅓	cup prepared horseradish
2	tablespoons olive oil
1	teaspoon coarsely ground pepper
1	teaspoon dried thyme, crushed
½	teaspoon salt
2	pounds tiny new potatoes
2	cups packaged, peeled baby carrots
¼	cup dry white wine or beef broth
1¼	cups beef broth
2	tablespoons all-purpose flour
¼	teaspoon dried thyme, crushed

[1] Place meat, fat side up, in a 15½×10½×2-inch roasting pan. Insert a meat thermometer into center of meat. In a large bowl combine horseradish, olive oil, pepper, the 1 teaspoon thyme, and the salt. Spoon half of the mixture over beef. Set remaining horseradish mixture aside. Roast beef in a 350° oven for 30 minutes.

[2] Meanwhile, peel a strip from the center of each potato; cut larger potatoes in half. Toss potatoes and carrots with reserved horseradish mixture. Arrange vegetables in pan around roast. Roast 1¼ to 1½ hours more or until the thermometer registers 145° for medium-rare, stirring vegetables once. Remove from pan. Cover with foil. Let stand 15 minutes before carving meat. (The meat's temperature will rise 5° during standing.)

[3] For sauce, add wine to roasting pan and stir up the brown bits. In a medium saucepan stir the 1¼ cups broth into the flour and ¼ teaspoon thyme until smooth. Stir in wine from roasting pan. Cook and stir until thickened and bubbly; cook and stir 1 minute more. Serve sauce with meat and vegetables. If desired, garnish with fresh thyme sprigs.

Nutrition Facts per serving: 421 cal., 18 g total fat (7 g sat. fat), 84 mg chol., 474 mg sodium, 31 g carbo., 3 g fiber, 32 g pro. Daily Values: 85% vit. A, 29% vit. C, 4% calcium, 34% iron

Cold Weather Osso Buco

[*Like an Italian osso buco, this dish is based on long-simmering veal shanks. But rather than the tomatoes and garlic traditionally found in that classic, we've added winter squash, potatoes, and Brussels sprouts to add comfort and color to a cold winter night.*]

Prep: *30 minutes* **Cook:** *8¾ hours* **Servings:** *4*

2	tablespoons olive oil
4	veal shank crosscuts (2 pounds) or 1½ pounds boneless beef short ribs
1	cup chopped onion
3	cloves garlic, minced
1	10¾-ounce can condensed chicken broth
8	new potatoes, halved
1	10-ounce package frozen Brussels sprouts
1½	cups cubed, peeled butternut squash (1- to 1½- inch cubes) (about 1 pound unpeeled)
1	tablespoon prepared horseradish
2	tablespoons cornstarch
2	tablespoons cold water

[1] In a large skillet heat oil over medium-high heat. Brown veal shanks or beef ribs, half at a time, in hot oil. Transfer meat to a 3½- or 4-quart electric crockery cooker, reserving drippings in skillet. Sprinkle meat with ¼ teaspoon pepper.

[2] Add onion and garlic to skillet. Add more oil if necessary. Reduce heat to medium; cook until onion is tender, stirring occasionally. Add broth, scraping bottom of skillet to loosen any brown bits. Transfer the onion mixture with juices to the crockery cooker. Add potatoes. Cover and cook on low-heat setting for 8 to 9 hours or on high-heat setting for 4 to 4½ hours or until meat is tender.

[3] If necessary, run Brussels sprouts under water to separate. Add sprouts, squash, and horseradish to crockery cooker, rearranging so vegetables are in cooking liquid. Stir together cornstarch and water; stir into crockery cooker. If using low-heat setting, turn to high-heat setting. Cover and cook for 45 to 60 minutes more or until vegetables are just tender. Transfer meat and vegetables to platter. If desired, sprinkle with snipped fresh parsley.

Nutrition Facts per serving: 474 cal., 14 g total fat (4 g sat. fat), 139 mg chol., 626 mg sodium, 42 g carbo., 7 g fiber, 46 g pro. Daily Values: 72% vit. A, 125% vit. C, 8% calcium, 29% iron

To Tote: After the food is completely cooked, wrap crockery cooker in heavy foil, several layers of newspaper, or a heavy towel. Then place the cooker in an insulated container. The food should stay hot for up to 2 hours (do not hold for longer than 2 hours). Serve as above.

Braised Short Ribs with Italian Vegetables

[*Short ribs are one of those less-tender meat cuts that require long, slow cooking in liquid (referred to as braising). So be sure the meat is tender before adding the vegetables for cooking.*]

Prep: *15 minutes* **Cook:** *1 hour 55 minutes* **Servings:** *4*

2½	to 3 pounds beef short ribs, cut into serving-size pieces
1	tablespoon olive oil
1	cup beef broth
1	cup dry red wine, apple cider, or apple juice
1	teaspoon dried oregano, crushed
½	teaspoon dried thyme, crushed
½	teaspoon pepper
¼	teaspoon salt
8	to 12 tiny new potatoes, halved (about ¾ pound)
1	9-ounce package frozen Italian green beans or cut green beans
1	medium tomato, chopped
4	teaspoons cornstarch
2	tablespoons cold water

[1] Trim fat from meat. In a Dutch oven heat oil. Brown meat in hot, oil turning to brown all sides. Drain fat. Combine broth, wine, oregano, thyme, pepper, and salt. Pour over ribs. Bring to boiling; reduce heat. Cover and simmer about 1½ hours or until meat is tender.

[2] Add potatoes, beans, and tomato. Return to boiling; reduce heat. Cover and simmer 15 to 20 minutes more or until potatoes are tender. Using a slotted spoon, transfer meat and vegetables to a platter; reserve cooking liquid in pan. Cover platter to keep warm.

[3] For gravy, skim fat from pan juices; measure juices. If necessary, add enough additional broth or water to equal 1½ cups liquid. (Discard remaining liquid.) Return juices to pan. In a small bowl stir cornstarch into cold water until smooth (or shake together in a screw-top jar). Stir into juices in pan. Cook and stir over medium heat until thickened and bubbly. Cook and stir for 2 minutes more. Serve gravy with meat and vegetables.

Nutrition Facts per serving: 481 cal., 20 g total fat (8 g sat. fat), 86 mg chol., 450 mg sodium, 28 g carbo., 1 g fiber, 38 g pro. Daily Values: 5% vit. A, 37% vit. C, 7% calcium, 38% iron

Mediterranean Mostaccioli

[*With chunky vegetables, ground lamb, and garlic-flavored tomatoes, this pasta sauce takes on a decidedly Mediterranean style, especially when it comes to the small amount of meat that's used. Stretching the meat is a defining characteristic of the Mediterranean diet.*]

Start to Finish: *30 minutes* **Servings:** *4*

6	ounces dried mostaccioli or gemelli
½	of a medium eggplant, cubed (about 3 cups)
2	cups sliced zucchini
8	ounces ground lamb or ground beef
2	14½-ounce cans diced tomatoes with basil, oregano, and garlic
½	cup raisins
¼	cup snipped fresh basil
½	teaspoon ground cinnamon
2	tablespoons balsamic vinegar

[1] Cook pasta according to package directions, adding eggplant and zucchini the last 2 minutes of cooking. Drain; keep warm.

[2] Meanwhile, for sauce, in a large skillet cook meat until brown; drain fat. Stir in undrained tomatoes, raisins, basil, and cinnamon. Bring to boiling; reduce heat. Cover and simmer for 5 minutes, stirring once or twice. Remove from heat; stir in vinegar.

[3] Transfer pasta mixture to a warm serving platter. Spoon sauce over pasta mixture. If desired, sprinkle with crumbled feta cheese.

Nutrition Facts per serving: 432 cal., 8 g total fat (3 g sat. fat), 38 mg chol., 939 mg sodium, 72 g carbo., 7 g fiber, 18 g pro. Daily Values: 14% vit. A, 48% vit. C, 5% calcium, 25% iron

Lamb and Polenta Bake

[*Ever wonder what to do with those tubes of refrigerated polenta you've spotted in supermarket produce aisles? Try this easy—yet impressive—recipe. Baked in individual casseroles, then inverted on dinner plates to serve, this layered dish makes a striking presentation.*]

Prep: *35 minutes*   **Bake:** *30 minutes*   **Servings:** *4*   **Oven:** *375°*

12	ounces ground lamb
½	cup chopped onion
1	small fennel bulb, chopped
4	cloves garlic, minced
1	tablespoon snipped fresh oregano or 1 teaspoon dried oregano, crushed
½	teaspoon coarsely ground pepper
1	14½-ounce can whole Italian-style tomatoes, cut up
1	16-ounce tube refrigerated cooked polenta
1	cup crumbled feta or garlic-and-herb feta cheese (4 ounces)
1	cup Italian-style tomato sauce

[1] In a large skillet cook lamb, onion, fennel, garlic, oregano, and pepper until lamb is brown and onion is tender. Drain fat. Add undrained tomatoes to mixture in skillet. Bring to boiling; reduce heat. Simmer, uncovered, for 10 to 15 minutes or until most of the liquid is evaporated, stirring occasionally.

[2] Meanwhile, cut polenta into ½-inch slices. Press or crumble half of the slices into bottoms of four 10- to 12-ounce greased casseroles or soufflé dishes, overlapping slices as necessary. Divide lamb mixture among casseroles on top of polenta. Sprinkle cheese over lamb mixture, reserving ¼ cup of the cheese. Firmly press or crumble remaining polenta on top. Bake in a 375° oven about 30 minutes or until heated through. Let stand 10 minutes.

[3] Meanwhile, in a saucepan heat tomato sauce just until boiling. Loosen edges of casseroles and invert onto serving plates; gently remove dish. Spoon sauce around casseroles. Sprinkle remaining cheese on top. If desired, garnish with cherry tomatoes cut into quarters and fresh parsley sprigs.

Nutrition Facts per serving: 414 cal., 18 g total fat (9 g sat. fat), 82 mg chol., 1,551 mg sodium, 39 g carbo., 13 g fiber, 24 g pro. Daily Values: 19% vit. A, 43% vit. C, 17% calcium, 15% iron

To Make Ahead: Prepare casseroles as directed, except do not bake. Cover and freeze up to 3 months. Thaw casseroles overnight in refrigerator. To serve, bake, covered with foil, in a 350° oven for 45 to 50 minutes or until heated through, uncovering the last 10 minutes of baking. Let stand 10 minutes before loosening edges and inverting onto plates.

Greek Skillet Supper

[*Take the simplicity of a skillet-macaroni supper and combine it with some wonderfully complex Greek-style flavors—lamb, cinnamon, and feta cheese—for results that are worldly, but still very easy.*]

Prep: *20 minutes*   **Cook:** *15 minutes*   **Servings:** *4*

8	ounces lean ground lamb or ground beef
¾	cup chopped onion
2	cloves garlic, minced
1	14½-ounce can beef broth
1½	cups dried medium shell macaroni
2	cups frozen mixed vegetables
1	14½-ounce can tomatoes, cut up
2	tablespoons tomato paste
2	teaspoons snipped fresh marjoram or 1 teaspoon dried marjoram, crushed
⅛	teaspoon ground cinnamon
⅛	teaspoon ground nutmeg
½	cup crumbled feta cheese (2 ounces)
1	teaspoon snipped fresh marjoram

[1] In a large skillet cook meat, onion, and garlic over medium heat until meat is brown and onion is tender. Drain fat. Stir in broth and macaroni. Bring to boiling; reduce heat. Cover and simmer for 10 minutes.

[2] Stir in vegetables, undrained tomatoes, tomato paste, dried marjoram (if using), cinnamon, and nutmeg. Return to boiling; reduce heat. Simmer, uncovered, for 5 to 10 minutes more or until vegetables are tender. Stir in the 2 teaspoons fresh marjoram (if using). Sprinkle with feta cheese and the 1 teaspoon fresh marjoram.

Nutrition Facts per serving: 400 cal., 12 g total fat (6 g sat. fat), 50 mg chol., 783 mg sodium, 51 g carbo., 3 g fiber, 22 g pro. Daily Values: 39% vit. A, 38% vit. C, 12% calcium, 28% iron

Tuscan Lamb Chop Skillet

[*Here white kidney beans are flavored with rosemary and garlic, then topped with lamb chops for a dish that is the very essence of the fresh and simple Tuscan style of cooking. Served with Italian bread and a mixed baby-greens salad, the dish will impress even the most well-traveled guest.*]

Start to Finish: *20 minutes*   **Servings:** *4*

- 8 lamb rib chops, cut 1 inch thick (1½ pounds)
- 2 teaspoons olive oil
- 3 cloves garlic, minced
- 1 19-ounce can white kidney (cannellini) beans, rinsed and drained
- 1 8-ounce can Italian-style stewed tomatoes
- 1 tablespoon balsamic vinegar
- 2 teaspoons snipped fresh rosemary

[1] Trim fat from chops. In a large skillet heat oil. Cook chops in hot oil over medium heat about 8 minutes for medium doneness, turning once. Transfer to a plate; keep warm.

[2] Stir garlic into drippings in skillet. Cook and stir for 1 minute. Stir in beans, undrained tomatoes, vinegar, and snipped rosemary. Bring to boiling; reduce heat. Simmer, uncovered, for 3 minutes.

[3] Spoon bean mixture onto four dinner plates; arrange two chops on each serving. If desired, garnish with fresh rosemary sprigs.

Nutrition Facts per serving: 272 cal., 9 g total fat (3 g sat. fat), 67 mg chol., 466 mg sodium, 24 g carbo., 6 g fiber, 30 g pro. Daily Values: 4% vit. A, 13% vit. C, 4% calcium, 21% iron

Sweet Potato Shepherd's Pie

[Shepherd's pie originated as a way to use up the leftovers of a Sunday roast. We've added a little American innovation to the Old English standard by crowning the mixture with mounds of mashed sweet potatoes instead of regular mashed potatoes.]

Start to Finish: *1¼ hours* **Servings:** *6*

1	tablespoon olive oil or cooking oil
1¼	pounds lean boneless lamb, cut into ½-inch cubes
1	cup chopped onion
1	clove garlic, minced
½	teaspoon dried savory, crushed
¼	teaspoon ground cinnamon
1	cup thinly sliced carrots
1	cup frozen cut green beans
2	large sweet potatoes, peeled and cubed (about 1 pound)
2	tablespoons margarine or butter
⅛	teaspoon ground nutmeg
	Milk
¼	cup cold water
2	tablespoons cornstarch

[1] In a large skillet heat oil. Brown lamb pieces, half at a time, in hot oil. Return all meat to pan. Stir in onion and garlic; cook for 1 minute more. Add 1½ cups water, savory, cinnamon, ½ teaspoon salt, and ¼ teaspoon pepper. Bring to boiling; reduce heat. Cover and simmer about 45 minutes or until meat is nearly tender. Add carrots and green beans. Cover and simmer about 10 minutes more or until vegetables are tender.

[2] Meanwhile, in a medium saucepan cook sweet potatoes in a small amount of boiling water for 20 to 25 minutes or until tender. Drain. Return potatoes to pan; add margarine, nutmeg, and ¼ teaspoon salt. Mash cooked sweet potato mixture with a potato masher or with an electric mixer on low speed. If mixture seems dry, gradually stir in enough milk (about 2 to 3 tablespoons) to make potatoes fluffy. Set aside.

[3] Combine the ¼ cup cold water and the cornstarch. Add water-cornstarch mixture to mixture in skillet. Cook and stir until thickened and bubbly. Spoon mashed sweet potato mixture in six mounds on top of the mixture in the skillet. Simmer, uncovered, about 5 minutes more or until potatoes are heated through. Serve immediately.

Nutrition Facts per serving: 336 cal., 19 g total fat (6 g sat. fat), 63 mg chol., 391 mg sodium, 23 g carbo., 3 g fiber, 18 g pro. Daily Values: 191% vit. A, 30% vit. C, 5% calcium, 12% iron

Lamb with Sausage and Beans

[*Serve this South-of-France inspired main dish alongside a simple vinaigrette-dressed salad; then follow the main course as the French might—with an array of cheeses and baguette slices.*]

Prep: *25 minutes*   **Soak:** *1 hour*   **Cook:** *8½ hours*   **Servings:** *6*

- 1   cup dry Great Northern beans or navy beans
- 1   tablespoon cooking oil
- 12   ounces lamb stew meat, cut into 1-inch cubes
- 2   cups beef broth
- 8   ounces cooked kielbasa, cut into ¼-inch slices
- 1   tablespoon snipped fresh thyme or 1 teaspoon dried thyme, crushed
- 3   cloves garlic, minced
- ¼   teaspoon whole black peppercorns
- 1   bay leaf
- 1   small eggplant, peeled and chopped
- 1   large green or red sweet pepper, coarsely chopped
- 1   6-ounce can tomato paste
- 3   cups hot cooked couscous

[1] Rinse beans. In a large saucepan add enough water to cover beans by 2 inches. Bring to boiling; reduce heat. Simmer, uncovered, for 10 minutes. Remove from heat. Cover and let stand for 1 hour. (Or, place beans in water in a large saucepan. Cover and let soak in a cool place overnight.) Drain and rinse beans.

[2] In a large skillet heat oil. Brown lamb in hot oil. Drain fat. In a 3½-, 4-, or 5-quart electric crockery cooker combine the beans, lamb, broth, kielbasa, dried thyme (if using), garlic, peppercorns, and bay leaf.

[3] Cover and cook on low-heat setting for 8 to 10 hours or on high-heat setting for 4 to 5 hours. If using low-heat setting, turn to high-heat setting. Stir in the eggplant, sweet pepper, and tomato paste. Cover and cook for 30 minutes more. Discard bay leaf. Stir in fresh thyme (if using). Season to taste with salt and black pepper. Serve over couscous.

Nutrition Facts per serving: 405 cal., 19 g total fat (2 g sat. fat), 33 mg chol., 959 mg sodium, 37 g carbo., 7 g fiber, 23 g pro. **Daily Values:** 8% vit. A, 45% vit. C, 4% calcium, 21% iron

Braised Lamb Shanks

[*This is the type of creatively combined dish you'd find—and pay top dollar for—in those clever little bistros that are popping up all over the country. When looking for the celeriac (sometimes called celery root), choose small, firm bulbs, as larger ones tend to be woody and tough.*]

Prep: *30 minutes* **Cook:** *2 hours* **Servings:** *4*

- 2 tablespoons all-purpose flour
- 4 meaty lamb shanks (about 4 pounds)
  Salt and pepper
- 6 leeks, sliced (2 cups)
- 2 tablespoons cooking oil
- 1 14½-ounce can reduced-sodium chicken broth
- 1 14½-ounce can stewed tomatoes
- 8 cloves garlic, crushed
- 2 teaspoons dried rosemary, crushed
- 8 ounces celeriac, peeled and cut into 1-inch pieces
- 8 ounces turnips, peeled and cut into 1-inch pieces
- 8 ounces small whole carrots, peeled, or packaged, peeled baby carrots

[1] Place flour in a large plastic bag. Add lamb shanks, one or two at a time, shaking to coat. Repeat with remaining shanks. Season lamb with salt and pepper; set aside.

[2] In a 4-quart Dutch oven cook leeks in hot oil until tender, but not brown. Remove from Dutch oven. Brown shanks on all sides, two at a time, in hot oil in Dutch oven. Return all shanks and leeks to Dutch oven.

[3] Add broth, undrained tomatoes, garlic, and rosemary. Bring to boiling; reduce heat. Cover and simmer for 1½ hours. Add celeriac, turnips, and carrots. Cover and simmer for 15 to 20 minutes more or until the vegetables and lamb are tender. Transfer lamb to a serving platter. Using a slotted spoon, transfer vegetables to platter; cover to keep warm.

[4] For sauce, skim fat from pan juices; measure juices. If necessary, add enough water to equal 2½ cups. Return mixture to Dutch oven. Bring juices to boiling; reduce heat. Simmer, uncovered, for 15 minutes or until sauce is reduced by half. Season to taste with salt and pepper. To serve, spoon sauce over vegetables and lamb. If desired, sprinkle with parsley.

Nutrition Facts per serving: 449 cal., 15 g total fat (4 g sat. fat), 119 mg chol., 872 mg sodium, 40 g carbo., 10 g fiber, 41 g pro. Daily Values: 132% vit. A, 46% vit. C, 12% calcium, 40% iron

Florentine Lasagna

[*A traditional lasagna in most respects—except for the colorful addition of spinach—this classic Italian casserole will taste great alongside a salad of cooked and chilled green beans tossed with a vinaigrette.*]

Prep: *25 minutes*   **Bake:** *30 minutes*   **Stand:** *10 minutes*   **Servings:** *8*   **Oven:** *375°*

12	ounces Italian sausage or uncooked turkey Italian sausage
½	cup chopped onion
1	8-ounce can tomato sauce
1	7½-ounce can tomatoes, cut up
2	teaspoons dried Italian seasoning, crushed
6	dried lasagna noodles
1	slightly beaten egg
1	15-ounce container ricotta cheese or 2 cups cream-style cottage cheese, drained
⅓	cup grated Parmesan cheese
½	of a 10-ounce package frozen chopped spinach, thawed and well drained
8	ounces sliced mozzarella cheese

[1] Remove casings from sausage, if present. For meat sauce, in a medium saucepan cook sausage and onion until sausage is no longer pink and onion is tender. Drain fat. Stir in tomato sauce, undrained tomatoes, and Italian seasoning. Bring to boiling; reduce heat. Simmer, uncovered, for 15 to 20 minutes or until desired consistency.

[2] Meanwhile, cook noodles in boiling, lightly salted water for 10 to 12 minutes or until tender, but still firm. Drain. Rinse with cold water; drain well. For filling, in a bowl stir together egg, ricotta cheese, ¼ cup of the Parmesan cheese, and ¼ teaspoon coarsely ground pepper. Fold in spinach. In a 2-quart rectangular baking dish layer half of the cooked noodles. Spread with half of the filling. Top with half of the meat sauce and half of the mozzarella cheese. Repeat layers. Sprinkle with remaining Parmesan cheese.

[3] Bake, uncovered, in a 375° oven about 30 minutes or until heated through. Let stand for 10 minutes before serving.

Nutrition Facts per serving: 343 cal., 19 g total fat (9 g sat. fat), 87 mg chol., 796 mg sodium, 19 g carbo., 2 g fiber, 24 g pro. Daily Values: 27% vit. A, 13% vit. C, 36% calcium, 14% iron

To Make Ahead: **Prepare through Step 2 above. Cover; refrigerate up to 24 hours. Bake, covered, in a 375° oven 40 minutes. Uncover; bake about 20 minutes more or until hot.**

To Tote: **Prepare lasagna just before leaving home. Cover with foil and wrap in several layers of newspaper. Then place in an insulated container. Do not hold for longer than 2 hours.**

Mexican Skillet Dinner

[*Chorizo, a spicy sausage made of coarsely ground pork, can be found in stores specializing in Mexican foods. The Mexican version of the sausage, made of fresh pork, is what you want for this recipe; Spanish chorizo is made of smoked pork.*]

Start to Finish: *25 minutes*   **Servings:** *6*

12	ounces chorizo or pork sausage
2	cups frozen whole kernel corn
1	14½-ounce can diced tomatoes
1	cup uncooked instant rice
½	cup water
2	teaspoons chili powder
½	teaspoon ground cumin
1	15-ounce can pinto beans, rinsed and drained
¾	cup shredded Mexican-blend cheeses or Colby and Monterey Jack cheese (3 ounces)

[1] Remove casing from sausage, if present. In a large skillet cook sausage over medium heat for 10 to 15 minutes or until brown. Drain in a colander; set aside.

[2] Add corn, undrained tomatoes, uncooked rice, water, chili powder, and cumin to skillet. Bring to boiling; reduce heat. Cover and simmer for 5 minutes or until liquid is absorbed and rice is tender. Stir in beans and cooked sausage; heat through. Sprinkle with cheese; cover and let stand 2 to 3 minutes until cheese is slightly melted.

Nutrition Facts per serving: 230 cal., 27 g total fat (11 g sat. fat), 13 mg chol., 585 mg sodium, 38 g carbo., 5 g fiber, 23 g pro. **Daily Values:** 9% vit. A, 22% vit. C, 11% calcium, 18% iron

Meat

Layered Polenta Casserole

[*Polenta is a northern Italian staple made of cornmeal that can be served soft, like mashed potatoes, or chilled and shaped, as it is here. It's easy enough to prepare your own homemade polenta, but if you're short on time, check out the recipe variation that calls on prepared refrigerated polenta.*]

Prep: *35 minutes* **Bake:** *30 minutes* **Chill:** *2 hours* **Stand:** *10 minutes* **Servings:** *6* **Oven:** *400°*

   Nonstick cooking spray
1   cup yellow cornmeal
1   tablespoon snipped fresh basil or ¾ teaspoon dried basil, crushed
¼   cup finely shredded Parmesan cheese
8   ounces Italian sausage or uncooked turkey Italian sausage
½   cup chopped carrot
1⅓ cups tomato-and-herb pasta sauce
1   cup shredded provolone or mozzarella cheese (4 ounces)
¼   cup grated or shredded Parmesan cheese

[1] Coat a 2-quart rectangular baking dish with cooking spray; set aside. For polenta, in a saucepan bring 2¾ cups water to boiling. Meanwhile, in a mixing bowl combine cornmeal, 1 cup cold water, basil, and ½ teaspoon salt. Slowly add the cornmeal mixture to the boiling water, stirring constantly. Cook and stir until the mixture returns to boiling. Reduce heat to low. Cook, uncovered, for 10 to 15 minutes or until mixture is very thick, stirring constantly. Stir in the ¼ cup Parmesan cheese, stirring until melted. Spread polenta in prepared baking dish. Cover and chill 2 hours or overnight.

[2] Remove casings from sausage, if present. In a medium saucepan cook sausage and carrot until sausage is no longer pink. Drain fat. Reserve ¾ cup of the pasta sauce; cover and refrigerate. Stir remaining pasta sauce into sausage mixture. Cool slightly; cover and chill. When ready to assemble, remove polenta from baking dish; cut into 24 triangles or squares. Spread reserved ¾ cup sauce in bottom of same rectangular baking dish. Arrange polenta on top of sauce. Spoon chilled sausage mixture over polenta. Sprinkle with provolone.

[3] Cover dish with foil. Bake in a 400° oven for 25 minutes. Remove foil. Sprinkle ¼ cup Parmesan cheese over top. Bake, uncovered, 5 to 10 minutes more or until cheese is bubbly and begins to brown. Let stand for 10 minutes. If desired, garnish with celery leaves.

Nutrition Facts per serving: 340 cal., 16 g total fat (6 g sat. fat), 42 mg chol., 932 mg sodium, 31 g carbo., 2 g fiber, 17 g pro. Daily Values: 44% vit. A, 21% vit. C, 21% calcium, 14% iron

Easy Layered Polenta Casserole: Substitute one and one-half 16-ounce tubes refrigerated herb-flavored or plain cooked polenta for water, cornmeal, basil, and salt. Cut polenta into ½-inch slices; arrange on the ¾ cup sauce spread in baking dish. Spoon sausage mixture over polenta. Sprinkle with provolone cheese. Continue at Step 3 above.

Deep Dish Pizza

[*Windy city winters demand hearty and filling foods, so it figures that Chicago is where the deep-dish pizza pie was invented. We've stuck to traditional toppings, but feel free to tailor the pizza toppings to your own tastes.*]

Prep: *25 minutes*   **Rise:** *30 minutes*   **Bake:** *25 minutes*   **Servings:** *6*   **Oven:** *425°*

1	tablespoon olive oil
1	16-ounce loaf frozen white bread dough, thawed
8	ounces Italian sausage
1½	cups shredded mozzarella cheese (6 ounces)
3	to 4 Roma tomatoes, thinly sliced
⅓	cup thinly sliced onion*
⅓	cup short, thin green sweet pepper strips*
1	teaspoon dried Italian seasoning, crushed
½	cup finely shredded Parmesan cheese

[1] For crust, with oiled fingers stretch and pat thawed dough in the bottom of a lightly greased 13×9×2-inch baking pan. Brush dough with remaining oil. Cover and let rise in a warm place until nearly double (30 to 45 minutes). Bake in a 425° oven for 10 minutes or until crust is lightly browned.

[2] Meanwhile, remove casings from sausage, if present. In a skillet cook sausage until no longer pink, breaking up the sausage. *(If desired, cook onion and green pepper with sausage until vegetables are desired doneness.) Drain fat. Remove crust from oven. If necessary, carefully push down the bubble of dough in the center of pan with a spatula. Sprinkle with mozzarella cheese. Top with cooked sausage, sliced tomato, sliced onion, and green pepper strips. Sprinkle with Italian seasoning and Parmesan cheese.

[3] Return pizza to oven and bake 15 to 20 minutes more or until crust is golden and topping is bubbly.

Nutrition Facts per serving: 410 cal., 16 g total fat (6 g sat. fat), 44 mg chol., 496 mg sodium, 37 g carbo., 1 g fiber, 22 g pro. **Daily Values:** 8% vit. A, 29% vit. C, 28% calcium, 6% iron

Mafalda with Sausage and Mushrooms

[*Mafalda is a long, ruffle-edged noodle that resembles a lasagna noodle, only narrower. If you can't find it, use fettuccine or spaghetti instead.*]

Prep: *15 minutes*   **Cook:** *6 hours*   **Servings:** *6 to 8*

- 12   ounces sweet Italian sausage
- 2   cups sliced fresh crimini and/or button mushrooms
- 1   28-ounce can crushed tomatoes
- 1   8-ounce can tomato sauce
- 1   6-ounce can tomato paste
- ½   cup chopped onion
- 1   tablespoon sugar
- 1   teaspoon dried rosemary, crushed, or 1 tablespoon snipped fresh rosemary
- 2   cloves garlic, minced
- 9   to 12 ounces dried mafalda, fettuccine, or spaghetti
  Freshly shredded or grated Parmesan cheese (optional)

[1] Remove casings from sausage, if present. In a large skillet brown sausage. Drain fat. In a 3½- or 4-quart electric crockery cooker combine mushrooms, undrained tomatoes, tomato sauce, tomato paste, ⅔ cup water, onion, sugar, rosemary, garlic, and ¼ teaspoon pepper. Stir in cooked sausage. Cover and cook on low-heat setting for 6 to 8 hours or on high-heat setting for 3 to 4 hours.

[2] Just before serving, cook pasta according to package directions; drain. Serve sausage mixture over pasta. If desired, sprinkle with freshly shredded Parmesan cheese.

Nutrition Facts per serving: 358 cal., 10 g total fat (3 g sat. fat), 22 mg chol., 938 mg sodium, 54 g carbo., 4 g fiber, 14 g pro. Daily Values: 19% vit. A, 47% vit. C, 4% calcium, 28% iron

Keep a Lid on It!
When cooking foods in your electric crockery cooker, resist the urge to lift the cover unless absolutely necessary. Cookers cook at such low temperatures, lost heat is not easily or quickly recovered. In fact, an uncovered cooker can lose up to 20 degrees of cooking heat in as little as two minutes, so if you need to lift the cover to add ingredients to your crockery cooker, replace the lid as quickly as possible, especially when cooking on the low-heat setting.

Rotini-Kielbasa Skillet

[*For this colorful dish, we chose rotini—the corkscrew-shaped pasta. Or, you can use rotelle pasta with its wagon-wheel shape. Both will add a little kid-pleasing whimsy to this flavorful skillet meal.*]

Start to Finish: *35 minutes*   **Servings:** *6*

2	cups dried rotini or rotelle pasta (about 6 ounces)
1	tablespoon olive oil
1	medium onion, cut into wedges
2	cloves garlic, minced
1	pound cooked kielbasa, halved lengthwise and sliced diagonally
1	small zucchini, cut into matchstick-size strips
1	yellow or orange sweet pepper, cut into small strips
1	teaspoon dried Italian seasoning, crushed
1/8	teaspoon ground red pepper
8	Roma tomatoes, cored and chopped (about 1 pound)

[1] Cook pasta according to package directions; drain. Meanwhile, in a very large skillet heat oil over medium-high heat. Add onion and garlic and cook for 1 minute. Add kielbasa; cook until onion is tender, stirring frequently.

[2] Add zucchini, sweet pepper, Italian seasoning, and ground red pepper; cook and stir for 5 minutes. Stir in tomatoes and cooked pasta. Heat through, stirring occasionally. If desired, garnish with fresh herbs.

Nutrition Facts per serving: 410 cal., 26 g total fat (0 g sat. fat), 0 mg chol., 714 mg sodium, 31 g carbo., 2 g fiber, 14 g pro. Daily Values: 5% vit. A, 65% vit. C, 1% calcium, 10% iron

Meats to Keep on Hand

Some meats store longer than others. This makes them a good choice for hectic, ever-changing schedules because if you don't cook them on the day you planned, they'll usually keep until you can get to them. Next time you shop, check out the "sell by" and "use by" dates of meats like pepperoni, kielbasa, and packaged corned beef. You'll notice that these selections usually have a longer shelf life, when refrigerated. Flag the recipes on this page and 127 and keep these meats and a handful of ingredients on hand. That way, you can get started on dinner without a time-eating trip to the store. (When it comes to cooking, isn't a trip to the store sometimes half the battle?)

Pork and Mango Picadillo

[*Pronounced pee-kah-DEE-yoh, this dish can be found in many Spanish-speaking countries. While most versions contain the tomatoes, spices, onions, garlic, and ground meat found here, our version includes mango for an enticing sweetness with spicy flavors.*]

Start to Finish: *30 minutes* **Servings:** *4*

1	pound lean ground pork
⅓	cup thinly sliced green onions
2	cloves garlic, minced
1	teaspoon ground cinnamon
1	teaspoon ground coriander
1	teaspoon ground cumin
1	teaspoon dried oregano, crushed
1	teaspoon dried thyme, crushed
1	cup thick-and-chunky salsa
1	mango, peeled, pitted, and cubed
2	tablespoons smoked almonds or whole almonds, chopped
2	tablespoons snipped fresh cilantro

[1] In a large skillet cook meat until no longer pink. Drain fat. Stir in onions, garlic, cinnamon, coriander, cumin, oregano, and thyme. Cook and stir for 2 minutes more. Gently stir in salsa and mango.

[2] Cover and cook for 1 to 2 minutes or until heated through. Spoon into serving dish. Sprinkle with almonds and cilantro. If desired, serve with hot cooked rice.

Nutrition Facts per serving: 223 cal., 12 g total fat (4 g sat. fat), 53 mg chol., 268 mg sodium, 16 g carbo., 2 g fiber, 16 g pro. Daily Values: 30% vit. A, 58% vit. C, 5% calcium, 20% iron

The Scoop on Skillets

Today's take on the skillet supper has moved well beyond chicken-and-rice dinners of the '50s—and the skillets themselves have come a long way, too! Today's options call on a variety of materials—from the tried-and-true cast-iron skillets our grandmothers stood by to the nonstick or oven-safe cookware many of today's home cooks swear by. You'll find a variety of sizes—here's how to match them up with recipes in this book:
▮ When a medium skillet is called for, use a skillet with an 8-inch diameter
▮ When a large skillet is called for, use a skillet with a 10-inch diameter
▮ When a very large skillet is called for, use a skillet with a 12-inch diameter

Ham Calzones

[*While the spinach greens wilt in a bowl of boiling water, you have time to start rolling out the easy-to-do crust that starts with thawed white bread dough.*]

Prep: *25 minutes*   **Bake:** *20 minutes*   **Servings:** *4*   **Oven:** *375°*

4   cups torn fresh spinach with stems removed
1   16-ounce loaf frozen white bread dough, thawed
3   cloves garlic, minced
1   teaspoon dried Italian seasoning, crushed
1   cup fat-free ricotta cheese or fat-free cottage cheese, well drained
4   ounces thinly sliced ham, chopped (1 cup)
4   ounces thinly sliced, reduced-fat Swiss cheese
1   cup tomato and herb pasta sauce, heated

[1] Pour enough boiling water over spinach to cover. Let stand for 5 minutes. Drain well, squeezing out the excess liquid; set aside.

[2] Divide bread dough into four equal portions. On a lightly floured surface roll each portion of dough into a 7-inch circle. Brush circles with the minced garlic. Sprinkle with seasoning. Divide ricotta cheese evenly among circles, spreading only on half of each crust and to within ½ inch of edges. Layer spinach, ham, and Swiss cheese over ricotta cheese.

[3] Moisten edges of dough with water. Fold dough in half over filling. Seal edges with the tines of a fork. Prick tops three or four times with the tines of the fork. Place calzones on a lightly greased baking sheet.

[4] Bake in a 375° oven about 20 minutes or until golden. Serve warm pasta sauce alongside the baked calzones.

Nutrition Facts per serving: 484 cal., 6 g total fat (2 g sat. fat), 32 mg chol., 802 mg sodium, 64 g carbo., 2 g fiber, 32 g pro. Daily Values: 39% vit. A, 30% vit. C, 70% calcium, 12% iron

To Make Ahead: Prepare calzones as above. Cool. Cover and chill the calzones overnight. To reheat, place calzones on a baking sheet. Bake calzones, uncovered, in a 375° oven for 12 to 15 minutes or until heated through.

Meat

Ham-and-Cheese Quiche

[See the word "quiche" and you probably think you'll need to fuss with a pie crust. Not with this recipe! Refrigerated biscuits are the shortcut solution here. Remember this page when summer's bumper crop of zucchini arrives.]

Prep: *30 minutes*   **Bake:** *25 minutes*   **Stand:** *10 minutes*   **Servings:** *6*   **Oven:** *375°*

2	cups thinly sliced zucchini and/or yellow summer squash
1	cup chopped onion
½	cup sliced fresh mushrooms
½	cup chopped red sweet pepper
1	tablespoon margarine or butter
¼	cup snipped fresh parsley or 1 tablespoon dried parsley
2	tablespoons snipped fresh basil or 1 teaspoon dried basil, crushed
1	teaspoon snipped fresh oregano or ¼ teaspoon dried oregano, crushed
¼	teaspoon garlic powder
⅛	teaspoon black pepper
2	beaten eggs
1	cup diced cooked ham
1	cup shredded mozzarella cheese (4 ounces)
½	cup shredded fontina cheese (2 ounces)
1	17.3-ounce package (8) refrigerated large biscuits

[1] Grease a 10-inch tart pan with removable bottom or a quiche dish; set aside. For filling, in a large skillet cook the zucchini, onion, mushrooms, and sweet pepper in hot margarine about 6 minutes or just until tender, stirring occasionally. Remove from heat. Stir in parsley, basil, oregano, garlic powder, and black pepper. Stir in eggs, ham, mozzarella, and fontina cheese; set aside.

[2] For crust, in prepared pan or quiche dish arrange seven slightly flattened biscuits around edge, allowing dough to extend over sides. Place the remaining biscuit in bottom of dish. Pinch edges to seal securely. Flatten slightly to form an even crust. Spread filling evenly in crust. (If using tart pan, place on a shallow baking pan.)

[3] Bake in a 375° oven about 25 minutes or until a knife inserted near center comes out clean; cover edge with foil the last 5 to 10 minutes of baking to prevent overbrowning. Let stand 10 minutes before cutting into wedges.

Nutrition Facts per serving: 438 cal., 23 g total fat (8 g sat. fat), 105 mg chol., 1,290 mg sodium, 39 g carbo., 2 g fiber, 20 g pro. Daily Values: 20% vit. A, 42% vit. C, 22% calcium, 18% iron

Fettuccine with Ham and Mushroom Sauce

[*This creamy and satisfying dish may remind you of a vegetable-studded Fettuccine Alfredo. However, an Alfredo sauce usually relies on butter, heavy cream, and Parmesan cheese for its richness. You'll find our sauce lighter, since it's made with evaporated milk and without butter.*]

Start to Finish: *30 minutes*   **Servings:** *4*

2	cups sliced fresh shiitake or button mushrooms
1	small red or green sweet pepper, cut into thin strips
½	cup chopped onion
1	clove garlic, minced
1	tablespoon cooking oil
1	12-ounce can (1½ cups) evaporated milk
2	tablespoons snipped fresh basil or ½ teaspoon dried basil, crushed
4	teaspoons cornstarch
¼	teaspoon black pepper
6	ounces cooked ham, cut into matchstick-size strips
1	9-ounce package refrigerated spinach fettuccine and/or plain fettuccine

[1] For sauce, in a skillet cook mushrooms, sweet pepper, onion, and garlic in hot oil until tender. In a mixing bowl combine evaporated milk, basil, cornstarch, and black pepper. Stir into vegetable mixture in skillet. Cook and stir over medium heat until bubbly. Cook and stir for 2 minutes more. Stir in ham. Remove from heat.

[2] Meanwhile, cook pasta according to package directions. Drain. Serve sauce over pasta. If desired, sprinkle with ¼ cup grated Parmesan cheese.

Nutrition Facts per serving: 475 cal., 15 g total fat (6 g sat. fat), 106 mg chol., 677 mg sodium, 58 g carbo., 3 g fiber, 27 g pro. Daily Values: 17% vit. A, 42% vit. C, 22% calcium, 20% iron

Quick Pepperoni Pasta

[*When you're craving pizza, but don't have time to make it yourself—or wait for the delivery truck— use your noodle! Try this super-quick pasta dish filled with the flavors of a traditional pie.*]

Start to Finish: *30 minutes*   **Servings:** *4*

- 6 ounces dried spaghetti, broken in half
- 3 cups sliced fresh mushrooms (8 ounces)
- ⅔ cup cubed pepperoni (3 ounces)
- 1 tablespoon margarine or butter
- 6 cups lightly packed torn fresh spinach
- ¼ cup grated Parmesan cheese
- 2 tablespoons snipped fresh basil
- 1 teaspoon lemon juice

[1] Prepare pasta according to package directions. Meanwhile, in a very large skillet cook mushrooms and pepperoni in margarine over medium heat for 5 minutes or until mushrooms are just tender. Drain fat. Stir in spinach. Cook and stir for 1 minute or until spinach begins to wilt. Remove from heat.

[2] Drain cooked pasta. In a large bowl combine pasta, pepperoni mixture, 3 tablespoons of the Parmesan cheese, the basil, and lemon juice. Toss to combine. Sprinkle with remaining Parmesan cheese. If desired, serve with breadsticks.

Nutrition Facts per serving: 344 cal., 14 g total fat (5 g sat. fat), 32 mg chol., 604 mg sodium, 39 g carbo., 2 g fiber, 15 g pro. Daily Values: 35% vit. A, 15% vit. C, 12% calcium, 29% iron

Jamaican Pork and Sweet Potato Stir-Fry

[*Lean pork, golden sweet potatoes, and jerk seasoning—we rolled three favorite ingredients of sunny Jamaica into one satisfying dish. To make this dish as easygoing as the island it's named after, slice the quartered potato and green onion in a food processor fitted with a thin slicing blade.*]

Start to Finish: *20 minutes* **Servings:** *4*

1½ cups uncooked instant rice
¼ cup thinly sliced green onions
1 large sweet potato (about 12 ounces)
1 medium tart apple (such as Granny Smith), cored
12 ounces lean boneless pork strips for stir-frying or pork tenderloin cut into thin strips
2 to 3 teaspoons purchased Jamaican jerk seasoning or Homemade Jamaican Jerk Seasoning*
1 tablespoon cooking oil
⅓ cup apple juice or water

[1] Prepare rice according to package directions. Stir half of the green onions into cooked rice; keep warm.

[2] Meanwhile, peel sweet potato. Cut into quarters lengthwise; then thinly slice crosswise. Place sweet potato slices in a microwave-safe pie plate or shallow dish. Cover with vented plastic wrap. Microwave on 100% power (high) for 3 to 4 minutes or until tender, stirring once. Cut apple into 16 wedges. Sprinkle pork strips with Jamaican jerk seasoning; toss to coat evenly.

[3] In a wok or large skillet heat oil over medium-high heat. (Add more oil, if necessary, during cooking.) Cook and stir seasoned pork in hot oil for 2 minutes. Add apple and remaining green onions; cook and stir for 1 to 2 minutes or until pork is no longer pink. Stir in sweet potato and apple juice. Bring to boiling; reduce heat. Simmer, uncovered, for 1 minute more. Serve over rice mixture. If desired, garnish with green onions.

Nutrition Facts per serving: 365 cal., 9 g total fat (2 g sat. fat), 38 mg chol., 131 mg sodium, 54 g carbo., 3 g fiber, 16 g pro. Daily Values: 150% vit. A, 32% vit. C, 3% calcium, 17% iron

Homemade Jamaican Jerk Seasoning: In a small bowl combine 1 teaspoon crushed red pepper; ½ teaspoon ground allspice; ¼ teaspoon curry powder; ¼ teaspoon coarsely ground black pepper; ⅛ teaspoon dried thyme, crushed; ⅛ teaspoon ground red pepper; and ⅛ teaspoon ground ginger.

Stir-Fried Pork with Peppers

[Long before American cooks came up with the one-dish meal, Asians were perfecting the concept in their stir-fries. Stir-frying is a cooking method that involves quickly frying foods over higher temperatures, with constant lifting and stirring. Today the speed of the method fits right into busy American lifestyles.]

Start to Finish: 35 *minutes*   **Servings:** 4

1	cup uncooked short grain rice
2	tablespoons dry sherry
2	tablespoons vinegar
2	tablespoons soy sauce
1	tablespoon cornstarch
1	tablespoon sugar
1/8	teaspoon crushed red pepper
3	teaspoons cooking oil
3	cloves garlic, minced
2	teaspoons grated fresh ginger
1/2	cup thinly sliced celery
1	cup coarsely chopped green sweet pepper
1	cup coarsely chopped red and/or yellow sweet pepper
1/2	cup thinly sliced green onions
12	ounces lean boneless pork, cut into small cubes
1/2	cup canned sliced bamboo shoots, rinsed and drained (about 1/2 of an 8-ounce can)
4	to 5 ears canned whole baby corn, drained and cut into 1½- to 2-inch pieces

[1] Cook rice according to package directions in lightly salted water; keep warm. Meanwhile, in a small bowl combine ½ cup water, the sherry, vinegar, soy sauce, cornstarch, sugar, and crushed red pepper; set aside.

[2] In a wok or large skillet heat 2 teaspoons of the oil over medium-high heat. Cook and stir garlic and ginger in hot oil for 30 seconds. Add celery and sweet peppers; cook and stir for 2 to 3 minutes. Add green onions; cook and stir for 1 minute or until vegetables are crisp-tender. Remove vegetables from wok.

[3] Add the remaining 1 teaspoon oil to the wok; heat until hot. Cook and stir pork for 3 to 4 minutes or until pork is tender and no longer pink. Stir cornstarch mixture; add to wok. Cook and stir until thickened and bubbly. Return vegetables to wok along with bamboo shoots and corn. Cook and stir until heated through. Serve over the rice.

Meat

Nutrition Facts per serving: 368 cal., 9 g total fat (3 g sat. fat), 38 mg chol., 565 mg sodium, 51 g carbo., 2 g fiber, 17 g pro. Daily Values: 22% vit. A, 106% vit. C, 2% calcium, 22% iron

Pork and Yellow Rice with Vegetables

[*Bursting with a confetti of vegetables—green onions, carrots, and cauliflower flowerets—and imbued with the uplifting hue of turmeric, this recipe is a colorful way to brighten up a cloudy day.*]

Prep: *15 minutes*　**Cook:** *15 minutes*　**Servings:** *5 or 6*

1	pound boneless pork loin
2	tablespoons cooking oil
¾	teaspoon cumin seed, crushed
1	medium onion, halved and sliced
2	cloves garlic, minced
1	cup packaged, peeled baby carrots
1½	cups cauliflower flowerets
1	14½-ounce can chicken broth
1	cup water
½	teaspoon ground turmeric
1⅓	cups uncooked long grain rice
¼	cup sliced green onions

[1] Trim fat from pork. Cut pork into 1-inch pieces. In a large skillet or Dutch oven heat oil over medium-high heat. Add pork and cumin. Cook and stir for 2 minutes. Add onion and garlic. Cook 2 minutes longer. Drain fat.

[2] Cut carrots in half lengthwise, if large. Add carrots, cauliflower, broth, water, and turmeric to skillet; mix gently. Stir in uncooked rice. Bring to boiling; reduce heat. Cover tightly and simmer for 15 to 20 minutes or until rice is tender. Stir mixture gently. Sprinkle with sliced green onions before serving.

Nutrition Facts per serving: 380 cal., 12 g total fat (3 g sat. fat), 41 mg chol., 318 mg sodium, 46 g carbo., 3 g fiber, 19 g pro. Daily Values: 69% vit. A, 38% vit. C, 4% calcium, 23% iron

Tinged with Turmeric

Made from the ground root of a tropical plant belonging to the ginger family, turmeric is a main ingredient in curry powder. However, cooks of many cuisines prize the spice for the yellow-orange hue it brings to foods, as well as its bittersweet, slightly musty flavor.

Pork Chops Smothered in Peppers and Onions

[*Move over, pepper steak! Pork chops lend themselves equally well to the treatment of colorful red, green, and yellow peppers and sweet onions. Enjoy it with a big slice of hearty bread to sop up the juices.*]

Start to Finish: *25 minutes*   **Servings:** *4*

1	tablespoon olive oil
4	pork loin or rib chops, cut ½ to ¾ inch thick (1¼ pounds)
1	red sweet pepper, cut into strips
1	green sweet pepper, cut into strips
1	yellow sweet pepper, cut into strips
1	large sweet onion, thinly sliced
¼	cup water
¼	cup dry white wine or chicken broth
1	teaspoon snipped fresh rosemary or ½ teaspoon dried rosemary, crushed
¼	teaspoon salt
4	slices crusty bread

[1] In a large skillet heat oil. Brown chops in hot oil over medium-high heat for 4 to 5 minutes, turning once. Remove chops from skillet; set aside. Add sweet peppers and onion to skillet. Cook, stirring frequently, about 10 minutes or until vegetables are tender.

[2] Return chops to skillet; add water, wine, rosemary, and salt. Bring to boiling; reduce heat. Cover and simmer for 5 to 6 minutes or until pork is no longer pink and juices run clear. Serve chops and vegetables with bread.

Nutrition Facts per serving: 273 cal., 12 g total fat (3 g sat. fat), 51 mg chol., 328 mg sodium, 20 g carbo., 1 g fiber, 19 g pro. Daily Values: 15% vit. A, 135% vit. C, 3% calcium, 10% iron

Rosemary Pork Chop Skillet

[*When was the last time you enjoyed a family-pleasing pork chop dinner? They haven't gone away—
they've just gotten better! This one brims with the heady flavors of sage and rosemary.*]

Start to Finish: *35 minutes*   **Servings:** *4*

1	pound boneless pork sirloin chops, cut ½-inch thick
½	teaspoon salt
½	teaspoon pepper
1	tablespoon olive oil
2	cups peeled winter squash cut into 1-inch cubes (such as butternut, banana, spaghetti, and/or acorn squash)
1	medium onion, cut into thin wedges
2	teaspoons snipped fresh rosemary
¼	cup chicken broth
¼	cup orange juice
2	medium zucchini, quartered lengthwise and cut into 1-inch pieces
1	teaspoon snipped fresh sage

[1] Trim fat from pork. Sprinkle chops with the salt and pepper. In a very large skillet heat oil over medium-high heat. Brown chops for about 4 minutes, turning once. Combine the winter squash, onion, and rosemary; spoon mixture over chops. Pour chicken broth and orange juice over vegetables. Bring to boiling; reduce heat. Cover and simmer for 10 minutes.

[2] Add zucchini and sage. Cover and cook about 5 minutes more or until chops are tender and no longer pink. Using a slotted spoon, transfer chops and vegetables to a serving platter. Cover with foil to keep warm.

[3] Bring reserved juices in skillet to boiling; reduce heat. Simmer, uncovered, about 5 minutes or until liquid is reduced to about ¼ cup. Spoon over chops and vegetables.

Nutrition Facts per serving: 192 cal., 9 g total fat (2 g sat. fat), 48 mg chol., 345 mg sodium, 12 g carbo., 3 g fiber, 16 g pro. Daily Values: 43% vit. A, 34% vit. C, 3% calcium, 9% iron

Summer Pasta with Pork

[*Flag this recipe for those precious months when the garden and farmer's market brim with fresh green beans and bright yellow summer squash. You'll love the way the recipe combines these summery flavors, quick-cooking boneless pork chops, and a few pantry staples for simple warm-weather cooking at its best.*]

Start to Finish: *30 minutes* **Servings:** *4*

2	tablespoons dried mushrooms such as shiitake or porcini
¼	cup dried tomatoes (not oil-packed)
6	ounces dried bow-tie pasta
2	cups green beans cut into 1-inch pieces
1	medium yellow summer squash, sliced (1¼ cups)
1	cup milk
¾	cup chicken broth
1	green onion, sliced
1	tablespoon cornstarch
½	teaspoon lemon-pepper seasoning
¼	teaspoon salt
1	pound boneless pork loin chops, cut ¾ to 1 inch thick
1	tablespoon olive oil

[1] Soak mushrooms and tomatoes for 5 minutes in enough boiling water to cover. Drain and snip, discarding mushroom stems; set aside. Cook pasta according to package directions, adding green beans to the water with the pasta. Add squash the last 2 minutes of cooking. Drain; keep warm.

[2] Meanwhile, in a mixing bowl stir together milk, broth, onion, cornstarch, lemon-pepper seasoning, and salt; set aside. Season pork lightly with additional salt and lemon-pepper seasoning. In a medium skillet heat oil. Cook pork in hot oil over medium heat for 5 to 6 minutes per side or until juices run clear. Remove meat from skillet; cut the meat into thin bite-size strips. Keep warm.

[3] For sauce, drain fat from skillet. Pour cornstarch mixture into skillet. Cook and stir until thickened and bubbly, scraping up any brown bits from bottom of skillet. Reduce heat; cook for 2 minutes more. Stir in mushrooms and tomatoes. Divide pasta mixture among four plates. Arrange pork strips on each plate; spoon sauce over all.

Nutrition Facts per serving: 435 cal., 13 g total fat (4 g sat. fat), 111 mg chol., 590 mg sodium, 44 g carbo., 5 g fiber, 35 g pro. Daily Values: 10% vit. A, 23% vit. C, 14% calcium, 20% iron

Pork with Pear, Fennel, and Cabbage

[Once relegated to home-style cooking, pork chops are appearing more and more on the menus of upscale restaurants. In this sophisticated recipe, the up-and-coming chop is enhanced by two of winter's best flavors—sweet pears and aromatic fennel.]

Start to Finish: *30 minutes*   **Servings:** *4*

2	fennel bulbs
4	boneless pork loin chops, cut 1½ inches thick
1	tablespoon olive oil
1	small onion, sliced
½	small head cabbage, coarsely chopped (2½ cups)
½	cup pear nectar or apple juice
¼	cup balsamic vinegar
½	teaspoon caraway seed
½	teaspoon dried thyme, crushed
¼	teaspoon salt
¼	teaspoon pepper
⅛	teaspoon ground nutmeg
	Pear nectar
1	tablespoon cornstarch
2	tablespoons cold water
1	large pear, cored and sliced

[1] Trim fennel, discarding the upper stalks, which tend to be tough. Remove feathery leaves; trim bottoms. Cut fennel into thin wedges. Season pork with salt and pepper. In a large skillet heat oil. Brown chops with onion in hot oil about 4 minutes per side. Drain fat.

[2] Arrange fennel wedges and chopped cabbage on top of meat. In a small bowl stir together the ½ cup nectar, vinegar, caraway seed, thyme, salt, pepper, and nutmeg; pour into skillet. Cover and simmer 12 to 15 minutes or until tender and pork is no longer pink. Using a slotted spoon, transfer pork and vegetables to platter. Cover with foil to keep warm.

[3] For sauce, measure pan juices. If necessary, add enough additional pear nectar to equal 1¼ cups. Return juices to skillet. In a small bowl stir cornstarch into cold water until smooth. Stir into skillet juices. Cook and stir over medium heat until thickened and bubbly. Stir in pear; heat through. Spoon sauce over meat and vegetables.

Nutrition Facts per serving: 344 cal., 15 g total fat (4 g sat. fat), 77 mg chol., 229 mg sodium, 25 g carbo., 2 g fiber, 26 g pro. Daily Values: 1% vit. A, 62% vit. C, 5% calcium, 14% iron

Spiced Fruit and Chops with Couscous

[Crockery cookers have long been a working mom's favorite for pot roasts, beef stews, and the like, but this intriguing recipe, sparked with contrasting sweet and peppery flavors, proves you can definitely teach an old appliance new tricks!]

Prep: *20 minutes*   **Cook:** *6 hours*   **Servings:** *4*

4	pork sirloin chops, cut ¾ inch thick (about 1½ pounds)
1	tablespoon cooking oil
1	6-ounce package dried apples
½	cup chopped onion
¼	cup golden raisins
¾	cup orange juice
¾	cup chicken broth
1	small jalapeño pepper, seeded and finely chopped (see tip, page 21)
1	clove garlic, minced
1	teaspoon grated fresh ginger
½	teaspoon apple pie spice
	Chicken broth
2	teaspoons cornstarch
1	recipe Orange-Almond Couscous

[1] Sprinkle chops with ¼ teaspoon salt and ¼ teaspoon black pepper. In a large skillet heat oil. Brown chops in hot oil, turning once. Transfer chops to a 3½- or 4-quart electric crockery cooker. Sprinkle apples, onion, and raisins over chops. In a bowl stir together orange juice, broth, jalapeño pepper, garlic, ginger, and apple pie spice. Pour over all.

[2] Cover and cook on low-heat setting for 6 to 8 hours or on high-heat setting for 3 to 4 hours. Transfer chops and fruit to a serving platter. Cover with foil to keep warm.

[3] For sauce, skim fat from juices; measure juices. If necessary, add enough additional broth to juices to equal 1 cup. Pour into a saucepan. In a small bowl combine ¼ cold water and cornstarch. Stir into juices in pan. Cook and stir until thickened and bubbly. Cook and stir for 2 minutes more. Serve chops and fruit with Orange-Almond Couscous. Pass sauce.

Orange-Almond Couscous: In a saucepan bring 1 cup water and ¼ teaspoon salt to boiling. Remove saucepan from heat. Stir in ⅔ cup quick-cooking couscous and 1 teaspoon finely shredded orange peel. Cover saucepan and let stand for 5 minutes. Stir in 2 tablespoons toasted slivered almonds.

Nutrition Facts per serving: 462 cal., 12 g total fat (3 g sat. fat), 48 mg chol., 531 mg sodium, 70 g carbo., 11 g fiber, 22 g pro. Daily Values: 1% vit. A, 55% vit. C, 4% calcium, 15% iron

Shanghai Pork Lo Mein

[Bok choy brings its emerald-green color, while mandarin oranges add more bits of brightness. Not only is this a beautiful, tasty dish, but it's ready in less time than it takes to order takeout. Serve it with hot jasmine or oolong tea and some fortune cookies from the grocery store.]

Start to Finish: *20 minutes*   **Servings:** *4*

- 6   ounces dried somen or fine egg noodles or angel hair pasta
- 2   teaspoons cooking oil
- 8   ounces pork tenderloin, halved lengthwise and sliced ¼ inch thick
- 2   cups sliced bok choy
- ¾   cup reduced-sodium chicken broth
- ¼   cup orange juice
- 3   tablespoons reduced-sodium soy sauce
- 2   teaspoons toasted sesame oil
- ¼   to ½ teaspoon crushed red pepper
- 1   11-ounce can mandarin orange sections, drained, or 2 large oranges, peeled, sectioned, and seeded

[1] Cook noodles according to package directions; drain. Meanwhile, in a wok or large skillet heat oil. Cook and stir pork in hot oil for 3 minutes, adding more oil if necessary. Add bok choy; cook and stir about 2 minutes more or until the pork is no longer pink and the bok choy is crisp-tender.

[2] Add chicken broth, orange juice, soy sauce, sesame oil, and crushed red pepper to wok; bring to boiling. Stir in cooked noodles. Cook for 1 minute, stirring occasionally. Stir in the orange sections.

Nutrition Facts per serving: 323 cal., 7 g total fat (1 g sat. fat), 40 mg chol., 1,337 mg sodium, 45 g carbo., 1 g fiber, 20 g pro. Daily Values: 5% vit. A, 30% vit. C, 3% calcium, 11% iron

So, Man — What's Somen?

With a very fine texture similar to that of angel hair pasta, dried Japanese somen noodles are made from wheat flour and are most often white. Look for them wherever Asian foods are sold, wrapped in bundles in such variations as plain, green tea (cha somen), egg yolk (tmago somen), or plum (ume somen).

[139]

Peppered Pork Chops and Pilaf

[*Tailor this quick recipe to whatever's looking good at the grocery store salad bar. Then combine the colorful vegetables with a few other convenient products—herb-pepper seasoning, bottled roasted red sweet peppers, and quick-cooking brown rice—for a skillet chop dish that's speedy and seasonal.*]

Start to Finish: *25 minutes* **Servings**: *4*

- 4   3-ounce boneless pork loin chops, cut ¾ inch thick
- 2   teaspoons herb-pepper seasoning
- 1   tablespoon olive oil
- 2   cups cut-up salad-bar vegetables, such as broccoli, carrots, mushrooms, onions, and/or sweet peppers
- 1   14½-ounce can chicken broth
- 2   cups uncooked instant brown rice
- ¼   cup roasted red sweet pepper strips

[1] Sprinkle both sides of meat with the herb-pepper seasoning. In a large skillet heat oil. Cook chops in hot oil for 5 minutes. Turn chops. Cook for 5 to 7 minutes more or until juices run clear. Remove chops from skillet; cover and keep warm.

[2] Meanwhile, cut vegetables into bite-size pieces. Add vegetables, broth, and uncooked rice to skillet. Bring to boiling; reduce heat. Cover and simmer for 5 to 7 minutes or until rice is done and vegetables are crisp-tender. Return pork chops to skillet; cover and heat through. Garnish with roasted red pepper strips.

Nutrition Facts per serving: 390 cal., 17 g total fat (5 g sat. fat), 70 mg chol., 492 mg sodium, 33 g carbo., 3 g fiber, 29 g pro. Daily Values: 49% vit. A, 65% vit. C, 4% calcium, 7% iron

Pork and Potato Skillet

[A potato skillet dinner usually means there's some peeling and chopping involved. Forget that! This recipe calls on frozen hash browns to keep things simple. The potatoes are studded with colorful carrots, peas, red peppers, and leeks, making an eye-catching base for the seasoned chops.]

Prep: *10 minutes*   **Cook:** *21 minutes*   **Servings:** *4*

4	4-ounce boneless pork loin chops
½	teaspoon seasoned salt
2	tablespoons cooking oil
1	leek, halved and sliced or ⅓ cup chopped onion
1	medium red sweet pepper, cut into ¾-inch pieces
3	cups frozen diced hash brown potatoes
2	cups frozen peas and carrots
1	teaspoon dried thyme, crushed
¼	teaspoon seasoned salt

[1] Sprinkle both sides of meat evenly with the ½ teaspoon seasoned salt. In a large skillet heat 1 tablespoon of the oil over medium-high heat. Cook chops in hot oil for 3 minutes. Turn chops. Cook for 3 minutes more or until brown. Remove chops from skillet.

[2] Carefully add remaining 1 tablespoon oil to skillet. Add leek and sweet pepper; cook 1 minute. Add potatoes, frozen peas and carrots, thyme, and ¼ teaspoon seasoned salt; mix well. Cook 7 minutes, stirring frequently.

[3] Place chops on top of potatoes in skillet; cover. Reduce heat to medium. Cook 7 to 9 minutes more or until pork chops are no longer pink and potatoes are brown.

Nutrition Facts per serving: 374 cal., 16 g total fat (4 g sat. fat), 51 mg chol., 363 mg sodium, 39 g carbo., 7 g fiber, 22 g pro. Daily Values: 68% vit. A, 85% vit. C, 4% calcium, 23% iron

Mexican Pork Tenderloin

[Chocolate? In a savory sauce? Sure—that's a hallmark ingredient of mole (MOH-lay), a rich, spicy sauce that hails from Mexico. This one's made with barbecue sauce, cocoa powder, and cinnamon, but you can substitute prepared mole, found in specialty stores, if you like.]

Prep: *15 minutes* **Chill:** *1 hour* **Roast:** *25 minutes* **Stand:** *15 minutes* **Servings:** *4* **Oven:** *425°/350°*

⅓	cup bottled hot-style barbecue sauce
1	tablespoon unsweetened cocoa powder
¼	teaspoon ground cinnamon
	Dash ground cloves
1	12-ounce pork tenderloin
2	medium green and/or red sweet peppers, cut into ½-inch-wide strips
1	large onion, cut into 6 wedges
8	7- to 8-inch flour tortillas

[1] Combine barbecue sauce, cocoa powder, cinnamon, and cloves; brush about half evenly over pork. Cover; refrigerate 1 to 2 hours. Place meat on rack in a shallow roasting pan. Insert a meat thermometer so tip of thermometer is in center of meat. Place pepper strips and onion around meat. Brush with remaining sauce. Roast in a 425° oven for 25 to 30 minutes or until thermometer registers 160°. Cover with foil and let stand 15 minutes before carving meat.

[2] Meanwhile, stack tortillas; wrap tightly in foil. Reduce oven temperature to 350°. Heat tortillas for 10 minutes to soften while roast is standing. Cut meat into bite-size strips. In a medium bowl toss together pork and vegetables. To serve, fill warmed tortillas with pork-and-vegetable mixture. If desired, add coarsely chopped avocado. Roll up tortillas.

Nutrition Facts per serving: 331 cal., 8 g total fat (2 g sat. fat), 60 mg chol., 455 mg sodium, 38 g carbo., 2 g fiber, 24 g pro. Daily Values: 4% vit. A, 50% vit. C, 8% calcium, 23% iron

Hot Thermometers

With today's concerns about cooking foods to proper temperatures for safety's sake, food thermometers are essential kitchen tools. Here are some available varieties:

▌Instant-read thermometers are used to check the internal temperature of food toward the end of cooking time. They should not be left in food as it cooks in the oven or microwave. Digital instant-read thermometers are also available and are useful for checking small cuts of meat such as ground meat patties.

▌Meat thermometers are generally made of glass and are used to check the internal temperature of meats such as roasts and whole poultry. They generally are left in the food while it cooks.

Spicy Orange Pork with Vegetables

[*Frozen stir-fry vegetables are the obvious time-saver here, but consider five-spice powder—an aromatic blend of pepper, cinnamon, cloves, fennel, and anise—a terrific convenience product, too.*]

Prep: *25 minutes*   **Cook:** *1 hour 7 minutes*   **Servings:** *6*

- 1   1½- to 2-pound boneless pork shoulder roast or pork sirloin roast
- 2   tablespoons cooking oil
- 1   14½-ounce can chicken broth
- ¼   cup frozen orange juice concentrate, thawed
- ½   teaspoon five-spice powder or Homemade Five-Spice Powder*
- ¼   teaspoon pepper
- 1   clove garlic, minced
- 1   16-ounce package frozen mixed stir-fry vegetables
- 2   tablespoons cornstarch
- 3   cups hot cooked rice, noodles, or orzo

[1] Trim fat from meat. Cut pork into 1-inch cubes. In a large saucepan or 4-quart Dutch oven heat oil. Brown pork, half at a time, in hot oil. Drain fat. Return all meat to pan; stir in broth, thawed concentrate, five-spice powder, pepper, and garlic. Bring mixture to boiling; reduce heat. Cover and simmer for 1 hour or until meat is just tender.

[2] Add frozen vegetables to saucepan or Dutch oven. Return to boiling; reduce heat. Cover and simmer for 5 to 10 minutes more or until meat and vegetables are tender.

[3] Stir together cornstarch and ¼ cup cold water. Add to mixture in saucepan or Dutch oven. Cook and stir until thickened and bubbly. Cook and stir 2 minutes more. Serve with rice, noodles, or orzo. If desired, garnish with a carrot fan.

Nutrition Facts per serving: 375 cal., 15 g total fat (4 g sat. fat), 75 mg chol., 289 mg sodium, 34 g carbo., 2 g fiber, 25 g pro. Daily Values: 16% vit. A, 70% vit. C, 4% calcium, 20% iron

Homemade Five-Spice Powder: In a blender container combine 3 tablespoons ground cinnamon; 2 teaspoons aniseed or 6 star anise; 1½ teaspoons fennel seed; 1½ teaspoons whole Szechwan peppers or whole black peppers; and ¾ teaspoon ground cloves. Cover; blend until powdery. Store tightly covered. Makes about ⅓ cup.

Pork and Mushroom Marengo

[Legend has it that the first Marengo was created by Napoleon's chef to celebrate the French army's victory at the Battle of Marengo, waged against the Austrians in 1800. While Napoleon's chef probably didn't use a crockery cooker, the concept here—meat braised in tomatoes and herbs—is much the same.]

Prep: *25 minutes*   **Cook:** *8¼ hours*   **Servings:** *4*

1½	pounds boneless pork shoulder
1	tablespoon cooking oil
8	ounces fresh mushrooms, sliced
½	cup chopped onion
1	14½-ounce can tomatoes, cut up
1	cup water
1	tablespoon snipped fresh marjoram or 1 teaspoon dried marjoram, crushed
1½	teaspoons snipped fresh thyme or ½ teaspoon dried thyme, crushed
1	teaspoon instant chicken bouillon granules
¼	teaspoon salt
	Dash pepper
⅓	cup cold water
3	tablespoons all-purpose flour
2	cups hot cooked rice

[1] Trim fat from meat. Cut pork into 1-inch cubes. In a large skillet heat oil. Brown meat, half at a time, in hot oil. Drain fat.

[2] In a 3½-, or 4-, or 5-quart electric crockery cooker place mushrooms and onion. Add meat. In a bowl combine undrained tomatoes, the 1 cup water, dried marjoram and thyme (if using), bouillon granules, salt, and pepper. Pour over all.

[3] Cover and cook on low-heat setting for 8 to 10 hours or on high-heat setting for 4 to 5 hours. If using low-heat setting, turn to high-heat setting. In a bowl stir together the ⅓ cup cold water and the flour; stir into pork mixture in crockery cooker. Cover and cook on high-heat setting for 15 to 20 minutes more or until thickened. Stir in fresh marjoram and thyme (if using). Serve over hot rice.

Nutrition Facts per serving: 481 cal., 22 g total fat (7 g sat. fat), 112 mg chol., 610 mg sodium, 36 g carbo., 2 g fiber, 35 g pro. Daily Values: 6% vit. A, 32% vit. C, 5% calcium, 32% iron

Mustard-Maple Pork Roast with Potatoes

[*We wouldn't suggest trying Dijon-style mustard and maple syrup over pancakes, but here the combo makes a wonderful glaze for pork. Let the roast stand for 15 minutes before carving—this allows the temperature to rise to 160° (an appropriate doneness for pork loin) and makes it easier to slice.*]

Prep: *20 minutes*　**Roast:** *1½ hours*　**Stand:** *15 minutes*　**Servings:** *8 to 10*　**Oven:** *325°*

1	2- to 2½- pound boneless pork loin roast (single loin)
2	tablespoons Dijon-style mustard
1	tablespoon maple-flavored syrup
2	teaspoons dried sage, crushed
1	teaspoon finely shredded orange peel
¼	teaspoon salt
¼	teaspoon pepper
20	to 24 tiny new potatoes (about 1¾ pounds)
16	ounces packaged, peeled baby carrots
1	tablespoon olive oil
¼	teaspoon salt

[1] Trim fat from meat. Stir together mustard, syrup, sage, orange peel, the ¼ teaspoon salt, and the pepper. Spoon mixture onto meat. Place roast, fat-side up, on a rack in a shallow roasting pan. Insert a meat thermometer. Roast, uncovered, in a 325° oven 45 minutes.

[2] Meanwhile, peel a strip of skin from the center of each potato. Cook potatoes in boiling salted water for 5 minutes. Add carrots; cook 5 minutes more. Drain.

[3] Toss together potatoes, carrots, olive oil, and the remaining ¼ teaspoon salt. Place in roasting pan around pork roast. Roast, uncovered, for 45 minutes to 1 hour more or until meat thermometer registers 155°. Cover with foil. Let stand for 15 minutes before carving. (The meat's temperature will rise 5° during standing.)

Nutrition Facts per serving: 281 cal., 10 g total fat (3 g sat. fat), 51 mg chol., 309 mg sodium, 29 g carbo., 3 g fiber, 19 g pro. Daily Values: 128% vit. A, 24% vit. C, 3% calcium, 17% iron

Pork Ribs with Apples and Cranberries

[*For something different, this fruit-studded recipe calls for either spaetzle or orzo to serve with the meat. Spaetzle, a German specialty, are tiny dumplings or egg noodles, while orzo, originally from Italy, is a rice-shaped pasta. Both can be found in the rice and pasta aisle of the supermarket.*]

Start to Finish: *1 hour* **Servings:** 6

2	pounds boneless pork country-style ribs
1	cup cranberry juice or cranberry-apple juice
½	cup sliced celery
1	teaspoon instant chicken bouillon granules
1	tablespoon snipped fresh sage or 1 teaspoon dried sage, crushed
¼	teaspoon ground cinnamon
¼	teaspoon ground ginger
¼	teaspoon pepper
3	medium red and/or green cooking apples, cored and cut into wedges
½	cup dried cranberries
¼	cup cranberry juice or cranberry-apple juice
2	teaspoons cornstarch
3	cups hot cooked spaetzle or orzo

[1] Preheat broiler. Place ribs on the unheated rack of a broiler pan. Broil 6 inches from the heat about 10 minutes or until brown, turning once.

[2] Place ribs in 4-quart Dutch oven. Add the 1 cup cranberry juice, celery, bouillon granules, dried sage (if using), cinnamon, ginger, and pepper. Bring to boiling; reduce heat. Cover and simmer for 25 minutes or until meat is tender. Add apple wedges, dried cranberries, and fresh sage (if using). Simmer, uncovered, 5 minutes or until apple wedges are tender. Transfer meat and fruit to serving platter; cover with foil to keep warm.

[3] For sauce, measure pan juices. If necessary, add enough additional cranberry juice to equal 1¼ cups. Return juices to Dutch oven. In a small bowl stir together the ¼ cup juice and cornstarch until smooth. Stir into pan juices in Dutch oven. Cook and stir until thickened and bubbly. Cook and stir for 2 minutes more. Serve meat and fruit over hot cooked spaetzle or noodles. Pass sauce. If desired, garnish with fresh sage leaves.

Nutrition Facts per serving: 434 cal., 21 g total fat (8 g sat. fat), 79 mg chol., 219 mg sodium, 40 g carbo., 3 g fiber, 22 g pro. Daily Values: 0% vit. A, 37% vit. C, 4% calcium, 15% iron

[Poultry]

Spanish-Style Chicken **Page 175**

[150]

Curried
Turkey and
Couscous
Pie
Page 183

Chicken
Braised
with Wine
and Tomatoes
Page 178

Lemon-Pepper Pasta and Chicken

[*If lemon-pepper pasta is not available at your local supermarket, use 2 cups plain cooked pasta. Then just before tossing the pasta with the chicken, add ¼ teaspoon freshly ground black pepper and ¼ teaspoon finely shredded lemon peel to the pasta.*]

Start to Finish: *20 minutes* **Servings:** *4*

- 8   ounces dried lemon-pepper linguine or penne pasta
- 1   cup shelled fresh or frozen baby peas
- 3   tablespoons olive oil
- 12   ounces skinless, boneless chicken breast halves, cut into thin, bite-size strips
- 1   medium red onion, cut into thin wedges
- 1   tablespoon snipped fresh marjoram or 1 teaspoon dried marjoram, crushed
- 4   cloves garlic, sliced
- 1   tablespoon lemon juice

[1] Prepare pasta according to package directions, adding peas during the last minute of cooking. Drain pasta mixture; toss with 1 tablespoon of the olive oil. Set aside.

[2] Meanwhile, in a large skillet heat remaining olive oil over medium heat. Cook chicken, onion, dried marjoram (if using), garlic, and ½ teaspoon salt in hot oil for 3 to 4 minutes or until chicken is no longer pink, stirring often. Stir in lemon juice. Cook and stir for 1 minute more, scraping up brown bits. Gently toss pasta with chicken mixture and fresh marjoram (if using). Serve immediately.

Nutrition Facts per serving: 446 cal., 14 g total fat (2 g sat. fat), 45 mg chol., 311 mg sodium, 54 g carbo., 4 g fiber, 26 g pro. **Daily Values:** 2% vit. A, 14% vit. C, 3% calcium, 23% iron

The Limits of Leftovers

Frozen leftovers will keep for a long time—but not forever! (See the tips on page 19 regarding the cooling and thawing of foods.) Be sure to label items with the date they were placed in the freezer. To prevent freezer burn, store food in freezer containers with tightly fitting lids, or wrap food tightly in freezer packaging material. Store soups and stews in the freezer up to 3 months and cooked meat casseroles up to 6 months.

Monterey Tortilla Casseroles

[There's something undeniably delightful about being served your own personal-size casserole. That's part of the beauty of this dish. The other part? It can be made ahead. Stash the individual casseroles in the freezer for up to two months, and family members can enjoy a homemade dinner in just moments.]

Prep: 25 minutes **Bake:** 35 minutes **Servings:** 4 **Oven:** 350°

Nonstick cooking spray
6   6-inch corn tortillas, each cut into six wedges
2   cups cubed cooked chicken
1   cup frozen whole kernel corn
1   16-ounce jar salsa verde
3   tablespoons light dairy sour cream
3   tablespoons snipped fresh cilantro
1   tablespoon all-purpose flour
1   cup crumbled Mexican Chihuahua cheese or farmer cheese (4 ounces)

[1] Lightly coat four 10- to 12-ounce baking dishes with nonstick spray. Place five tortilla wedges in the bottom of each dish. Place remaining tortilla pieces on a baking sheet. Bake in a 350° oven about 10 minutes or until crisp and golden.

[2] Meanwhile, combine chicken, corn, salsa verde, sour cream, cilantro, and flour. Divide mixture evenly among dishes.

[3] Bake, uncovered, in a 350° oven for 20 minutes. Arrange baked tortilla pieces on top of casseroles. Top with crumbled cheese; bake for 5 to 10 minutes more or until heated through. If desired, garnish with additional dairy sour cream, thinly sliced fresh jalapeño pepper, snipped fresh cilantro, and chopped tomato.

Nutrition Facts per serving: 479 cal., 21 g total fat (3 g sat. fat), 98 mg chol., 1,247 mg sodium, 45 g carbo., 7 g fiber, 34 g pro. Daily Values: 22% vit. A, 73% vit. C, 27% calcium, 11% iron

To Make Ahead: Assemble casseroles as directed through Step 2. Place baked tortilla pieces in a moisture- and vapor-proof plastic bag. Freeze casseroles and baked tortilla pieces up to two months. To bake frozen casseroles, cover and bake in a 350° oven for 25 minutes. Uncover and bake about 20 minutes more or until heated through. Top with tortilla pieces and cheese; bake for 5 to 10 minutes more or until heated through. If desired, garnish as above.

Poultry

Chicken and Broccoli Stir-Fry

[Thirty minutes to a fresh, hot, homemade stir-fry—that beats takeout any day! Especially when the results are seasoned with hoisin sauce and sesame oil—two super-convenient ways to bring complex, aromatic flavors to a dish.]

Start to Finish: *30 minutes*   **Servings:** *4*

½   cup water
2   tablespoons soy sauce
2   tablespoons hoisin sauce
2   teaspoons cornstarch
1   teaspoon grated fresh ginger
1   teaspoon toasted sesame oil
1   pound broccoli
1   yellow sweet pepper
2   tablespoons cooking oil
12 ounces skinless, boneless chicken, cut into bite-size pieces
2   cups chow mein noodles or hot cooked rice

[1] For sauce, in a small bowl stir together water, soy sauce, hoisin sauce, cornstarch, ginger, and sesame oil. Set aside.

[2] Cut flowerets from broccoli stems and separate flowerets into small pieces. Cut broccoli stems crosswise into ¼-inch slices. Cut pepper into short, thin strips.

[3] In a wok or large skillet heat 1 tablespoon of the cooking oil over medium-high heat. Cook and stir broccoli stems in hot oil for 1 minute. Add broccoli flowerets and sweet pepper; cook and stir for 3 to 4 minutes or until crisp-tender. Remove from wok; set aside.

[4] Add remaining oil to wok or skillet. Add chicken; cook and stir for 2 to 3 minutes or until no longer pink. Push chicken from center of wok. Stir sauce; pour into center of wok. Cook and stir until thickened and bubbly. Return cooked vegetables to wok. Stir together to coat. Cook and stir 1 minute more or until heated through. Serve over chow mein noodles or rice. If desired, garnish with toasted sesame seed and serve with additional hoisin sauce.

Nutrition Facts per serving: 378 cal., 16 g total fat (3 g sat. fat), 49 mg chol., 877 mg sodium, 31 g carbo., 6 g fiber, 29 g pro. Daily Values: 18% vit. A, 272% vit. C, 8% calcium, 13% iron

Chicken and Orzo Pilaf

[*When it comes to pilafs, two grains are better than one—especially when they both cook in the same amount of time, as do the orzo and brown rice here. This duo teams up for a wholly satisfying yet healthful recipe chock-full of stir-fried veggies and an intriguing mix of Mediterranean flavors.*]

Start to Finish: *30 minutes*   **Servings:** *2*

1	cup water
⅓	cup dried orzo (rosamarina)
⅓	cup uncooked instant brown rice
⅓	cup chopped onion
¼	cup sliced celery
2	teaspoons margarine or butter
¾	cup sliced fresh mushrooms
¼	cup chopped red sweet pepper
½	cup chicken broth
1½	teaspoons cornstarch
¼	teaspoon ground turmeric
⅛	teaspoon salt
⅛	teaspoon ground coriander
⅛	teaspoon ground cinnamon
⅛	teaspoon black pepper
¾	cup finely chopped cooked chicken or turkey
½	cup trimmed asparagus cut into 1-inch pieces

[1] In a small saucepan bring water to boiling. Add orzo and rice. Return to boiling; reduce heat. Cover and simmer for 10 minutes or until tender. Drain any excess water; rinse and drain again. Return to saucepan. Cover and keep warm.

[2] Meanwhile, in a medium skillet cook onion and celery in margarine over medium heat until vegetables are tender but not brown. Add mushrooms and sweet pepper. Cook about 2 minutes more or until sweet pepper is crisp-tender.

[3] In a small bowl stir together broth, cornstarch, turmeric, salt, coriander, cinnamon, and black pepper. Add to vegetable mixture in skillet. Cook and stir over medium heat until thickened and bubbly. Cook and stir for 2 minutes more. Stir in chicken and asparagus. Cook and stir 2 minutes. Serve over orzo-rice mixture.

Nutrition Facts per serving: 338 cal., 10 g total fat (2 g sat. fat), 51 mg chol., 438 mg sodium, 39 g carbo., 3 g fiber, 24 g pro. Daily Values: 17% vit. A, 54% vit. C, 3% calcium, 20% iron

Chicken Couscous

[*The term "couscous" can refer both to the quick-cooking pasta beads that serve as the base of this dish or to the entire dish itself. While a couscous dish is often a long-simmering stew, we've quickened the recipe by bringing stir-frying speed to the preparation.*]

Start to Finish: *30 minutes*   **Servings:** *4*

2	medium onions, cut into thin wedges
2	cloves garlic, minced
1	tablespoon olive oil
1	pound skinless, boneless chicken breast halves, cut into bite-size pieces
16	packaged, peeled baby carrots (about ¾ cup)
2	medium zucchini, quartered and cut into 2-inch pieces
½	cup raisins
½	cup chicken broth
2	to 3 teaspoons curry powder
½	teaspoon ground cinnamon
2	cups chicken broth
½	teaspoon ground cinnamon
1⅓	cups quick-cooking couscous

[1] In large saucepan cook onions and garlic in hot oil 3 minutes or until crisp-tender. Add chicken and carrots. Cook, uncovered, over medium heat 5 minutes, stirring often. Stir in zucchini, raisins, ½ cup broth, curry powder, ½ teaspoon cinnamon, and ½ teaspoon salt. Cover; cook 3 to 4 minutes or until chicken is no longer pink and vegetables are crisp-tender.

[2] Meanwhile, in a medium saucepan bring 2 cups chicken broth and remaining cinnamon to boiling. Stir in couscous; cover. Remove from heat; let stand 5 minutes. Fluff lightly with a fork before serving. To serve, divide couscous among four plates. Spoon chicken and vegetable mixture over couscous. If desired, garnish with ¼ cup toasted slivered almonds.

Nutrition Facts per serving: 500 cal., 8 g total fat (2 g sat. fat), 60 mg chol., 833 mg sodium, 72 g carbo., 13 g fiber, 34 g pro. Daily Values: 62% vit. A, 10% vit. C, 6% calcium, 20% iron

Couscous — Of Course!

Could it be a coincidence that couscous has gained in popularity in the last few years? We think not! While regular couscous can take up to 60 minutes to cook, the quick-cooking forms most widely available today are usually ready in about five minutes. A specialty of North Africa, the bead-shaped pieces are made from ground semolina and provide a mild yet texturally interesting side dish that goes with just about anything.

Chicken and Prosciutto Pasta

[*It's amazing the gourmet touch that prosciutto and capers can bring to a dish that's based on two super-simple refrigerated pasta sauces. Find prosciutto—a salt-cured, air-dried ham that's a specialty of Parma, Italy—in Italian specialty markets or at the deli counters of more extensive supermarkets.*]

Prep: *30 minutes* **Bake:** *25 minutes* **Servings:** *6* **Oven:** *350°*

Nonstick cooking spray
- 6 ounces dried penne pasta (about 2 cups)
- 1 tablespoon olive oil
- 12 ounces skinless, boneless chicken breast halves, cut into ½-inch-wide strips
- 2 cloves garlic, minced
- 4 ounces sliced prosciutto or ham, coarsely chopped
- ½ of a medium green sweet pepper, cut into bite-size strips
- ½ of a medium yellow sweet pepper, cut into bite-size strips
- 1 teaspoon dried basil, crushed
- 1 tablespoon drained capers (optional)
- 1 15-ounce container refrigerated marinara sauce
- 1 10-ounce container refrigerated Alfredo sauce
- ⅓ cup finely shredded Parmesan cheese

[1] Coat a 2-quart casserole with nonstick spray; set aside. Cook pasta according to package directions. Drain and return pasta to saucepan; set aside.

[2] Meanwhile, in large skillet heat oil over medium-high heat. Add chicken and garlic; cook and stir for 2 minutes. Add prosciutto, green and yellow pepper strips, basil, and capers (if desired). Cook and stir 2 to 3 minutes longer or until chicken is no longer pink and pepper is crisp-tender. Add to pasta in saucepan; mix well.

[3] Layer half of the pasta mixture in the prepared casserole. Top with 1 cup of the marinara sauce. Top with the remaining pasta mixture; then add the Alfredo sauce. Drizzle with remaining marinara sauce. Sprinkle with Parmesan cheese.

[4] Bake, uncovered, in a 350° oven for 25 to 35 minutes or until heated through. If desired, garnish with a sprig of fresh basil.

Nutrition Facts per serving: 465 cal., 26 g total fat (2 g sat. fat), 62 mg chol., 839 mg sodium, 30 g carbo., 1 g fiber, 28 g pro. Daily Values: 3% vit. A, 52% vit. C, 7% calcium, 8% iron

To Tote: Prepare casserole as above just before leaving home. Cover tightly; wrap in several layers of newspaper or a heavy towel. Then place the casserole in an insulated container. Do not hold for longer than 2 hours.

Chicken with Artichokes and Olives

[*If you think you've tried chicken every way under the sun, try this dish. Artichokes, olives, thyme, and curry lend worldly flavors, yet it's all cooked up in a crockery cooker—for American ease.*]

Prep: *20 minutes* **Cook:** *7 hours* **Servings:** *6*

2	cups sliced fresh mushrooms
1	14½-ounce can diced tomatoes
1	8- or 9-ounce package frozen artichoke hearts
1	cup chicken broth
½	cup chopped onion
½	cup sliced pitted ripe olives or ¼ cup capers, drained
¼	cup dry white wine or chicken broth
3	tablespoons quick-cooking tapioca
2	to 3 teaspoons curry powder
¾	teaspoon dried thyme, crushed
¼	teaspoon salt
¼	teaspoon pepper
1½	pounds skinless, boneless chicken breast halves and/or thighs
4	cups hot cooked couscous

[1] In a 3½- or 4-quart electric crockery cooker combine mushrooms, undrained tomatoes, frozen artichoke hearts, broth, onion, olives, and wine. Stir in tapioca, curry powder, thyme, salt, and pepper. Add chicken; spoon some tomato mixture over the chicken.

[2] Cover and cook on low-heat setting for 7 to 8 hours or on high-heat setting for 3½ to 4 hours. Serve with couscous.

Nutrition Facts per serving: 345 cal., 6 g total fat (1 g sat. fat), 60 mg chol., 531 mg sodium, 43 g carbo., 9 g fiber, 30 g pro. Daily Values: 5% vit. A, 27% vit. C, 6% calcium, 21% iron

Tapioca? For Dinner?

Tapioca is a starch extracted from the roots of the tropical cassava plant. Though we think "pudding" when we hear the word "tapioca," the starch often is used to thicken a variety of cooked dishes. In fact, it works better than cornstarch and flour for thickening foods in the crockery cooker for two reasons. First, it doesn't need to be stirred during cooking to prevent it from settling; second, it can withstand long cooking times without breaking down. Recipes thickened with tapioca also freeze well because tapioca mixtures, unlike flour or cornstarch mixtures, retain their thicknesses when reheated.

Chicken and Vegetables Alfredo with Rice

[*A 20-minute dish that calls on three convenience products—frozen stir-fry vegetables, refrigerated pasta sauce, and instant cooked rice—gives the phrase "easy does it" a whole delicious new meaning.*]

Start to Finish: *20 minutes*   **Servings:** *4*

1	tablespoon margarine or butter
12	ounces skinless, boneless chicken breasts or thighs
1	clove garlic, minced
2½	cups frozen stir-fry vegetables (such as broccoli, carrots, onion, and red sweet pepper)
1	10-ounce container refrigerated light Alfredo sauce
1	cup milk
1⅓	cups uncooked instant rice

[1] In a large skillet melt margarine over medium heat; add chicken and garlic. Cook for 3 to 4 minutes per side or until chicken is brown. Remove chicken from skillet.

[2] Add frozen vegetables, Alfredo sauce, milk, and uncooked rice to skillet. Bring to boiling, stirring occasionally; reduce heat. Top with chicken. Cover and cook over medium-low heat for 6 to 8 minutes or until chicken is no longer pink, stirring mixture once or twice. If desired, sprinkle with 2 tablespoons finely shredded Parmesan cheese.

Nutrition Facts per serving: 599 cal., 16 g total fat (8g sat. fat), 85 mg chol., 732 mg sodium, 77 g carbo., 2 g fiber, 35 g pro. Daily Values: 20% vit. A, 51% vit. C, 31% calcium, 11% iron

Pasta Pronto

Prepared pasta sauces—those found in cans and jars as well as those in refrigerated packages—provide a real boon to the time-pressed cook. Most have a long shelf life, so you can stock up to have on hand for a last-minute meal anytime. You can also use your imagination and dress them up with your favorite ingredients. A few ideas:

▌Add cooked ham pieces and frozen peas to a light Alfredo sauce; heat through. Serve over rotini or other pasta.

▌Toss grilled vegetables with prepared pesto sauce; toss with bow-tie pasta.

▌Add cooked Italian sausages and grilled red sweet peppers to a chunky marinara sauce and serve over linguine. Sprinkle snipped fresh basil over all.

Chicken in Peanut Sauce

[*Nutty and sweet—with a little heat—that's what you get when crossing peanut butter and coconut milk with curry powder, jalapeño pepper, and cilantro. What a great way to liven up quick-cooking chicken breasts and fresh green beans.*]

Prep: *20 minutes*　**Cook:** *12 minutes*　**Servings:** *6*

1	tablespoon cooking oil
1	pound skinless, boneless chicken breast halves, cut into bite-size strips
2	teaspoons curry powder
1	fresh jalapeño pepper, seeded and finely chopped (see tip, page 21)
1	pound fresh green beans, trimmed and cut into 2-inch pieces, or 3 cups frozen cut green beans
1	cup purchased light coconut milk*
¾	cup chunky peanut butter
2	tablespoons soy sauce
¼	cup snipped fresh cilantro
3	cups hot cooked cellophane noodles or rice

[1] In a large skillet heat oil over medium-high heat. In a medium bowl toss chicken with curry powder and jalapeño. Add to skillet; cook and stir for 2 minutes. Carefully add beans and ¾ cup water. Bring to boiling; reduce heat. Cover and simmer for 5 minutes.

[2] In a medium bowl stir together coconut milk, peanut butter, and soy sauce. Add to the skillet. Return to boiling; reduce heat. Simmer, uncovered, for 5 minutes more or until chicken is no longer pink and beans are tender, stirring occasionally. Stir in 2 tablespoons of the cilantro. Serve chicken mixture over noodles or rice and sprinkle with remaining cilantro.

Nutrition Facts per serving: 448 cal., 22 g total fat (5 g sat. fat), 44 mg chol., 524 mg sodium, 39 g carbo., 5 g fiber, 27 g pro. Daily Values: 7% vit. A, 22% vit. C, 6% calcium, 17% iron

*Coconut Milk
Adding nutty sweetness to Thai-inspired dishes such as the one above is as easy as opening a can of coconut milk. However, be sure to choose the right product. Canned coconut milk is made from equal parts of water and coconut, which has been strained. You can usually find it in the international sections of supermarkets. Coconut milk is not the milky liquid you find when you open a fresh coconut, nor should it be confused with cream of coconut, a sweetened coconut concoction that's often used for desserts and mixing drinks such as piña coladas.

Caribbean Chicken and Rice Casserole

[*Over time, a great variety of peoples have colonized the Caribbean, so it's no wonder the foods there are international in nature. This dish resembles Spain's paella (a classic seafood dish)—minus the seafood.*]

Prep: *25 minutes*   **Bake:** *35 minutes*   **Servings:** *4*   **Oven:** *350°*

- 2   tablespoons cooking oil
- 4   skinless, boneless chicken thighs (about 12 ounces)
- ½   cup chopped onion
- 1   medium green sweet pepper, seeded and chopped
- 1   10-ounce package Spanish yellow rice mix
- 1   cup frozen peas
- ½   cup diced cooked ham
- 2   tablespoons snipped fresh cilantro

[1] In a large skillet heat oil. Brown chicken in hot oil over medium-high heat about 5 minutes, turning once. Remove chicken from skillet. Add the onion and green pepper to drippings in skillet. Cook and stir for 3 to 5 minutes or until tender. Stir in the rice mix and 2½ cups water (or according to package directions); bring to boiling. Carefully transfer mixture to a 2-quart casserole. Arrange chicken on top.

[2] Bake, covered, in a 350° oven about 25 minutes or until most of the liquid is absorbed. Remove from oven and stir in the peas, ham, and, if desired, ½ cup sliced pimiento-stuffed green olives. Bake, covered, 10 minutes more. Sprinkle cilantro over the top.

Nutrition Facts per serving: 442 cal., 13 g total fat (3 g sat. fat), 50 mg chol., 1,443 mg sodium, 59 g carbo., 4 g fiber, 24 g pro. Daily Values: 5% vit. A, 43% vit. C, 6% calcium, 11% iron

Keeping Hot Foods Hot

One-dish meals make great potluck fare, but for food safety's sake, remember to keep hot foods hot. Here's how:

▌ Keep hot food in the oven until just before leaving home.

▌ If desired, transfer hot food (such as baked beans, soups, and casseroles) to an electric slow crockery cooker for extra insulation.

▌ Wrap the covered dish, container, or crockery cooker in heavy foil, several layers of newspaper, or a heavy towel and place in an insulated container to tote.

▌ The food should stay hot for up to two hours. If electricity is available at your dining venue, and you have a crockery cooker, your food will stay warm for hours on the low-heat setting (add additional liquid as needed).

Chicken and Dumplings

[*When was the last time you had a wonderfully comforting meal of chicken and dumplings? Perhaps back in the old days when someone had time to cook it! Try our up-to-date version that takes advantage of a couple of shortcuts, including condensed soup and ready-to-bake buttermilk biscuits.*]

Prep: *15 minutes*   **Cook:** *30 minutes*   **Servings:** *4*

1	tablespoon all-purpose flour
12	ounces skinless, boneless chicken breast halves or thighs, cut into 1-inch pieces
1	stalk celery, sliced
1	medium carrot, chopped
1	onion, cut into wedges
2	tablespoons margarine or butter
1¼	cups chicken broth
1	10¾-ounce can condensed cream of chicken with herbs soup
⅛	teaspoon pepper
1	4.5-ounce package (6) refrigerated buttermilk biscuits*
1	cup frozen peas

[1] Place flour in a plastic bag. Add chicken pieces and shake until coated. In large saucepan cook chicken, celery, carrot, and onion in hot margarine for 2 to 3 minutes or until chicken is brown. Stir in broth, condensed soup, and pepper. Bring to boiling; reduce heat. Cover and simmer about 20 minutes or until chicken and vegetables are tender.

[2] Meanwhile, separate biscuits. Cut each biscuit into quarters. Stir peas into chicken mixture; return to boiling. Place biscuit pieces on top of chicken mixture. Cover and simmer over medium-low heat 10 to 15 minutes or until a toothpick inserted in center of biscuit comes out clean. Serve in bowls.

Nutrition Facts per serving: 338 cal., 11 g total fat (2 g sat. fat), 56 mg chol., 1,194 mg sodium, 31 g carbo., 4 g fiber, 28 g pro. Daily Values: 53% vit. A, 13% vit. C, 5% calcium, 15% iron

*Note: If you like, substitute drop-biscuits for the refrigerated biscuits. To prepare biscuits, in a medium mixing bowl combine 1 cup packaged biscuit mix and ⅓ cup milk. Drop mixture by teaspoonfuls into 8 dumplings onto hot chicken mixture. Cover and cook as directed above.

Poultry

Two-Bean Cassoulet

[*To add a little American ease to this French country supper, we called on canned beans—no soaking required. The results are equally as "ooh-la-la" as the classic.*]

Prep: *25 minutes* **Bake:** *25 minutes* **Servings:** 6 **Oven:** *350°*

- 6   skinless, boneless chicken thighs (about 1¼ pounds)
- 1   tablespoon olive oil or cooking oil
- 3   medium carrots, thinly sliced
- ½   cup chopped onion
- 2   cloves garlic, minced
- 1   15-ounce can butter beans, rinsed and drained
- 1   15-ounce can black beans, rinsed and drained
- 1   8-ounce can tomato sauce
- ¼   cup dry red wine
- 1   teaspoon dried thyme, crushed
- ¼   teaspoon ground allspice
- 8   ounces smoked turkey sausage, cut into ½-inch slices

[1] In a large skillet brown chicken slowly in oil over medium-low heat about 10 minutes, turning occasionally. Remove chicken from skillet, reserving drippings. Add carrots, onion, and garlic to drippings in skillet. Cover and cook about 10 minutes or until carrots are just tender, stirring occasionally.

[2] Stir in the drained beans, tomato sauce, wine, thyme, and allspice. Stir in sausage. Transfer the mixture to a 2-quart casserole. Arrange chicken thighs on top.

[3] Bake, uncovered, in a 350° oven for 25 to 30 minutes or until chicken is no longer pink. If desired, sprinkle with seeded and chopped tomatoes and snipped fresh parsley; bake 5 minutes more or until tomatoes are just heated through.

Nutrition Facts per serving: 332 cal., 9 g total fat (2 g sat. fat), 101 mg chol., 1,022 mg sodium, 27 g carbo., 7 g fiber, 34 g pro. Daily Values: 101% vit. A, 10% vit. C, 8% calcium, 20% iron

To Tote: Prepare casserole as above just before leaving home, omitting the tomato and parsley garnish. Cover tightly; wrap in several layers of newspaper or a heavy towel. Then place the casserole in an insulated container. Do not hold for longer than 2 hours. If using tomato and parsley garnish, pack them separately and sprinkle on casserole before serving.

Braised Chicken with Beans and Squash

[*White kidney beans, sometimes called "cannellini beans," are very popular in the Tuscany region of Italy. As American chefs have become increasingly interested in Tuscan cooking, the beans are becoming much loved stateside, too.*]

Prep: *15 minutes* **Cook:** *20 minutes* **Servings:** *6*

6	skinless, boneless chicken thighs (about 1 pound)
1	tablespoon cooking oil or olive oil
½	cup dry white wine or water
2	cloves garlic, minced
1	teaspoon instant chicken bouillon granules
1	teaspoon dried oregano, crushed, or 1 tablespoon snipped fresh oregano
¾	teaspoon dried thyme, crushed, or 2 teaspoons snipped fresh thyme
½	teaspoon dried savory, crushed, or 1 teaspoon snipped fresh savory
⅛	teaspoon pepper
1	pound banana, buttercup, or butternut squash, peeled, seeded, and cut into ½-inch pieces (about 2½ cups)
1	15-ounce can white kidney (cannellini) beans, rinsed and drained
1	14½-ounce can diced tomatoes
2	tablespoons snipped fresh parsley

[1] In a large skillet brown chicken in hot oil, turning occasionally. Remove chicken from skillet. Drain fat. Add wine, garlic, and bouillon granules to skillet. Bring to boiling; reduce heat. Boil gently, uncovered, about 3 minutes or until liquid is reduced by about half, stirring to scrape up any brown bits.

[2] Stir in dried oregano, thyme, and savory (if using), and pepper. Return chicken to skillet. Add squash. Bring to boiling; reduce heat. Cover and simmer 15 to 20 minutes or until squash is just tender and chicken is no longer pink. Stir in beans, undrained tomatoes, and fresh herbs (if using).

[3] Simmer, uncovered, for 5 minutes more or until sauce thickens slightly. Spoon bean mixture into six individual bowls. Place chicken on bean mixture. Sprinkle with parsley.

Nutrition Facts per serving: 190 cal., 7 g total fat (1 g sat. fat), 36 mg chol., 454 mg sodium, 18 g carbo., 5 g fiber, 16 g pro. Daily Values: 39% vit. A, 32% vit. C, 5% calcium, 15% iron

Chicken Pot Pie in Puff Pastry

[*Elegant touches, such as white wine, tarragon, shallots, and a lovely golden-brown pastry that magically puffs and rises as it cooks, bring the humble pot pie to new gourmet heights.*]

Prep: *30 minutes* **Bake:** *20 minutes* **Servings:** *4* **Oven:** *425°*

- 1 sheet frozen puff pastry (½ of a 17¼-ounce package)
- 2 tablespoons margarine or butter
- 12 ounces skinless, boneless chicken breast halves, cut into ¾-inch pieces
- ¼ cup chopped red sweet pepper (optional)
- 2 medium shallots, thinly sliced
- 2 tablespoons all-purpose flour
- ¾ teaspoon salt
- ½ teaspoon dried tarragon, crushed
- ¼ teaspoon black pepper
- 1¼ cups milk
- ⅓ cup dry white wine or chicken broth
- ½ cup frozen peas

[1] Thaw puff pastry according to package directions. Meanwhile, in a large skillet melt margarine over medium-high heat. Add chicken, sweet pepper (if using), and shallots. Cook 4 to 5 minutes or until chicken is lightly brown and no longer pink, stirring frequently. Stir in flour, salt, tarragon, and black pepper. Add milk all at once. Cook and stir until thickened and bubbly. Stir in wine and peas; heat through. Keep warm while preparing topper.

[2] For topper, unfold and roll puff pastry sheet into an 11-inch square. Cut out a 10-inch circle from pastry.* Transfer the hot chicken mixture to a 1½-quart casserole. Place pastry on top of the casserole. Flute edges of pastry and cut slits in the top for steam to escape. Bake in a 425° oven for 20 to 25 minutes or until crust is puffed and golden brown.

*Note: Scraps of puff pastry may be trimmed into cutout shapes or discarded. If using cutouts, moisten with a little water and place on top of pastry before baking.

Nutrition Facts per serving: 490 cal., 29 g total fat (3 g sat. fat), 50 mg chol., 790 mg sodium, 31 g carbo., 1 g fiber, 23 g pro. Daily Values: 19% vit. A, 4% vit. C, 9% calcium, 7% iron

Poultry

Chipotle-Chicken Casserole

[*Chipotle chilies are actually smoked jalepeño peppers. Here they add a smoky-hot appeal to this family-style dish. Look for canned chipotles in adobo sauce in the international food aisle of your supermarket or at Hispanic food markets.*]

Prep: *20 minutes*   **Bake:** *20 minutes*   **Stand:** *3 minutes*   **Servings:** *4*   **Oven:** *375°*

   Nonstick cooking spray
- 2   **cups frozen or fresh whole kernel corn**
- 3   **cups frozen diced hash brown potatoes**
- 1   **14½-ounce can diced tomatoes with basil, garlic, and oregano**
- 2   **chipotle peppers in adobo sauce, chopped (see tip, page 21)**
- ½   **teaspoon chili powder**
- ½   **teaspoon ground cumin**
- ½   **teaspoon dried oregano, crushed**
- 1   **tablespoon olive oil**
- 4   **skinless, boneless chicken breast halves (1 pound)**
- ¼   **teaspoon chili powder**
- ¼   **teaspoon ground cumin**
- ¾   **cup shredded Colby and Monterey Jack cheese (3 ounces)**

[1] Coat a 2-quart round casserole with nonstick spray; set aside. Coat an unheated large nonstick skillet with nonstick spray. Heat skillet over medium-high heat. Add corn; cook about 5 minutes or until corn begins to lightly brown. Add potatoes; cook and stir 5 to 8 minutes longer or until potatoes begin to brown. Stir in tomatoes, chipotle peppers, ½ teaspoon chili powder, ½ teaspoon cumin, and the oregano. Remove from heat; transfer mixture to the prepared casserole.

[2] Wipe skillet clean. Add oil to skillet and heat over medium-high heat. Sprinkle chicken evenly with ¼ teaspoon salt, ¼ teaspoon chili powder, and ¼ teaspoon cumin. Brown chicken in hot oil, turning once to brown both sides (about 3 minutes on each side). Place chicken on top of potato mixture in casserole.

[3] Bake, uncovered, in a 375° oven for 20 minutes or until bubbly and chicken is no longer pink. Sprinkle with cheese.

Nutrition Facts per serving: 460 cal., 15 g total fat (6 g sat. fat), 79 mg chol., 939 mg sodium, 50 g carbo., 4 g fiber, 33 g pro. Daily Values: 27% vit. A, 53% vit. C, 18% calcium, 24% iron

To Tote: Prepare casserole as above just before leaving home. Cover tightly with foil; wrap in several layers of newspaper or a heavy towel. Place casserole in an insulated container. Do not hold for longer than 2 hours.

Chicken in Ale

[*Using beer to flavor cooking (a strategy you'll find here) isn't necessarily a new idea, but it's becoming increasingly popular with the appearance of brew pubs all over the country. Since this dish cooks up quickly, be sure to start the water boiling for the fettuccine before you put the chicken on to cook.*]

Start to Finish: *35 minutes* **Servings:** *6*

4	teaspoons cooking oil
6	skinless, boneless chicken breast halves (about 1½ pounds)
⅓	cup chopped onion
2½	cups chopped mixed mushrooms (such as white, chanterelle, crimini, and/or shiitake)
1¼	cups chicken broth
⅓	cup brown ale or beer or amber nonalcoholic beer
4	teaspoons white wine Worcestershire sauce
1	tablespoon snipped fresh thyme or ½ teaspoon dried thyme, crushed
12	ounces dried fettuccine
3	tablespoons all-purpose flour

[1] In a large skillet heat oil. Brown chicken and onion in hot oil over medium-high heat, turning chicken once to brown both sides (about 2 minutes per side). Add mushrooms, ¾ cup of the broth, the ale, Worcestershire sauce, thyme, ¼ teaspoon each salt and pepper. Bring to boiling; reduce heat. Cover; cook about 5 minutes or until chicken is no longer pink.

[2] Meanwhile, cook fettuccine according to package directions. Drain well. Set aside and keep warm. Remove chicken breasts to serving platter; cover with foil and keep warm. In a screw-top jar shake together flour and remaining broth; add to skillet. Cook and stir until thickened and bubbly. Cook and stir for 1 minute more. Serve chicken and sauce over fettuccine. If desired, garnish with sprigs of fresh thyme.

Nutrition Facts per serving: 413 cal., 8 g total fat (2 g sat. fat), 60 mg chol., 336 mg sodium, 52 g carbo., 1 g fiber, 32 g pro. Daily Values: 0% vit. A, 3% vit. C, 2% calcium, 26% iron

Talk Turkey (and Chicken, Too!)

Next time a question about cooking or handling meat or poultry has you stumped, contact the U.S. Department of Agriculture's Meat and Poultry Hotline. Recorded messages cover a variety of topics, including safe cooking methods; safe use of cooking equipment; information on preparing meat and poultry products; food storage, refrigeration, and freezing; handling and serving food; food-borne bacteria and illnesses; recalls and advisories; problems related to power failure or natural disasters; and labeling and nutrition of meat and poultry products. The toll-free number is: 1-800-535-4555. Website address for Food Safety and Inspection Service is www.fsis.usda.gov.

Old World Chicken

[*While too bitter to eat out of hand, juniper berries often are dried and used for flavoring savory dishes, such as meats and sauces. Teetotalers may not immediately recognize their aroma, but martini-lovers may—juniper berries are used to flavor gin.*]

Prep: *30 minutes*   **Cook:** *6 hours 5 minutes*   **Servings:** *4*

- 2 slices bacon
- 1 teaspoon whole juniper berries
- 3 medium carrots, cut into ½-inch pieces
- ¼ cup chopped shallots or onions
- ¼ cup coarsely chopped celery
- 2½ to 3 pounds meaty chicken pieces (breasts, thighs, and drumsticks)
- ½ cup chicken broth
- ¼ cup dry red wine or port
- 2 tablespoons quick-cooking tapioca
- 1½ teaspoons snipped fresh thyme or ½ teaspoon dried thyme, crushed
- 1 teaspoon snipped fresh rosemary or ¼ teaspoon dried rosemary, crushed
- ¼ teaspoon salt
- ⅛ teaspoon pepper
- 1 cup frozen peas
- 2 tablespoons currant jelly
- 2 cups hot cooked rice

[1] In a small skillet cook bacon until crisp; drain on paper towels. Crumble bacon; set aside. For spice bag, place juniper berries on a double-thick, 6-inch square of 100-percent-cotton cheesecloth. Bring corners together and tie with clean cotton string.

[2] In a 3½-, 4-, or 5-quart electric crockery cooker place carrots, shallots, celery, and spice bag. Remove skin from chicken. Add chicken to crockery cooker. Sprinkle with bacon. In a small bowl combine broth, wine, tapioca, dried thyme and dried rosemary (if using), salt, and pepper. Pour over ingredients in crockery cooker.

[3] Cover and cook on low-heat setting for 6 to 7 hours or on high-heat setting for 3 to 3½ hours or until chicken is tender. Using a slotted spoon, transfer chicken and carrots to a serving platter; keep warm. If using low-heat setting, turn to high-heat setting. Stir in peas and fresh thyme and rosemary (if using). Cook for 5 minutes more. Remove spice bag. Skim fat. Add currant jelly; stir until smooth. Pour over chicken mixture. Serve with rice.

[173]

Nutrition Facts per serving: 474 cal., 11 g total fat (3 g sat. fat), 118 mg chol., 500 mg sodium, 45 g carbo., 3 g fiber, 43 g pro. Daily Values: 144% vit. A, 11% vit. C, 5% calcium, 25% iron

Poultry

Spanish-Style Chicken

[*An old Spanish saying claims that in Spain, food is generally fried in the south, roasted in the middle of the country, and stewed in the north. If so, that means this dish, a quick version of stew, is reminiscent of northern Spain.*]

Prep: *15 minutes*   **Cook**: *47 minutes*   **Servings**: *6*

1	3- to 3½-pound cut-up broiler-fryer chicken
¼	cup all-purpose flour
½	teaspoon salt
¼	teaspoon ground red pepper
2	tablespoons olive oil
1	28-ounce can whole Italian-style tomatoes, cut up
4	medium potatoes, cut into ½-inch pieces (4 cups)
1	medium onion, sliced (½ cup)
½	cup halved pitted ripe olives
½	cup dry red wine
2	tablespoons capers (optional)
1	tablespoon snipped fresh basil or 1 teaspoon dried basil, crushed
2	teaspoons snipped fresh oregano or ½ teaspoon dried oregano, crushed
2	cloves garlic, minced
1	tablespoon cold water
2	teaspoons cornstarch

[1] Remove skin from chicken. In a large plastic bag combine flour, salt, and ground red pepper. Add chicken, a few pieces at a time; shake to coat. In a 4-quart Dutch oven heat oil. Cook chicken in hot oil over medium heat about 10 minutes or until chicken is lightly browned, turning to brown evenly.

[2] Add undrained tomatoes, potatoes, onion, olives, wine, capers (if using), dried basil and dried oregano (if using), and garlic to Dutch oven. Bring to boiling; reduce heat. Cover and simmer for 35 to 45 minutes or until chicken is tender and no longer pink. Remove chicken to a serving dish; cover and keep warm.

[3] In a small bowl combine the water and cornstarch; add to potato mixture in Dutch oven. Cook and stir until thickened and bubbly. Cook and stir for 2 minutes more. Stir in fresh basil and oregano (if using). Pour thickened mixture over chicken in dish. If desired, garnish with a sprig of fresh basil or oregano.

[175]

Nutrition Facts per serving: 354 cal., 12 g total fat (3 g sat. fat), 77 mg chol., 566 mg sodium, 28 g carbo., 4 g fiber, 29 g pro. Daily Values: 10% vit. A, 57% vit. C, 8% calcium, 18% iron

Rosemary Chicken Dinner

[Balsamic vinegar lends its sharp, sweet flavor and rich mahogany hue to this dish, while rosemary and thyme bring the delightful aromas of sunny Provence. All this with just ten minutes of preparation time.]

Prep: *10 minutes* **Cook:** *47 minutes* **Servings:** *4*

1	3- to 3½-pound cut-up broiler-fryer chicken
2	tablespoons olive oil
½	cup chicken broth
3	tablespoons balsamic vinegar or dry white wine
2	medium shallots, chopped
1	tablespoon snipped fresh rosemary
1	teaspoon snipped fresh thyme
1	clove garlic, minced
¼	teaspoon salt
¼	teaspoon pepper
1	pound tiny new potatoes, halved
2	cups packaged, peeled baby carrots
2	teaspoons cornstarch

[1] If desired, remove skin from chicken. In a very large skillet heat oil. Cook chicken in hot oil over medium heat about 10 minutes or until chicken is lightly brown, turning to brown evenly. Drain fat. Add broth, vinegar, shallots, rosemary, thyme, garlic, salt, and pepper to skillet. Add potatoes and carrots. Bring to boiling; reduce heat. Cover and simmer for 35 to 40 minutes or until chicken is no longer pink and vegetables are tender. Remove chicken and vegetables to a platter; cover and keep warm. Reserve pan juices.

[2] For sauce, skim fat from juices; measure juices. If necessary, add water to equal 1 cup. Return juices to skillet. In a bowl combine 1 tablespoon cold water and cornstarch; add to juices in skillet. Cook and stir until bubbly. Cook 2 minutes more. Spoon over all.

Nutrition Facts per serving: 550 cal., 26 g total fat (6 g sat. fat), 119 mg chol., 397 mg sodium, 38 g carbo., 4 g fiber, 41 g pro. Daily Values: 184% vit. A, 31% vit. C, 5% calcium, 31% iron

Herbed Chicken and Roasted Vegetables

[*Roast chicken and vegetables may sound like Sunday dinner fare, but this lovely herb-infused version calls on cut-up chicken (rather than the whole bird) to save roasting time. It's too good—and too quick—to save for weekends only!*]

Prep: *15 minutes*   **Roast:** *35 minutes*   **Servings:** *6*   **Oven:** *425°*

- 3   **tablespoons olive oil or cooking oil**
- 2   **teaspoons dried basil, crushed**
- 2   **teaspoons dried marjoram, crushed**
- 1   **teaspoon dried rosemary, crushed**
- 2   **cloves garlic, minced**
- ½   **teaspoon salt**
- ¼   **teaspoon pepper**
- 4   **medium carrots, peeled and cut into 1½-inch pieces**
- 1   **large onion, cut into wedges**
- 1   **3- to 3½-pound cut-up broiler-fryer chicken**

[1] In a small bowl combine oil, basil, marjoram, rosemary, garlic, salt, and pepper. In a shallow roasting pan combine carrots and onion. Drizzle half of the oil mixture over the vegetables; toss to combine and push to edges of pan. Brush the remaining oil mixture on the chicken pieces. Place chicken in the prepared pan.

[2] Roast, uncovered, in a 425° oven for 35 to 45 minutes or until chicken is no longer pink and vegetables are tender.

Nutrition Facts per serving: 308 cal., 19 g total fat (4 g sat. fat), 79 mg chol., 283 mg sodium, 8 g carbo., 2 g fiber, 25 g pro. Daily Values: 119% vit. A, 4% vit. C, 3% calcium, 12% iron

To Tote: Prepare roast chicken and vegetables as above just before leaving home. Cover roasting pan tightly with foil; wrap in several layers of newspaper or a heavy towel. Then place the pan in an insulated container. Do not hold for longer than 2 hours.

Chicken Braised with Wine and Tomatoes

[*Braising—the method of cooking food slowly in a small amount of liquid in a tightly covered pan—results in moist, tender, and flavorful foods. The method is best for less-tender cuts of meat, which is why we chose chicken thighs rather than breasts for this dish.*]

Prep: *15 minutes* **Cook:** *40 minutes* **Servings:** *4*

8	small or 4 large chicken thighs (about 2 pounds)
1	tablespoon cooking oil
⅔	cup chicken broth
¼	cup dry white wine or chicken broth
2	cloves garlic, minced
2	teaspoons snipped fresh rosemary or ¾ teaspoon dried rosemary, crushed
¼	teaspoon salt
¼	teaspoon black pepper
2	cups chopped Roma tomatoes (6 medium)
1	medium yellow sweet pepper, cut into ½-inch-wide strips
1	medium green sweet pepper, cut into ½-inch-wide strips
1½	cups sliced fresh mushrooms
2	tablespoons cornstarch
2	tablespoons cold water
2	cups hot cooked noodles or rice

[1] Remove skin from chicken. In a large skillet heat oil. Brown chicken in hot oil over medium heat about 5 minutes, turning chicken to brown evenly. Drain fat. Add broth, wine, garlic, dried rosemary (if using), salt, and black pepper to chicken in skillet. Bring to boiling; reduce heat. Cover and simmer about 20 minutes.

[2] Add tomatoes, sweet peppers, and mushrooms to skillet. Simmer, covered, 15 minutes more or until chicken is tender and no longer pink. Transfer chicken to a serving dish, reserving vegetables and cooking liquid in skillet. Cover chicken with foil to keep warm.

[3] In a small bowl combine the cornstarch, water, and fresh rosemary (if using); stir into mixture in skillet. Cook and stir until thickened and bubbly. Cook and stir for 2 minutes more. Spoon vegetables and sauce around chicken. Serve with noodles or rice.

Nutrition Facts per serving: 355 cal., 10 g total fat (2 g sat. fat), 117 mg chol., 408 mg sodium, 34 g carbo., 3 g fiber, 29 g pro. Daily Values: 11% vit. A, 218% vit. C, 4% calcium, 19% iron

Roasted Chicken and Sweet Potatoes

[*When crushed just before adding to a recipe, cumin seed and caraway seed add exciting bursts of flavor. Whole spices, such as these seeds, keep up to two years; store tightly covered in a cool, dry place. On the other hand, ground spices such as turmeric generally lose freshness after six months.*]

Prep: *15 minutes* **Roast:** *1 hour* **Stand:** *10 minutes* **Servings:** *6* **Oven:** *375°*

1   tablespoon caraway seed, crushed
2   teaspoons dried oregano, crushed
1   teaspoon cumin seed, crushed
1   teaspoon ground turmeric
½   teaspoon salt
¼   teaspoon garlic powder
⅛   to ¼ teaspoon ground red pepper
1   2½- to 3-pound whole broiler-fryer chicken
3   tablespoons olive oil
4   medium sweet potatoes, peeled and sliced
1   cup apple juice

[1] In a small bowl combine caraway seed, oregano, cumin seed, turmeric, salt, garlic powder, and ground red pepper. Skewer neck skin of chicken to back; tie legs to tail and twist wings under back. Place chicken, breast side up, on a rack in a shallow roasting pan. Brush chicken with 2 tablespoons of the olive oil.

[2] Set aside 2 teaspoons of the spice mixture. Rub chicken with remaining spice mixture. Insert a meat thermometer into center of an inside thigh muscle. Do not allow thermometer bulb to touch bone. Roast, uncovered, in a 375° oven for 20 minutes.

[3] Meanwhile, toss sweet potatoes with remaining 1 tablespoon olive oil and the reserved spice mixture. Pour apple juice into roasting pan around chicken. Add potatoes. Continue roasting for 40 to 55 minutes or until meat thermometer registers 180° to 185°, drumsticks move easily in their sockets, and potatoes are tender. Remove from oven. Let chicken stand, covered, for 10 minutes before carving. Spoon potatoes into a serving bowl.

Nutrition Facts per serving: 346 cal., 17 g total fat (4 g sat. fat), 66 mg chol., 249 mg sodium, 25 g carbo., 3 g fiber, 22 g pro. Daily Values: 175% vit. A, 33% vit. C, 4% calcium, 14% iron

To Tote: Prepare roast chicken and sweet potatoes as above just before leaving home. Cover roasting pan tightly with foil; wrap in several layers of newspaper or a heavy towel. Then place the pan in an insulated container. Do not hold for longer than 2 hours.

Popover Pizza Casserole

[Here a saucy mix of ground turkey (or beef) and pepperoni is topped with a layer of mozzarella cheese and then a popover batter that puffs as it bakes. It has all the beloved flavors of pizza.]

Prep: *30 minutes* **Bake:** *30 minutes* **Servings:** *8* **Oven:** *400°*

1   pound uncooked ground turkey meat or ground beef
1   cup chopped onion
1   cup chopped green sweet pepper
½   of a 3½-ounce package sliced pepperoni
1   15-ounce can or one 15½-ounce jar pizza sauce
1   4-ounce can mushroom stems and pieces, drained
½   teaspoon fennel seed, crushed
½   teaspoon dried oregano, crushed
½   teaspoon dried basil, crushed
2   eggs
1   cup milk
1   tablespoon cooking oil
1   cup all-purpose flour
6   ounces thinly sliced mozzarella cheese
¼   cup grated Parmesan cheese

[1] In a large skillet cook turkey, onion, and green pepper until meat is brown and vegetables are tender. Drain fat. Cut pepperoni slices in half. Stir pepperoni, pizza sauce, mushrooms, fennel seed, oregano, and basil into meat mixture. Bring to boiling; reduce heat. Simmer, uncovered, for 10 minutes, stirring occasionally.

[2] Meanwhile, for topping, in a medium bowl combine eggs, milk, and oil. Beat with an electric mixer on medium speed for 1 minute. Add flour; beat 1 minute more or until smooth. Grease the sides of a 3-quart rectangular baking dish; spoon meat mixture into dish. Arrange cheese slices over hot meat mixture. Pour topping over cheese, covering completely. Sprinkle with Parmesan cheese.

[3] Bake in a 400° oven about 30 minutes or until topping is puffed and golden brown. Serve immediately.

Nutrition Facts per serving: 328 cal., 16 g total fat (7 g sat. fat), 124 mg chol., 683 mg sodium, 22 g carbo., 2 g fiber, 22 g pro. Daily Values: 15% vit. A, 34% vit. C, 23% calcium, 13% iron

Curried Turkey and Couscous Pie

[*Phyllo dough can be found in the frozen food aisles of most grocery stores. You've probably experienced the paper-thin layers in the classic Greek dessert, baklava, but the dough often is used in savory dishes as well. Here the dough makes an elegant, golden crust for this hearty (and surprisingly low-fat) pie.*]

Prep: *40 minutes*　**Bake:** *30 minutes*　**Stand:** *5 minutes*　**Servings:** *6 to 8*　**Oven:** *350°*

　　Nonstick cooking spray
1　pound turkey breast tenderloin or skinless, boneless chicken breasts, cut into ½-inch pieces
2　cloves garlic, minced
1½　teaspoons curry powder
⅛　teaspoon salt
⅛　teaspoon ground red pepper
1　14½-ounce can chicken or vegetable broth
1　cup frozen peas
1　cup uncooked couscous
¼　cup snipped fresh cilantro
6　sheets frozen phyllo dough, thawed

[1] Coat an unheated large nonstick skillet with nonstick spray. Heat over medium heat. Add turkey and garlic; cook and stir for 1 minute. Sprinkle curry powder, salt, and ground red pepper over turkey; cook and stir 1 to 2 minutes more or until turkey is no longer pink. Add broth and peas; bring to boiling. Remove from heat; stir in couscous. Cover and let stand 5 minutes or until liquid is absorbed. Stir in cilantro, fluffing the couscous with a fork.

[2] Place one phyllo sheet on a work surface; spray lightly with nonstick spray. Top with two more phyllo sheets, spraying each layer with cooking spray. Coat a 9-inch springform pan with cooking spray. Place the layered sheets in the pan, allowing the ends to extend up and over the sides of the pan. Repeat layering three more phyllo sheets as above; place in pan across the first three sheets to cover the bottom and edges of pan. Spoon turkey mixture into pan, spreading evenly. Fold the overhanging phyllo dough over the top to cover the filling. Spray top of pie with nonstick spray.

[3] Bake in a 350° oven for 30 to 35 minutes or until golden brown. If phyllo is browning too quickly, tent with aluminum foil. Let stand 5 minutes before cutting into wedges. If desired, serve with plain low-fat yogurt and cranberry or mango chutney.

Nutrition Facts per serving: 278 cal., 4 g total fat (1 g sat. fat), 33 mg chol., 406 mg sodium, 38 g carbo., 6 g fiber, 22 g pro. Daily Values: 1% vit. A, 4% vit. C, 2% calcium, 14% iron

White Bean and Sausage Rigatoni

[Busy day tomorrow? Assemble this casserole tonight, then store it in the refrigerator. The next evening when you get home, pop it in the oven to heat through. Then relax, pour yourself a refreshing beverage, and savor the hearty Italian aromas that will soon fill the house.]

Prep: *25 minutes* **Bake:** *30 minutes* **Servings:** *4 to 6* **Oven:** *375°*

8	ounces dried rigatoni (5 cups)
8	ounces cooked turkey kielbasa
1	10-ounce package frozen chopped spinach, thawed
2	14½-ounce cans diced tomatoes with basil, oregano, and garlic
1	15-ounce can Great Northern beans, rinsed and drained
½	of a 6-ounce can Italian-style tomato paste
¼	cup dry red wine or reduced-sodium chicken broth
⅓	cup shredded or grated Parmesan cheese

[1] In a large saucepan cook pasta according to package directions; drain and return to saucepan. Cut kielbasa into bias slices. Drain thawed spinach well.

[2] Add kielbasa, spinach, undrained tomatoes, beans, tomato paste, and wine to the cooked pasta. Stir to mix. Spoon into an ungreased 3-quart rectangular baking dish.

[3] Cover with foil and bake in a 375° oven for 25 minutes. Uncover and sprinkle with Parmesan cheese. Bake, uncovered, 5 minutes more or until hot.

Nutrition Facts per serving: 579 cal., 9 g total fat (3 g sat. fat), 43 mg chol., 1,368 mg sodium, 91 g carbo., 10 g fiber, 32 g pro. Daily Values: 73% vit. A, 73% vit. C, 35% calcium, 38% iron

To Make Ahead: **Prepare as above through Step 2. Cover casserole with plastic wrap; chill overnight. Remove plastic wrap. Bake, covered with foil, in a 375° oven about 55 minutes or until hot. Top with cheese.**

What a Dish!

What are the differences in a baking dish, a baking pan, and a casserole?
▌ A casserole is a round or oval covered dish used for cooking in the oven; it may be glass, ceramic, or metal. A casserole frequently has curved sides.
▌ Baking dishes and baking pans are coverless utensils used for cooking in the oven; a baking dish is made of glass or ceramic, while a baking pan is made of metal.
▌ Casseroles are measured by volume. If you're not sure what size casserole or baking dish you have, measure the amount of water it holds when filled to the top. Baking pans are measured across the top of the container from inside edge to inside edge.

Skillet-Style Lasagna

[*Lasagna—traditionally a time-consuming, calorie-laden recipe—gets with today's program with a lighter fat and calorie profile and a no-fuss top-of-the-range method. Never fear—all the traditional flavors of this family favorite are still delightfully present.*]

Start to Finish: *40 minutes*   **Stand:** *10 minutes*   **Servings:** *6*

8	ounces uncooked ground turkey sausage
½	cup chopped onion
2	cups light spaghetti sauce
1	cup water
1½	cups coarsely chopped zucchini
2	cups dried wide noodles
½	cup fat-free ricotta cheese
2	tablespoons grated Parmesan or Romano cheese
1	tablespoon snipped fresh parsley
½	cup shredded reduced-fat mozzarella cheese (2 ounces)

[1] Remove casings from sausage, if present. In a large skillet cook sausage and onion until meat is brown, breaking up meat during cooking. Drain fat. Stir in spaghetti sauce and water. Bring to boiling. Stir in zucchini and uncooked noodles. Return to boiling; reduce heat. Cover and simmer for 12 minutes or until pasta is tender, stirring occasionally.

[2] Meanwhile, in a small mixing bowl stir together ricotta cheese, Parmesan cheese, and parsley. Drop cheese mixture by spoonfuls into six mounds over the sausage-pasta mixture in the skillet. Sprinkle each mound with mozzarella. Cover and cook over low heat for 4 to 5 minutes or until cheese mixture is heated through. Let stand 10 minutes before serving.

Nutrition Facts per serving: 235 cal., 8 g total fat (2 g sat. fat), 38 mg chol., 418 mg sodium, 26 g carbo., 2 g fiber, 18 g pro. Daily Values: 9% vit. A, 16% vit. C, 7% calcium, 13% iron

Know What You're Buying

Ground turkey or chicken may sound like a leaner alternative to ground beef, but be careful! Some products contain dark meat and/or skin, which are less lean than breast meat. When a recipe calls for ground chicken or turkey, look for the leanest meat you can find. If you can't find packages that are specifically labeled as breast meat only, ask the butcher to skin, bone, and grind chicken or turkey breasts for you. Or, grind it yourself in a food grinder, using a coarse blade.

Poultry

Smoked Turkey and Wild Rice Pilaf

[*All the ingredients for this apple-studded pilaf simmer in a single skillet. And talk about versatile— while the autumnal flavors make it perfect for a brisk fall day, should the weather turn Indian-summer warm, you can chill it overnight and serve on lettuce leaves for a picnic-perfect main-dish salad.*]

Prep: *15 minutes* **Cook:** *43 minutes* **Servings:** *4*

- 1 tablespoon margarine or butter
- 1 cup sliced celery
- ¼ cup chopped onion
- ⅓ cup uncooked wild rice, rinsed and drained
- 1 14½-ounce can reduced-sodium chicken broth
- ⅓ cup uncooked long grain rice
- 12 ounces cooked smoked turkey, cubed
- 2 medium red-skinned apples, chopped
- 1 large carrot, peeled and cut into matchstick-size strips
- 2 tablespoons snipped fresh parsley

[1] In a large skillet melt margarine. Add celery and onion and cook about 10 minutes or until tender. Add uncooked wild rice; cook and stir for 3 minutes. Add broth. Bring to boiling; reduce heat. Cover and simmer for 20 minutes. Stir in long grain rice. Return to boiling; reduce heat. Cover and simmer about 20 minutes more or until wild rice and long grain rice are tender and most of the liquid is absorbed.

[2] Stir in turkey, apple, and carrot. Cook, uncovered, for 3 to 4 minutes more or until heated through and liquid is absorbed. Stir in parsley.

Nutrition Facts per serving: 289 cal., 7 g total fat (2 g sat. fat), 44 mg chol., 1,231 mg sodium, 37 g carbo., 3 g fiber, 21 g pro. Daily Values: 65% vit. A, 14% vit. C, 3% calcium, 12% iron

To Tote: Prepare the dish as above. Cool slightly and transfer to a storage container. Cover and chill thoroughly, up to 24 hours. Just before leaving home, place in an insulated container. Do not hold for longer than 2 hours.

Sweet 'n' Spicy Turkey

[*Now that you can buy turkey parts, the festive bird isn't just for the holidays anymore! Here just two thighs make up to six servings.*]

Prep: *15 minutes*   **Cook:** *5 hours*   **Servings:** *6*

2	turkey thighs (2½ to 2¾ pounds)
⅔	cup chopped onion
¾	cup cranberry juice
¼	cup Dijon-style mustard
¼	teaspoon ground red pepper
½	cup dried cranberries or cherries
1	tablespoon cold water
2	teaspoons cornstarch
3	cups hot cooked barley
1	medium nectarine or pear, cored and chopped

[1] Remove skin from turkey thighs. Place turkey in bottom of a 3½- or 4-quart electric crockery cooker. Add onion. In a mixing bowl combine cranberry juice, mustard, and ground red pepper. Pour over all in crockery cooker. Cover and cook on low-heat setting for 5 to 6 hours or on high-heat setting for 2½ to 3 hours. Remove turkey; cover to keep warm.

[2] For sauce, strain cooking juices. Measure juices. If necessary, add enough water to equal 1½ cups. In a small saucepan combine juices and cranberries. In a small bowl combine the water and cornstarch; stir into mixture in saucepan. Cook and stir over medium heat until thickened and bubbly. Cook and stir for 2 minutes more. To serve, toss hot cooked barley with chopped nectarine. Serve turkey and sauce over barley mixture.

Nutrition Facts per serving: 436 cal., 11 g total fat (3 g sat. fat), 116 mg chol., 365 mg sodium, 41 g carbo., 6 g fiber, 42 g pro. Daily Values: 2% vit. A, 22% vit. C, 5% calcium, 29% iron

Poultry: Handle with Care
When working with raw poultry, keep these food-safety tips in mind:
▌ Refrigerate chicken in the coldest section, placing it on a tray to catch drips.
▌ Thaw frozen, wrapped chicken in the refrigerator—never at room temperature.
▌ It's a good idea to designate one cutting board for raw poultry and meats and a separate one for chopping vegetables.
▌ Always wash hands, work surfaces, and utensils in hot soapy water after handling raw poultry to prevent bacteria from spreading to other foods. Never put cooked meat on the same plate that held raw poultry unless the plate has been sanitized.

Turkey Enchiladas

[Yes, you can have the whole enchilada and honor your aim to eat healthfully, too. Light and reduced-fat dairy products allow you to save 5 grams of fat per enchilada.]

Prep: *40 minutes* **Bake:** *44 minutes* **Servings:** *12* **Oven:** *350°*

½ cup chopped onion
½ of an 8-ounce package reduced-fat cream cheese (Neufchâtel), softened
1 teaspoon ground cumin
4 cups chopped cooked turkey or chicken breast
¼ cup chopped pecans, toasted
12 7- to 8-inch flour tortillas
    Nonstick cooking spray
1 10¾-ounce can reduced-sodium condensed cream of chicken soup
1 8-ounce carton light dairy sour cream
1 cup skim milk
2 to 4 tablespoons finely chopped pickled jalapeño peppers (see tip, page 21)
½ cup shredded reduced-fat sharp cheddar cheese (2 ounces)

[1] In a small saucepan cook onion, covered, in a small amount of water over medium heat until tender; drain. In a medium bowl stir together cream cheese, 1 tablespoon water, cumin, ¼ teaspoon black pepper, and ⅛ teaspoon salt. Stir in cooked onion, turkey, and pecans. Stack tortillas; wrap in foil. Heat in a 350° oven for 10 to 15 minutes to soften.

[2] Meanwhile, coat a 3-quart rectangular baking dish with nonstick spray. For each enchilada, spoon about ¼ cup of the turkey mixture onto a tortilla; roll up. Place tortilla, seam side down, in the baking dish. Repeat with remaining filling and tortillas.

[3] For sauce, in a medium bowl stir together soup, sour cream, milk, and jalapeño peppers; pour mixture over enchiladas. Bake, covered, in a 350° oven about 40 minutes or until heated through. Sprinkle enchiladas with the shredded cheddar cheese. Bake enchiladas, uncovered, for 4 to 5 minutes more or until the cheese is melted. If desired, top with snipped fresh cilantro or parsley, chopped tomatoes, and chopped sweet pepper.

Nutrition Facts per serving: 272 cal., 10 g total fat (3 g sat. fat), 57 mg chol., 398 mg sodium, 22 g carbo., 1 g fiber, 22 g pro. Daily Values: 10% vit. A, 1% vit. C, 11% calcium, 13% iron

To Tote: Prepare casserole as above just before leaving home. Cover tightly; wrap in several layers of newspaper or a heavy towel. Then place the casserole in an insulated container. Do not hold for longer than 2 hours.

Turkey Breast with Roasted Asparagus

[*Remember this recipe when spring's first tender shoots of asparagus begin to appear at farmers' markets and in produce aisles. You'll love the perfect flavor-pairing of tarragon and Dijon-style mustard, and the bright, vibrant colors of the asparagus, parsley, and red peppers.*]

Prep: *30 minutes* **Roast:** *1½ hours* **Stand:** *15 minutes* **Servings:** *10 to 12*

¼	cup margarine or butter, softened
2	teaspoons Dijon-style mustard
¾	teaspoon dried tarragon, crushed
¼	teaspoon salt
⅛	teaspoon black pepper
2	boneless turkey breast halves (with skin on) (2½ to 3 pounds total)
1	7-ounce jar roasted red sweet peppers, drained and coarsely chopped
½	cup snipped fresh parsley
1½	pounds asparagus spears
1	tablespoon olive oil
¼	teaspoon salt

[1] In a small bowl combine margarine, mustard, tarragon, the ¼ teaspoon salt, and the black pepper; set aside.

[2] Remove skin from turkey; set aside. Lay one turkey breast half, boned side up, on work surface. Make 4 to 5 shallow cuts in the thickest portion of breast (do not cut through). Place turkey breast between two pieces of plastic wrap. Using the flat side of a meat mallet, lightly pound turkey breast to an even thickness (about ¾ inch). Remove plastic wrap. Repeat with remaining turkey breast. Dot breast halves with half of the margarine mixture; set remaining mixture aside. Top turkey evenly with red peppers and parsley. Starting with a short side, roll up each turkey breast into a spiral. Wrap reserved skin around each roll. Tie with 100-percent-cotton string. Place on a rack in a shallow roasting pan.

[3] Melt remaining margarine mixture and brush over surface of turkey. Insert a meat thermometer into the center of one of the turkey rolls. Roast in a 325° oven for 1½ to 1¾ hours or until juices run clear and the thermometer registers 170°.

[4] Meanwhile, snap off and discard woody bases from asparagus. If desired, scrape off scales. Toss asparagus, oil, and the ¼ teaspoon salt together in a large bowl. Add asparagus to the roasting pan around the turkey the last 15 to 20 minutes of roasting time. Cover turkey and asparagus; let stand 15 minutes before slicing. Serve turkey with asparagus.

Nutrition Facts per serving: 212 cal., 9 g total fat (2 g sat. fat), 80 mg chol., 220 mg sodium, 2 g carbo., 1 g fiber, 28 g pro. Daily Values: 14% vit. A, 91% vit. C, 3% calcium, 11% iron

Thai Turkey

[*Thanks to precooked turkey breast, this curry-flavored dish will come together quickly. So quickly, in fact, that you should put the rice on to boil before you stir up the sauce or slice the turkey breast.*]

Start to Finish: *30 minutes*   **Servings:** *4*

2	tablespoons soy sauce
1	tablespoon honey
2	teaspoons toasted sesame oil
2	teaspoons curry powder
1	teaspoon cornstarch
1/8	to 1/4 teaspoon crushed red pepper
	Nonstick cooking spray
1	small onion, cut into thin wedges
1	red sweet pepper, cut into thin strips
12	ounces cooked turkey, cut into bite-size strips (about 3 cups)
1	clove garlic, minced
2	cups hot cooked rice

[1] For sauce, in a small bowl combine ⅔ cup water, the soy sauce, honey, sesame oil, curry powder, cornstarch, and crushed red pepper; set aside.

[2] Coat a large skillet or wok with nonstick spray. Cook and stir onion wedges and sweet pepper strips over medium heat until tender. Stir in the turkey strips and garlic. Stir in sauce. Cook and stir until thickened and bubbly. Cook and stir for 2 minutes more. Serve over rice. If desired, garnish with sliced serrano peppers.

Nutrition Facts per serving: 335 cal., 11 g total fat (3 g sat. fat), 81 mg chol., 576 mg sodium, 31 g carbo., 1 g fiber, 27 g pro. Daily Values: 20% vit. A, 53% vit. C, 3% calcium, 21% iron

Micro-Heating Leftover Rice

Next time you're cooking rice, cook some extra and refrigerate it in an airtight container for up to one week. To reheat the chilled cooked rice, place rice in a microwave-safe container and cover with vented plastic wrap. For 2 cups chilled rice, add 1 tablespoon water and micro-cook on 100% power (high) for 2 to 3 minutes or until heated through, stirring once. For 3 cups chilled cooked rice, add 2 tablespoons water and micro-cook on high for 3 to 4 minutes or until heated through, stirring once. After the rice is heated, fluff gently with a fork.

Roasted Game Hens Moroccan

[Game hens are as easy to prepare as chicken, but quite elegant. Try this recipe for a special occasion or for an intimate dinner party.]

Prep: *40 minutes* **Roast:** *1 hour* **Servings:** *4* **Oven:** *375°*

Nonstick cooking spray
2 1¼- to 1½-pound Cornish game hens
½ teaspoon salt
½ teaspoon ground cinnamon
¼ teaspoon ground cumin
⅛ teaspoon ground red pepper
2 teaspoons olive oil
½ cup chopped carrot
½ cup sliced celery
⅓ cup chopped onion
2 teaspoons olive oil
1 cup chicken broth
⅓ cup raisins
⅓ cup toasted pine nuts
⅔ cup quick-cooking couscous

[1] Lightly coat a 3-quart rectangular baking dish with nonstick spray; set aside. Use a long heavy knife or kitchen shears to cut Cornish hens in half lengthwise; cut through the breast bone, just off center, and cut through the center of the backbone. Twist wing tips under back. Place hen halves, cut sides down, in prepared baking dish.

[2] Combine salt, cinnamon, cumin, and ground red pepper. Set aside half of the spice mixture. Combine remaining spice mixture with the 2 teaspoons olive oil. Brush hens with oil mixture. Roast, covered, in a 375° oven for 35 minutes.

[3] Meanwhile, cook carrot, celery, and onion in the 2 teaspoons olive oil until almost tender. Add broth, raisins, pine nuts, and reserved spice mixture. Bring to boiling; remove from heat. Stir in the couscous. Cover and let stand for 5 minutes.

[4] Uncover baking dish and carefully drain off drippings. Spoon couscous mixture around hens in baking dish. Roast, uncovered, about 25 minutes more or until hens are tender and no longer pink.

[193]

Nutrition Facts per serving: 631 cal., 35 g total fat (7 g sat. fat), 120 mg chol., 581 mg sodium, 39 g carbo., 6 g fiber, 45 g pro. Daily Values: 40% vit. A, 4% vit. C, 3% calcium, 16% iron

Charleston
Crab Pot Pie
Page 215

Dilled Shrimp
with Rice
Page 206

[194]

[*Fish and Seafood*]

Pecan-Crusted Fish
with Peppers and Squash
Page 199

Deviled Fish and Pasta

[*While we usually think "eggs" when we hear the word "deviled," this recipe shows that chicken can go to the devil, too! To devil a dish means to add spicy seasonings, such as the red pepper and mustard you see here. Paradoxically the results are actually quite heavenly!*]

Prep: *30 minutes* **Bake:** *15 minutes* **Servings:** *4* **Oven:** *400°*

12	ounces fresh or frozen cod, orange roughy, or flounder fillets
1½	cups dry white wine or chicken broth
1	cup dried small shell macaroni
1	8-ounce carton plain low-fat yogurt
½	cup thinly sliced celery
1	tablespoon Worcestershire sauce
2	teaspoons Dijon-style mustard
¼	teaspoon salt
	Dash ground red pepper
¼	cup grated Parmesan or Romano cheese
2	tablespoons fine dry bread crumbs
1	tablespoon snipped fresh chives
1	tablespoon butter or margarine, melted
	Paprika

[1] Thaw fish, if frozen. Rinse fish and pat dry with paper towels. Measure thickness of fish fillets. In a large skillet bring white wine to boiling; add fish. Return to boiling; reduce heat. Cover and simmer until fish just begins to flake with a fork (allow 4 to 6 minutes per ½-inch thickness of fish). Drain fish; discarding liquid. Cut fish into bite-size pieces.

[2] Meanwhile, cook pasta according to package directions. Drain pasta; rinse with cold water. Drain again.

[3] In a large mixing bowl stir together yogurt, celery, Worcestershire sauce, Dijon-style mustard, salt, and ground red pepper. Add fish and pasta, tossing lightly to coat. Spoon pasta mixture into four au gratin dishes.

[4] In a small bowl toss together the Parmesan cheese, bread crumbs, chives, and butter. Sprinkle the crumb mixture over pasta mixture. Sprinkle with paprika. Bake in a 400° oven about 15 minutes or until heated through and crumbs are golden. If desired, garnish with additional snipped chives.

Nutrition Facts per serving: 290 cal., 7 g total fat (4 g sat. fat), 53 mg chol., 521 mg sodium, 28 g carbo., 1 g fiber, 25 g pro. Daily Values: 7% vit. A, 6% vit. C, 23% calcium, 10% iron

Poached Orange Roughy with Lemon Sauce

[*No fish out of water here! Poaching the popular fish in a lemon- and pepper-infused broth preserves its delicate flavor and texture. Notice, too, how this fry-free method requires no added oil, resulting in a light, flavorful low-fat dish.*]

Start to Finish: *20 minutes*   **Servings:** *4*

1   **pound fresh orange roughy or red snapper, ½ inch thick**
1   **pound asparagus spears**
1   **14½-ounce can reduced-sodium chicken broth**
2   **teaspoons finely shredded lemon peel**
1   **medium yellow sweet pepper, cut into bite-size strips**
4   **teaspoons cornstarch**
2   **tablespoons snipped fresh chives**
2   **cups hot cooked couscous or rice**

[1] Rinse fish; pat dry. Cut fish into four serving-size pieces; set aside. Snap off and discard woody bases from asparagus. Cut asparagus in half; set aside. In a large skillet combine 1 cup of the chicken broth, the lemon peel, and ⅛ teaspoon black pepper. Bring to boiling; reduce heat. Carefully add fish and asparagus. Cover; cook over medium-low heat for 4 minutes. Add sweet pepper. Cover; cook 2 minutes more or until fish flakes easily. Transfer fish and vegetables to a platter, reserving liquid in skillet. Keep fish and vegetables warm.

[2] For sauce, stir together remaining broth and cornstarch. Stir into liquid in skillet. Cook and stir until thickened and bubbly. Cook and stir for 2 minutes more. Stir in chives. To serve, arrange fish and vegetables on top of couscous. Spoon sauce over fish and vegetables.

Nutrition Facts per serving: 249 cal., 2 g total fat (0 g sat. fat), 60 mg chol., 390 mg sodium, 29 g carbo., 6 g fiber, 28 g pro. **Daily Values:** 8% vit. A, 96% vit. C, 3% calcium, 8% iron

Nose Knows—and the Eyes Have It

When buying seafood, trust your nose and eyes to help you make the best selection.

Look for fish with
▌ Clear, bright bulging eyes
▌ Shiny, taut bright skin
▌ Red gills that are not slippery
▌ Flesh that feels firm and elastic
▌ Moist, clean-cut fillets and steaks
▌ Packages that are solidly frozen

Avoid fish with
▌ Strong, fishy odor
▌ Dull, bloody, or sunken eyes
▌ Fading skin and gill color
▌ Ragged-cut fillets and steaks
▌ Frozen packages that have torn wrappers, frost, or blood inside or out

Fish and
Seafood

Pecan-Crusted Fish with Peppers and Squash

[Catfish is a great choice for this quick-fix recipe, as it's a gutsy fish that stands up to a crunchy and flavorful treatment. A confetti of colorful vegetables rounds out the dinner. For a heartier menu, try serving with a packaged Creole-seasoned rice mix.]

Prep: 20 minutes   **Bake:** 20 minutes   **Servings:** 4   **Oven:** 425°

12	ounces skinless catfish fillets, white fish, or orange roughy, ½ inch thick
½	cup finely chopped pecans
⅓	cup yellow cornmeal
½	teaspoon onion salt
¼	cup all-purpose flour
¼	teaspoon ground red pepper
1	egg
1	tablespoon water
2	small red and/or orange sweet peppers, seeded and quartered
1	medium zucchini, cut into ½-inch diagonal slices
1	medium yellow summer squash, cut into ½-inch diagonal slices
1	tablespoon cooking oil
¼	teaspoon seasoned salt

[1] Line a 15×10×1-inch baking pan with foil. Lightly grease the foil; set aside. Rinse fish and pat dry with paper towels. Cut fish into four serving-size pieces; set aside.

[2] In a shallow dish stir together pecans, cornmeal, and onion salt. In another shallow dish stir together flour and ground red pepper. In a small bowl beat together egg and water. Dip one piece of fish in flour mixture to coat lightly, shaking off any excess. Dip fish in egg mixture, then in pecan mixture to coat. Place the coated fish in the prepared pan. Repeat with the remaining fish pieces.

[3] In a large bowl combine sweet peppers, zucchini, and yellow summer squash. Add cooking oil and seasoned salt, tossing to coat. Arrange peppers and squash next to fish, overlapping vegetables as needed to fit onto pan. Bake, uncovered, in 425° oven for 20 to 25 minutes or until fish flakes easily with a fork and vegetables are tender.

[4] To serve, divide fish pieces and vegetables among four dinner plates. If desired, garnish with fresh oregano leaves.

Nutrition Facts per serving: 302 cal., 15 g total fat (2 g sat. fat), 98 mg chol., 367 mg sodium, 21 g carbo., 3 g fiber, 21 g pro. Daily Values: 241% vit. A, 74% vit. C, 42% calcium, 12% iron

Tuna and Pasta Alfredo

[It takes only minutes to prepare fresh tuna for this recipe, but if time prohibits a trip to the seafood market, a can of tuna will do. Either will create a luscious dish that's ready in minutes.]

Start to Finish: 25 minutes   **Servings:** 6

- 3 cups dried mini lasagna, broken mafalda, or medium noodles
- 1 tablespoon margarine or butter
- 2 cups chopped broccoli rabe or broccoli
- 1 medium red sweet pepper, chopped
- 1 10-ounce container refrigerated light Alfredo sauce
- 2 teaspoons snipped fresh dill
- 1 to 2 tablespoons milk
- 8 ounces flaked, cooked tuna* or one 9½-ounce can tuna (water pack), drained and broken into chunks
- ½ cup sliced almonds, toasted (optional)

[1] Cook pasta according to package directions; drain. Meanwhile, in a large saucepan melt margarine. Cook the broccoli rabe and sweet pepper in hot margarine until tender. Stir in Alfredo sauce and dill. If necessary, add milk to make desired consistency. Gently stir in cooked pasta and tuna. Heat through. To serve, transfer pasta to a warm serving dish. If desired, sprinkle with almonds.

*Note: To broil tuna, place on the greased rack of a broiler pan. Broil 4 inches from the heat for 4 to 6 minutes per ½-inch thickness or until fish flakes easily with fork. If fish is more than 1 inch thick, turn it over halfway through cooking. To poach tuna, add 1½ cups water to a large skillet. Bring to boiling; add fish. Simmer, uncovered, for 4 to 6 minutes per ½-inch thickness or until fish flakes easily with fork.

Nutrition Facts per serving: 324 cal., 12 g total fat (5 g sat. fat), 39 mg chol., 461 mg sodium, 35 g carbo., 1 g fiber, 19 g pro. Daily Values: 49% vit. A, 69% vit. C, 11% calcium, 12% iron

Broccoli's Slender Cousin
Though the broccoli rabe is much-loved in Italy, Americans are just getting to know this vegetable. Akin to broccoli, only much thinner, broccoli rabe is also known as rapini; it has a leafy green stalk with small clusters of florets, a pleasantly bitter flavor, and a crunchy texture. Find it at many supermarkets and specialty food stores during the fall through the spring of the year.

Coriander-Crusted Salmon with Tropical Rice

[*The taste of complexly flavored coriander seeds—a cross between caraway and sage, with a little lemon bite—adds a pleasantly crisp layer to the salmon fillet. Keep in mind that it takes so little time to snip, shred, and crush the lively ingredients in this quick supper that you should put the rice on to cook first.*]

Prep: *15 minutes* **Bake:** *12 minutes* **Servings:** *4* **Oven:** *450°*

- 1 1½-pound fresh or frozen salmon fillet
- 2 tablespoons coriander seed, coarsely crushed
- 1 tablespoon brown sugar
- 1 teaspoon lemon-pepper seasoning
- 1 tablespoon margarine or butter, melted
- 2 cups cooked rice
- 1 medium mango, peeled, seeded, and chopped
- 1 tablespoon snipped fresh cilantro
- 1 teaspoon finely shredded lemon peel

[1] Thaw salmon, if frozen. Rinse fish and pat dry with paper towels. Measure thickness of fish. Place fish, skin side down, in a greased shallow baking pan. In a small bowl stir together coriander seed, brown sugar, and lemon-pepper seasoning. Brush top and sides of fish with melted margarine. Sprinkle fish with coriander mixture, pressing in slightly.

[2] Stir together rice, mango, cilantro, and lemon peel. Spoon rice mixture around fish. Bake, uncovered, in a 450° oven for 4 to 6 minutes per ½-inch thickness of fish.

[3] To serve, cut fish into four serving-size pieces. Serve fish on top of rice mixture. If desired, garnish each serving with additional shredded lemon peel and cilantro sprigs.

Nutrition Facts per serving: 336 cal., 9 g total fat (2 g sat. fat), 31 mg chol., 406 mg sodium, 36 g carbo., 1 g fiber, 27 g pro. Daily Values: 26% vit. A, 24% vit. C, 4% calcium, 18% iron

Managing a Mango
Because the meat from the mango holds tightly to the seed, these fruits require a little effort before yielding their fragrant spicy-peach meat. An easy way to remove the meat is to make a cut through the mango, sliding a sharp knife next to the seed along one side. Repeat on other side of the seed, resulting in two large pieces. Then cut away all of the meat that remains around the seed. Remove peel on all pieces; cut up or puree the meat.

[201]

Salmon with Fresh Tomato and Olive Sauce

[*Here salmon gets along swimmingly with a Mediterranean-style treatment of tomatoes, garlic, olive oil, and black olives. Like much cooking from that region, the dish showcases fresh foods simply prepared— and a hallmark touch of olive oil.*]

Start to Finish: *40 minutes*　**Servings:** *4*

4	fresh or frozen salmon fillets, about 1 inch thick
¼	teaspoon salt
¼	teaspoon pepper
4	large ripe tomatoes, peeled, seeded, and chopped
¼	cup halved, pitted kalamata olives
1	tablespoon olive oil
3	cloves garlic, minced
2	cups hot cooked tiny bow-tie pasta, orzo, or couscous
2	tablespoons shredded fresh basil

[1] Thaw salmon, if frozen. Rinse fish and pat dry with paper towels. Sprinkle fish with salt and pepper; set aside.

[2] In a large skillet combine tomatoes, olives, olive oil, and garlic. Bring to boiling; add salmon fillets. Cover and simmer for 8 to 12 minutes or until fish flakes easily with a fork. Remove fish from skillet; cover and keep warm.

[3] Return tomato mixture to boiling; reduce heat. Simmer, uncovered, about 5 minutes or until slightly reduced. To serve, divide pasta among four dinner plates. Top each serving with a piece of fish and some sauce. Sprinkle with shredded basil.

Nutrition Facts per serving: 402 cal., 17 g total fat (3 g sat. fat), 87 mg chol., 318 mg sodium, 26 g carbo., 3 g fiber, 35 g pro. Daily Values: 16% vit. A, 41% vit. C, 3% calcium, 13% iron

Peel Out
You needn't always peel the skin off the tomato; in fact, when using tomatoes uncooked in salads or sandwiches, the skin helps the tomato slices hold their shape. However, when the tomatoes will be cooked, as in the above recipe, it's best to peel them. Otherwise, the skins can be difficult to eat. The quickest way to peel tomatoes is to plunge them into boiling water for 30 seconds, then rinse them in cold water. Loosen the skin with the tip of a paring knife and slip off the skin.

Asian Salmon and Vegetable Stir-Fry

[*If snow pea pods are not available, you can substitute fresh asparagus—either will bring a crunchy texture and vibrant-green hue to this speedy dish.*]

Start to Finish: *25 minutes*   **Servings:** *4*

1	pound fresh or frozen salmon fillets or steaks
2	tablespoons rice vinegar
2	tablespoons soy sauce
1	teaspoon toasted sesame oil
½	to 1 teaspoon red chili paste
1	cup thinly sliced red, yellow, and/or green sweet pepper
1	teaspoon grated fresh ginger
2	cloves garlic, minced
1	teaspoon peanut oil
2	medium cucumbers, peeled, halved lengthwise, seeded, and cut into ¼-inch-thick slices
1	cup fresh snow pea pods, strings removed, or 8 ounces thin asparagus, cut into 1-inch pieces
2	cups cooked rice noodles or rice

[1] Thaw salmon, if frozen. Rinse fish and pat dry. Remove skin and bones; discard. Cut fish into 1-inch pieces; set aside. In a small bowl combine rice vinegar, soy sauce, sesame oil, and red chili paste; set aside.

[2] In a large nonstick skillet cook sweet pepper, ginger, and garlic in hot peanut oil until tender. Add salmon. Cook and stir for 3 to 5 minutes or until salmon flakes easily, being careful not to break up pieces. Add cucumber and pea pods; cook and stir about 1 minute or until heated through. Stir in vinegar mixture. Serve salmon and vegetable mixture over cooked rice noodles. If desired, sprinkle with 1 sliced green onion.

Nutrition Facts per serving: 362 cal., 7 g total fat (1 g sat. fat), 20 mg chol., 1,650 mg sodium, 49 g carbo., 3 g fiber, 25 g pro. Daily Values: 22% vit. A, 97% vit. C, 17% iron

The Fish Switch

If a variety of fish called for in a recipe isn't available, consider these substitutions:
- Cod: substitute haddock, halibut, pike, or pollack
- Orange roughy: substitute cod, flounder, sea bass, or sole
- Catfish: substitute cusk, red snapper, or sea trout
- Tuna: substitute mackerel, salmon, or swordfish
- Salmon: substitute swordfish or tuna

Pad Thai

[*No wonder Pad Thai is one of Thailand's most famous noodle dishes—its multifaceted mixture of nutty, salty, sweet, hot, and fresh flavors is singularly addictive. Find the hot sauce, fish sauce, and rice noodles in Asian specialty stores or in the Asian food aisle of the supermarket.*]

Start to Finish: *40 minutes*   **Servings:** *4*

- 1   pound fresh or frozen shrimp in shells
- 6   ounces wide rice noodles
- 1   cup shredded carrot
- 3   tablespoons lime juice
- 3   tablespoons fish sauce
- 2   teaspoons sugar
- 1   tablespoon Thai hot sauce
- 1   cup bean sprouts
- 6   green onions, chopped
- 1   tablespoon cooking oil
- 2   cloves garlic, minced
- ¼   cup dry roasted peanuts, finely chopped

[1] Thaw shrimp, if frozen. Peel and devein shrimp. Rinse shrimp and pat dry with paper towels; set aside.

[2] Meanwhile, soak rice noodles in cold water for 30 minutes. Drain noodles. Cook noodles in boiling water about 5 minutes or just until tender and opaque. Stir in carrot; drain and set aside.

[3] For dressing, in a small bowl stir together lime juice, fish sauce, sugar, and hot sauce. In a large mixing bowl toss together cooked noodles and carrots, dressing, bean sprouts, and green onions.

[4] In a wok or large skillet heat cooking oil over medium heat. Cook and stir shrimp and garlic in hot oil for 2 to 3 minutes or until shrimp turn opaque. Add shrimp to the noodle mixture, tossing to combine.

[5] To serve, transfer mixture to a serving dish. Sprinkle with peanuts and 1 tablespoon snipped fresh cilantro, if desired.

Nutrition Facts per serving: 388 cal., 9 g total fat (1 g sat. fat), 131 mg chol., 908 mg sodium, 53 g carbo., 3 g fiber, 24 g pro. Daily Values: 86% vit. A, 29% vit. C, 5% calcium, 24% iron

[205]

Dilled Shrimp with Rice

[*The sprightly marriage of lemon and dill is a match made in heaven, and three certainly isn't a crowd when sweet pink shrimp are added to the mix. More and more supermarkets are offering fully cooked, peeled shrimp—rely on this convenience product to get this dish to the table in less than half an hour.*]

Start to Finish: *25 minutes* **Servings:** *4*

1	tablespoon margarine or butter
⅔	cup thinly sliced leeks
1½	cups shredded carrots
1	cup fresh pea pods, cut in half
1	teaspoon instant chicken bouillon granules
12	ounces fully cooked peeled shrimp
2	cups hot cooked rice
1	teaspoon finely shredded lemon peel
1	tablespoon snipped fresh dillweed or ½ teaspoon dried dillweed

[1] In a large skillet melt margarine over medium-high heat. Cook and stir leeks, carrots, and pea pods in hot margarine for 2 to 3 minutes or until vegetables are crisp-tender.

[2] Dissolve bouillon granules in ¼ cup water. Stir shrimp, rice, lemon peel, and dissolved granules into skillet. Cook about 5 minutes or until heated through, stirring occasionally. Stir in dillweed. To serve, divide rice mixture among four bowls. If desired, garnish with fresh dill sprigs.

Nutrition Facts per serving: 268 cal., 4 g total fat (1 g sat. fat), 166 mg chol., 478 mg sodium, 35 g carbo., 5 g fiber, 22 g pro. Daily Values: 136% vit. A, 31% vit. C, 7% calcium, 34% iron

Stir-Fries Forever

An Asian cooking technique, stir-frying involves cooking pieces of meat, poultry, seafood, and/or vegetables quickly over high heat with a constant stirring motion. These days, many American cooks appreciate the method for both its speed and because it requires little oil. While a wok is traditionally used in stir-frying, you can also use a large, deep skillet. The high sides will make it easy to stir and toss foods—without tossing them out of the pan. Don't overload the skillet, however, because when too much food is added at once, the wok may cool, causing the food to stew rather than fry. Because stir-frying involves quick cooking, be sure to have all vegetables prepared as directed, as well as all seasonings and spices measured and combined as directed, before you start the cooking process.

Fish and
Seafood

Shrimp and Couscous Jambalaya

[Jambalaya, that lively Creole dish of rice and just about anything, is hardly a sleepy dish to begin with. But here we've stirred things up even more by calling on couscous for a textural change—and also because it cooks quickly right in the same skillet along with the rest of the ingredients.]

Start to Finish: *25 minutes*   **Servings:** *4*

12	ounces fresh or frozen medium shrimp in shells
1	cup sliced celery
¾	cup chopped green sweet pepper
½	cup chopped onion
½	teaspoon Cajun seasoning
¼	teaspoon dried oregano, crushed
2	tablespoons cooking oil
1	14½-ounce can reduced-sodium chicken broth
1	cup quick-cooking couscous
½	cup chopped ripe tomato

[1] Thaw shrimp, if frozen. Peel and devein shrimp. Rinse shrimp and pat dry with paper towels; set aside. In a large skillet cook and stir celery, sweet pepper, onion, seasoning, and oregano in hot oil until vegetables are tender. Carefully add broth; bring to boiling.

[2] Stir in the shrimp and remove from heat. Stir in the couscous and tomato. Cover and let stand for 5 minutes. To serve, fluff mixture with a fork. Transfer mixture to a shallow serving bowl. If desired, serve with bottled hot pepper sauce and lemon wedges.

Nutrition Facts per serving: 317 cal., 8 g total fat (1 g sat. fat), 98 mg chol., 462 mg sodium, 42 g carbo., 9 g fiber, 18 g pro. Daily Values: 8% vit. A, 39% vit. C, 4% calcium, 16% iron

Shrimp Smarts

Sure, you can make life easier by buying peeled and deveined shrimp, but don't be daunted if you can't find a market that will do this for you. Here's how it's done:
▮ To peel, use your fingers to open the shell lengthwise down the body's underside. Starting at the head end, peel the shell back from the body. Then gently pull on the tail portion of the shell and remove it.
▮ To devein, use a sharp knife to make a shallow slit along the shrimp's back from the head end to the tail. Rinse under cold running water to remove the vein, using the tip of knife, if necessary.

Greek Leeks and Shrimp Stir-Fry

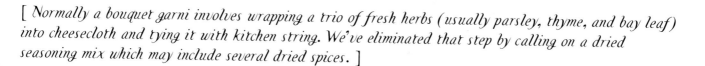

[*Normally a bouquet garni involves wrapping a trio of fresh herbs (usually parsley, thyme, and bay leaf) into cheesecloth and tying it with kitchen string. We've eliminated that step by calling on a dried seasoning mix which may include several dried spices.*]

Start to Finish: *30 minutes* **Servings:** *4*

1¼	pounds fresh or frozen peeled, deveined medium shrimp
⅔	cup water
⅓	cup lemon juice
2	teaspoons cornstarch
¼	teaspoon bouquet garni seasoning or dried oregano, crushed
1	cup quick-cooking couscous
½	teaspoon bouquet garni seasoning or dried oregano, crushed
¼	teaspoon salt
1½	cups boiling water
1	tablespoon olive oil
1⅓	cups thinly sliced leeks
½	cup crumbled feta cheese (2 ounces)
10	pitted kalamata olives, quartered

[1] Thaw shrimp, if frozen. Rinse shrimp and pat dry with paper towels; set aside. In a small bowl combine the ⅔ cup water, lemon juice, cornstarch, and ¼ teaspoon of the bouquet garni seasoning or oregano. Set the mixture aside.

[2] In a small bowl combine couscous, the ½ teaspoon bouquet garni, and salt. Pour boiling water over couscous. Cover and let stand for 5 minutes.

[3] Meanwhile, heat oil in wok or large skillet over medium-high heat. Cook and stir leeks in hot oil for 2 to 3 minutes or until leeks are tender. Remove leeks from wok; set aside. Stir lemon juice mixture. Add to wok and bring to boiling. Add shrimp and cook about 3 minutes or until shrimp turn pink. Stir in cooked leeks and ¼ cup of the feta cheese.

[4] To serve, fluff couscous mixture with a fork. Transfer couscous mixture to a serving platter. Spoon shrimp mixture over couscous and sprinkle with kalamata olives and remaining feta cheese. If desired, garnish with whole kalamata olives.

Nutrition Facts per serving: 412 cal., 10 g total fat (3 g sat. fat), 230 mg chol., 609 mg sodium, 49 g carbo., 11 g fiber, 33 g pro. Daily Values: 11% vit. A, 28% vit. C, 14% calcium, 36% iron

Fish and
Seafood

Linguine with Scallops, Spinach, and Lemon

[*Sweet scallops get a sprightly spark from lemon in this quick dish that's worthy of serving at a casual gathering of friends. Because there's no cheese in the dish, a varied cheese platter would make a perfect appetizer. After dinner, linger into the evening with a fruity sorbet and a tray of dainty sugar cookies.*]

Start to Finish: *25 minutes* **Servings:** *4*

8	ounces dried linguine or spaghetti
1	pound fresh sea scallops
2	tablespoons butter
3	cloves garlic, minced
½	teaspoon finely shredded lemon peel
¼	teaspoon crushed red pepper
2	tablespoons lemon juice
2	cups shredded fresh spinach
1	cup coarsely shredded carrot

[1] Cook pasta in lightly salted water according to package directions. Drain and return pasta to hot pan.

[2] Meanwhile, rinse scallops and pat dry with paper towels. Halve any large scallops. In a large skillet melt butter over medium heat. Cook scallops, garlic, lemon peel, and red pepper in hot butter for 3 to 4 minutes or until scallops turn opaque. Add lemon juice, tossing to coat. Add scallop mixture, spinach, and carrot to cooked pasta, tossing lightly to combine.

[3] To serve, divide the pasta mixture among four dinner plates. If desired, garnish with lemon wedges or slices.

Nutrition Facts per serving: 370 cal., 8 g total fat (4 g sat. fat), 49 mg chol., 262 mg sodium, 52 g carbo., 2 g fiber, 24 g pro. Daily Values: 102% vit. A, 24% vit. C, 10% calcium, 34% iron

Buy-the-Sea Scallops
Sea scallops are the larger of the two most widely available varieties of this kind of shellfish. Bay scallops, the smaller variety, have a sweet flavor similar to sea scallops. Scallops should be firm, sweet smelling, and free of excess cloudy liquid. Chill shucked scallops covered with their own liquid in a closed container for up to 2 days. Or, freeze freshly shucked scallops with their own liquid in a freezer container. Leave ½-inch headspace at top of the freezer container. Seal, label, and freeze the scallops. Thaw frozen scallops in the refrigerator.

Pan-Seared Scallops

[*Though scallops are quickly seared and everything's cooked in one skillet, this recipe's no mere flash in the pan. With its sophisticated melding of balsamic vinegar-dressed spinach and crisp-cooked bacon, you'll enjoy it for years to come. Serve it with corn bread and cold beer for a meal that's homey and elegant.*]

Start to Finish: *20 minutes* **Servings:** *4*

1	pound fresh sea scallops
2	tablespoons all-purpose flour
1	to 2 teaspoons blackened steak seasoning or Cajun seasoning
1	tablespoon cooking oil
1	10-ounce package prewashed spinach
1	tablespoon water
2	tablespoons balsamic vinegar
¼	cup cooked bacon pieces

[1] Rinse scallops and pat dry with paper towels. In a plastic bag combine flour and seasoning. Add scallops, shaking to coat. In a large skillet heat cooking oil over medium heat. Cook scallops in hot oil about 6 minutes or until brown and opaque, turning once. Remove scallops from skillet.

[2] Add spinach to hot skillet; sprinkle with water. Cover and cook over medium-high heat about 2 minutes or until spinach is wilted. Add vinegar, tossing to coat evenly. Return scallops to skillet and heat through. Sprinkle with bacon.

Nutrition Facts per serving: 158 cal., 6 g total fat (1 g sat. fat), 37 mg chol., 323 mg sodium, 9 g carbo., 2 g fiber, 18 g pro. Daily Values: 49% vit. A, 37% vit. C, 12% calcium, 29% iron

Fish and Seafood

Beyond Ice Cream

Don't desert dessert for lack of time! Consider these no-recipe ideas next time you want to serve something sweet to someone special:

❚ Slice a purchased angel food cake in half horizontally; fill with a thin layer of purchased lemon curd and frost with sweetened whipped cream. Serve immediately.

❚ Toss strawberries with a little sugar; let stand about 1 hour or until a syrup forms. Toss with a small amount of balsamic vinegar, and top with a dollop of mascarpone cheese.

❚ Remember, too, the simple pleasures of in-season fruits—such as peaches, nectarines, and plums, tossed with a little honey. Add some chopped, toasted almonds or pecans, if you wish.

Trattoria Pasta Shells with Clams

[Trattorias are the small, one-of-a-kind family restaurants tucked into neighborhoods throughout Italy. This dish, with its heady garlic flavor and sprightly white wine and lemon aromas, resembles "spaghetti alla vongole," a similar dish you might find at a trattoria in a coastal Italian village.]

Prep: 50 minutes   **Cook:** 15 minutes   **Servings:** 4

1	pound small clams in shells (about 16)
8	ounces dried medium shell pasta
1	zucchini, cut in half lengthwise and thinly sliced
1	cup chicken broth
⅓	cup dry white wine
6	cloves garlic, coarsely chopped
1	tablespoon cornstarch
1	tablespoon chicken broth
1	cup cherry tomatoes, halved
2	tablespoons lemon-flavored olive oil or 2 tablespoons olive oil plus ½ teaspoon finely shredded lemon peel
1	tablespoon snipped fresh tarragon
¼	teaspoon crushed red pepper

[1] Scrub clamshells under cold running water, using a stiff brush. In a large bowl combine 4 quarts cold water and ⅓ cup salt; add clams. Soak clams for 15 minutes; drain and rinse, discarding water. Repeat soaking and rinsing twice.

[2] Meanwhile, cook pasta according to package directions, adding the zucchini the last 2 minutes of cooking time. Drain and set aside.

[3] In a large skillet combine the 1 cup chicken broth, the white wine, and garlic. Bring to boiling; add clams. Cover and cook clams about 5 minutes or until clams open. Discard any clams that do not open. Remove clams from skillet and cover to keep warm. Strain the liquid to remove sand. Measure 1⅓ cups cooking liquid and return it to the skillet.

[4] In a small bowl stir together cornstarch and the 1 tablespoon chicken broth. Add mixture to liquid in skillet. Cook and stir over medium heat until thick and bubbly. Cook and stir for 2 minutes more. Add the cooked pasta, cherry tomatoes, olive oil, tarragon, crushed red pepper, and enough salt to taste to liquid mixture in skillet. Heat through. Arrange clams on top of pasta mixture in skillet. Cover and cook for 1 to 2 minutes more to heat clams. If desired, pass grated Parmesan cheese.

[213]

Nutrition Facts per serving: 437 cal., 10 g total fat (1 g sat. fat), 48 mg chol., 330 mg sodium, 55 g carbo., 3 g fiber, 28 g pro. Daily Values: 17% vit. A, 48% vit. C, 8% calcium, 151% iron

Fish and
Seafood

Charleston Crab Pot Pie

[Like the famous dance named after this Southern city, this recipe for pot pie is full of twists and kicks! The Cajun seasoning in the luscious crab-and-leek filling is sure to raise a few eyebrows, and ultrathin layers of crisp phyllo dough will add another delightfully unexpected dimension.]

Prep: *35 minutes* **Bake:** *25 minutes* **Servings:** *6* **Oven:** *375°*

3	**tablespoons butter**
4	**leeks, chopped**
⅓	**cup all-purpose flour**
2½	**cups milk**
1	**pound crabmeat, flaked and cartilage removed**
1	**cup frozen peas**
¼	**cup dry sherry (optional)**
1½	**teaspoons Cajun seasoning**
2	**tablespoons butter, melted**
1	**teaspoon Dijon-style mustard (optional)**
2	**sheets frozen phyllo dough (17×12-inch rectangles), thawed**

[1] In a large skillet melt the 3 tablespoons butter over medium heat. Cook and stir leeks in hot butter for 2 to 3 minutes or until tender. Add the flour to the skillet; cook and stir about 1 minute. Stir in the milk; cook and stir until mixture begins to boil. Stir in the crabmeat, peas, dry sherry (if desired), Cajun seasoning, and, if desired, ⅛ to ¼ teaspoon ground red pepper. Spoon the crab mixture into a 2-quart square baking dish.

[2] In a small bowl stir together the 2 tablespoons melted butter and, if desired, the Dijon-style mustard. Brush one sheet of phyllo dough with butter mixture; fold in half crosswise. Repeat with other sheet. Stack the two sheets. Using a sharp knife, trim phyllo to about a 9-inch square. Place phyllo stack over crab mixture; tuck edges under. Brush any remaining butter mixture over top. Bake in a 375° oven for 25 to 30 minutes or until heated through. Serve immediately.

Nutrition Facts per serving: 297 cal., 13 g total fat (7 g sat. fat), 109 mg chol., 461 mg sodium, 23 g carbo., 4 g fiber, 22 g pro. Daily Values: 19% vit. A, 15% vit. C, 20% calcium, 17% iron

Indian-Style
Vegetables
and Rice
Page 221

Lasagna
with Zucchini
and Walnuts
Page 230

[Vegetarian]

Tortilla Bean-and-Rice Bake **Page 224**

Corn and Tomato Bread Pudding

[*Here the classic bread pudding dessert gets reinvented as a luscious vegetarian main course. If using the French bread option, cut cubes from only firm, dry bread, as fresh bread is too soft to soak up all the milk and eggs and hold its shape.*]

Prep: *20 minutes* **Bake:** *30 minutes* **Servings:** *6* **Oven:** *375°*

- 3 tablespoons snipped dried tomatoes (not oil-packed)
- 4 beaten eggs
- 1½ cups milk, half-and-half, or light cream
- 1 tablespoon snipped fresh basil or 1 teaspoon dried basil, crushed
- 4 cups torn English muffins or dry French bread
- 1½ cups fresh or frozen whole kernel corn
- 1 cup shredded reduced-fat cheddar cheese or hot pepper cheese (4 ounces)

[1] Place dried tomatoes in a small bowl; add enough hot water to cover. Let stand about 15 minutes or until softened; drain. Meanwhile, in a medium bowl beat together eggs, milk, and basil; set aside. In an ungreased 2-quart square baking dish toss together torn English muffins, corn, cheese, and the softened tomatoes.

[2] Carefully pour egg mixture evenly over muffin mixture in the baking dish. Bake, uncovered, in a 375° oven about 30 minutes or until a knife inserted near the center comes out clean. Cool slightly. If desired, serve bread pudding on top of thin tomato wedges.

Nutrition Facts per serving: 275 cal., 9 g total fat (4 g sat. fat), 160 mg chol., 486 mg sodium, 32 g carbo., 3 g fiber, 16 g pro. Daily Values: 14% vit. A, 6% vit. C, 23% calcium, 11% iron

To Make Ahead: Prepare Step 1. Cover and refrigerate the egg mixture and the English muffin mixture separately for up to 24 hours. When ready to bake, combine the two mixtures and bake, uncovered, as directed above.

Drying Bread Cubes

You can dry bread cubes following either of the methods below. You'll need about 5 cups fresh bread cubes to make 4 cups dry cubes.

▮ Cut bread into ½-inch-thick pieces; then cut into cubes. Spread in a single layer in a shallow baking pan. Bake in a 300° oven for 10 to 15 minutes or until dry, stirring twice; cool. (Bread will continue to dry and crisp as it cools.)

▮ Or, let bread cubes stand, loosely covered, at room temperature for 8 to 12 hours.

[218]
Vegetarian

Mushroom and Asparagus Strata

[*This layered baked strata showcases spring's tender asparagus well. Remember it as a great make-ahead brunch or lunch dish for any springtime event, such as Easter, Mother's Day, or a bridal luncheon.*]

Prep: *25 minutes* **Chill:** *2 hours* **Bake:** *45 minutes* **Stand:** *10 minutes* **Servings:** *6 to 8* **Oven:** *325°*

1	pound thin asparagus spears
1	tablespoon olive oil
4	cups sliced fresh variety mushrooms (such as button and/or shiitake) (about 12 ounces)
2	cloves garlic, minced
¼	teaspoon salt
¼	teaspoon freshly ground white or black pepper
2	cups shredded Swiss and/or Edam cheese (8 ounces)
2	tablespoons snipped fresh dillweed or 1 teaspoon dried dillweed
6	slices French or Italian bread, cut into 4×1×1-inch sticks
6	eggs
2¼	cups half-and-half, light cream, or whole milk
¼	cup grated Romano, Parmesan, or other hard grating cheese

[1] Clean asparagus; snap off woody bases. If spears are thick, cut in half lengthwise. Cut spears into 3-inch pieces. In a large saucepan bring a small amount of water to boiling. Add asparagus. Cook, uncovered, 1 minute. Drain; rinse with cold water. Drain on paper towels.

[2] Lightly grease a 2-quart rectangular baking dish; set aside. In a large skillet heat oil. Add mushrooms, garlic, salt, and pepper. Cook, uncovered, over medium-high heat for 4 to 5 minutes or until nearly all of the liquid has evaporated, stirring often; set aside. In a bowl toss together the Swiss cheese and dillweed. Arrange half the bread in the bottom of the baking dish. Top with half of the mushrooms, half of the cheese mixture, and half of the asparagus. Repeat with remaining mushrooms, cheese mixture, and asparagus. Top with remaining bread pieces.

[3] In a bowl beat together eggs and half-and-half. Pour mixture over layers in dish. Press lightly with back of a spoon to thoroughly moisten bread. Sprinkle grated cheese over top. Cover and chill 2 hours. Bake, uncovered, in a 325° oven about 45 minutes or until a knife inserted near center comes out clean. Remove from oven; let stand 10 minutes before cutting.

Nutrition Facts per serving: 484 cal., 31 g total fat (16 g sat. fat), 284 mg chol., 521 mg sodium, 27 g carbo., 2 g fiber, 27 g pro. Daily Values: 35% vit. A, 26% vit. C, 48% calcium, 23% iron

To Make Ahead: Layer the strata and pour the egg mixture over layers. Cover and chill up to 24 hours. Bake, uncovered, as directed above.

Indian-Style Vegetables and Rice

[*Don't be daunted by the length of the ingredient list—many of the items called for are seasonings that require little work aside from measuring. In fact, this dish takes just 30 minutes from start to finish.*]

Start to Finish: *30 minutes* **Servings:** *4*

¾	cup uncooked regular brown rice
	Nonstick cooking spray
1	large red onion, cut into strips
2	cloves garlic, minced
¾	cup water
½	cup apple juice
2	medium potatoes, cut into ½-inch chunks
1	medium carrot, cut into ¼-inch slices
2	tablespoons reduced-sodium soy sauce
2	to 3 teaspoons curry powder
1	teaspoon grated fresh ginger
½	teaspoon ground cardamom
¼	teaspoon ground cinnamon
2	cups cauliflower flowerets
1	medium zucchini, halved lengthwise and cut into ½-inch slices
1	cup frozen peas
⅓	cup golden raisins

[1] Cook rice according to package directions, except omit any salt. Meanwhile, coat an unheated 4½-quart Dutch oven with nonstick spray. Preheat over medium-high heat. Add onion and garlic; cook and stir until onion is tender. Carefully add the water, apple juice, potatoes, carrot, soy sauce, curry powder, ginger, cardamom, and cinnamon. Bring to boiling; reduce heat. Cover and simmer for 10 minutes.

[2] Add the cauliflower, zucchini, peas, and raisins to the Dutch oven. Cover and simmer for 10 minutes more or until cauliflower is tender. Serve over the cooked rice. If desired, serve with chutney.

Nutrition Facts per serving: 330 cal., 2 g total fat (0 g sat. fat), 0 mg chol., 320 mg sodium, 72 g carbo., 8 g fiber, 9 g pro. Daily Values: 42% vit. A, 89% vit. C, 6% calcium, 24% iron

Butternut Squash Risotto with Pumpkin Seeds

[*A popular ingredient in Mexican cooking, pumpkin seeds (also known as pepitas) can be found in supermarkets, health food stores, and Hispanic markets. The seeds won't resemble the white seeds you pull from pumpkins when making a jack-o'-lantern because their white hulls have been removed.*]

Prep: *45 minutes* **Cook:** *25 minutes* **Servings:** *4*

2	dried pasilla or chipotle chili peppers* (see tip, page 21)
1½	cups cubed peeled butternut or acorn squash
1	bunch green onions, sliced (about ½ cup)
2	cloves garlic, minced
2	tablespoons olive oil or cooking oil
1	cup uncooked arborio or medium grain rice
3	cups vegetable broth or chicken broth
1	cup shredded fontina or Muenster cheese (4 ounces)
¼	cup grated Parmesan cheese
¼	cup toasted pumpkin seeds

[1] Cut chili peppers open and discard stems and seeds. Cut into small pieces. Place in a small bowl and pour boiling water over peppers. Let stand for 45 to 60 minutes until softened. Drain, chop, and set aside. Place squash and a small amount of water in a medium saucepan. Bring to boiling; reduce heat. Cover and simmer about 10 minutes or until just tender. Drain and set aside. In a large saucepan cook green onions and garlic in oil over medium heat until tender. Stir in rice. Cook and stir for 4 to 5 minutes or until rice is lightly golden.

[2] Meanwhile, in another saucepan bring broth to boiling; reduce heat to keep broth simmering. Slowly add about 1 cup of the broth to the rice mixture, stirring constantly. Continue to cook and stir until liquid is absorbed. Add remaining broth, about ½ cup at a time, stirring constantly until all of the broth has been absorbed. The rice should be slightly creamy and just tender. This should take about 15 minutes. Stir in chili peppers and cheeses until fontina is melted. Fold in squash. Turn into a serving dish and sprinkle with pumpkin seeds.

*Note:** For a milder dish, try ancho or New Mexico chili peppers for one or both peppers.

Nutrition Facts per serving: 496 cal., 24 g total fat (8 g sat. fat), 37 mg chol., 1,045 mg sodium, 59 g carbo., 3 g fiber, 17 g pro. Daily Values: 65% vit. A, 23% vit. C, 30% calcium, 14% iron

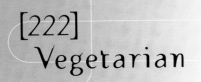

The Right Rice for Risotto
If possible, choose arborio rice, a short-grained rice, for making risotto. Its higher starch content helps bring about the hallmark creaminess so loved about the dish.

Triple Mushroom and Rice Fajitas

[*This recipe proves that the age-old comfort and satisfaction derived from roasting works equally well with an array of colorful vegetables. Think of it next time you're headed out to a Saturday farmer's market in search of a windfall of fresh vegetables, and you'll be set for a new Sunday tradition.*]

Start to Finish: *1 hour* **Servings:** *4* **Oven:** *350°*

½ cup uncooked regular brown rice

¼ cup water

2 tablespoons lime juice

1 tablespoon olive oil or cooking oil

2 large cloves garlic, minced

½ teaspoon ground cumin

½ teaspoon dried oregano, crushed

¼ teaspoon salt

3 ounces fresh portobello mushrooms, stemmed and thinly sliced

3 ounces fresh chanterelle or oyster mushrooms, thinly sliced

3 ounces fresh shiitake mushrooms, stemmed and thinly sliced

1 medium green and/or red sweet pepper, cut into thin strips

4 green onions, cut into 1½-inch pieces

8 7- to 8-inch flour tortillas

¼ cup slivered almonds, toasted

[1] Cook rice according to package directions, except omit any salt. Meanwhile, for marinade, in a large plastic bag set in a deep bowl combine the water, lime juice, oil, garlic, cumin, oregano, and salt. Add mushrooms, sweet pepper strips, and green onions. Seal the bag; turn bag to coat vegetables. Marinate at room temperature for 15 to 30 minutes. Stack tortillas; wrap in foil. Heat in a 350° oven for 10 minutes to soften.

[2] For filling, in a large nonstick skillet cook undrained mushroom mixture over medium-high heat for 6 to 8 minutes or until peppers are tender and all but about 2 tablespoons of the liquid has evaporated, stirring occasionally. Stir in cooked rice and almonds; heat through. To serve, spoon mushroom-rice mixture onto warmed tortillas; roll up. If desired, tie a green onion top around each rolled tortilla.

Nutrition Facts per serving: 331 cal., 9 g total fat (2 g sat. fat), 0 mg chol., 380 mg sodium, 55 g carbo., 4 g fiber, 9 g pro. Daily Values: 3% vit. A, 35% vit. C, 9% calcium, 27% iron

Tortilla Bean-and-Rice Bake

[Some like it hot—but others don't! No problem—you can adjust the spice kick in this layered, low-fat casserole by choosing mild, medium, or hot salsa.]

Prep: *30 minutes* **Bake:** *25 minutes* **Servings:** *6* **Oven:** *350°*

1½	cups water
⅔	cup uncooked long grain rice
6	6-inch corn tortillas
¾	cup fat-free dairy sour cream
1	tablespoon all-purpose flour
1	tablespoon skim milk
1	14½-ounce can Mexican-style stewed tomatoes
1	8-ounce jar salsa
1	15-ounce can kidney beans or small red beans, rinsed and drained
	Nonstick cooking spray

[1] In a medium saucepan bring water to boiling. Add rice and return to boiling; reduce heat. Cover and simmer for 20 minutes or until rice is tender. Meanwhile, stack tortillas; wrap in foil. Heat in a 350° oven for 10 minutes to soften.

[2] In a bowl stir together the sour cream, flour, and milk; set aside. In a medium bowl combine the tomatoes and salsa. Stir drained beans into cooked rice. Coat a 2-quart casserole or baking dish with nonstick spray. Cut softened tortillas into quarters and arrange half of them in the bottom of the casserole. Layer half of the rice-bean mixture over tortillas, then half of the tomato mixture, and half of the sour cream mixture. Repeat layers.

[3] Bake, covered, in a 350° oven for 25 to 30 minutes or until heated through. If desired, garnish with jalapeño slices and shredded reduced-fat Monterey Jack cheese.

Nutrition Facts per serving: 269 cal., 1 g total fat (0 g sat. fat), 0 mg chol., 540 mg sodium, 56 g carbo., 6 g fiber, 11 g pro. Daily Values: 11% vit. A, 26% vit. C, 12% calcium, 21% iron

To Tote: Prepare casserole as above just before leaving home. Omit the optional garnishes. Cover tightly; wrap in several layers of newspaper or a heavy towel. Then place the casserole in an insulated container. Do not hold for longer than 2 hours.

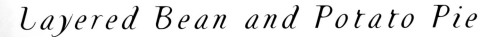

Layered Bean and Potato Pie

[*If you're trying to cut down on meat, try this two-bean casserole featuring garbanzo beans as well as red beans. Layer them in a sauce between a bottom and top covering of thinly sliced potatoes.*]

Prep: *25 minutes*   **Bake:** *45 minutes*   **Servings:** *5*   **Oven:** *350°*

1	**pound small red potatoes**
1	**tablespoon cooking oil**
1	**cup chopped onion**
2	**stalks celery, sliced**
4	**cloves garlic, minced**
¼	**teaspoon cracked black pepper**
1	**15-ounce can garbanzo beans, rinsed and drained**
1	**15-ounce can small red beans, rinsed and drained**
1	**cup frozen peas**
1	**cup chopped green sweet pepper**
1	**10¾-ounce can condensed cream of potato soup**
¼	**cup skim milk**
½	**teaspoon ground cumin**
½	**teaspoon ground coriander**
½	**cup shredded reduced-fat Monterey Jack cheese (2 ounces)**

[1] Scrub potatoes; thinly slice. Cook, covered, in enough boiling water to cover for 4 to 5 minutes or until nearly tender. Drain. Run cold water over potatoes in colander. Drain; set aside. In a large saucepan heat oil. Add onion, celery, garlic, and black pepper; cook for 5 minutes or until vegetables are tender. Mash ½ cup of the garbanzo beans; add to vegetable mixture along with remaining garbanzo beans, red beans, peas, sweet pepper, soup, milk, cumin, and coriander. Gently stir to combine. Grease a 2-quart casserole. Place a single layer of potato slices in casserole. Spoon bean mixture on top and cover with remaining potato slices in layers, overlapping if necessary.

[2] Bake, covered, in a 350° oven for 35 minutes. Uncover and sprinkle with cheese. Bake about 10 minutes more or until the cheese melts.

Nutrition Facts per serving: 376 cal., 8 g total fat (2 g sat. fat), 11 mg chol., 1,073 mg sodium, 63 g carbo., 12 g fiber, 19 g pro. Daily Values: 6% vit. A, 41% vit. C, 16% calcium, 35% iron

To Make Ahead: Prepare as directed through Step 1. Cover tightly and chill overnight. To serve, cover and bake in a 350° oven about 1 hour or until heated through. Uncover and sprinkle with the cheese. Bake, uncovered, 5 minutes more or until the cheese melts.

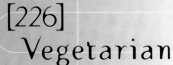

Vegetable Pastitsio

[*Meat isn't the only thing we've omitted from the traditional Greek dish. By calling on refrigerated egg product and skim milk, we've omitted some of the fat, too.*]

Prep: *40 minutes*   **Bake:** *35 minutes*   **Stand:** *5 minutes*   **Servings:** *6*   **Oven:** *350°*

	Nonstick cooking spray
8	ounces dried penne pasta or elbow macaroni
½	cup refrigerated egg product
½	teaspoon ground nutmeg
2	cups fresh spinach leaves
½	cup chopped onion
1	clove garlic, minced
1	tablespoon chicken broth or water
4	teaspoons margarine or butter
1	8-ounce can tomato sauce
1	cup frozen whole kernel corn
1	cup cubed, cooked potatoes
¾	teaspoon dried mint, crushed
½	teaspoon dried oregano, crushed
¼	teaspoon ground cinnamon
3	tablespoons all-purpose flour
1½	cups fat-free milk
¼	cup grated Parmesan cheese

[1] Coat a 2-quart square baking dish with nonstick spray; set aside. Cook pasta according to package directions; drain, reserving hot water. Rinse pasta with cold water; drain. In a large bowl stir together pasta, egg product, ¼ teaspoon of the nutmeg, and ¼ teaspoon salt. Spread mixture evenly in dish. Add spinach to reserved cooking water; let stand 2 minutes or until spinach is wilted. Drain well. Spread spinach on top of pasta mixture. In a large nonstick skillet cook onion and garlic in broth and 1 teaspoon of the margarine over medium heat for 3 minutes or until onion is tender. Add tomato sauce, corn, potatoes, mint, oregano, cinnamon, ¼ teaspoon salt, and ¼ teaspoon pepper; cook and stir until heated through. Spread vegetable mixture over spinach leaves.

[2] In saucepan melt remaining margarine. Stir in flour. Add milk. Cook and stir until bubbly; cook 1 minute more. Stir in Parmesan and remaining nutmeg. Spread on top. Bake in a 350° oven for 35 minutes or until top is firm. Let stand 5 minutes before serving.

[227]

Nutrition Facts per serving: 321 cal., 6 g total fat (2 g sat. fat), 5 mg chol., 602 mg sodium, 54 g carbo., 3 g fiber, 14 g pro. Daily Values: 28% vit. A, 26% vit. C, 187% calcium, 22% iron

Pasta with Marinara Sauce

[*Every cook needs his or her own version of a homemade marinara sauce. Consider this one yours. Sure, it's great over pasta, but once you've tasted it, you'll think of even more great ways to use it.*]

Prep: *30 minutes*   **Cook:** *8 hours*   **Servings:** *6*

2	cups coarsely chopped carrots
1½	cups sliced celery
1	cup chopped onion
1	cup chopped green sweet pepper
3	cloves garlic, minced
2	tablespoons olive oil
1	28-ounce can whole Italian-style tomatoes, cut up
1	6-ounce can tomato paste
1	tablespoon dried Italian seasoning, crushed
2	teaspoons sugar
1	bay leaf
12	ounces dried pasta, cooked and drained

[1] In a skillet cook carrots, celery, onion, pepper, and garlic in oil 5 minutes. In a 3½- or 4-quart electric crockery cooker combine undrained tomatoes, paste, seasoning, sugar, bay leaf, ½ cup water, ½ teaspoon black pepper, and ¼ teaspoon salt. Stir in vegetable mixture.

[2] Cover and cook on low-heat setting for 8 to 10 hours or on high-heat setting for 4 to 5 hours. Discard bay leaf. Serve over hot cooked pasta.

Nutrition Facts per serving: 365 cal., 6 g total fat (1 g sat. fat), 0 mg chol., 387 mg sodium, 68 g carbo., 7 g fiber, 11 g pro. Daily Values: 131% vit. A, 81% vit. C, 8% calcium, 32% iron

To Make Ahead: Cook sauce as directed. Divide into freezer containers. Seal, label, and freeze up to 3 months. Thaw in the refrigerator overnight. To serve, heat in a saucepan until boiling. Meanwhile, cook pasta according to package directions. Serve sauce over pasta.

Marinara — the Marvelous Leftover

The uses for leftover marinara are myriad. Some of our favorites:
▎ Serve over broiled or sautéed chicken breasts. If desired, add sautéed mushrooms.
▎ Transform it into pizza sauce. Spread it on a prepared pizza crust and add toppings.
▎ Try it over grilled or sautéed vegetables and polenta.
▎ Use it as a sauce to perk up your favorite meat-loaf recipe.

Spicy Tomato and Cheese Macaroni

[*Macaroni and cheese grows up! With a sophisticated medley of cheeses, a selection of colorful vegetables, and even a little red-pepper kick, this casserole transcends memories of school cafeteria fare and gives the baked Italian classic back its good name.*]

Prep: *30 minutes* **Bake:** *30 minutes* **Stand:** *10 minutes* **Servings:** *5*

1½	cups dried elbow macaroni
2	cups broccoli flowerets
⅓	cup dried tomatoes (not oil-packed)
⅓	cup sliced green onions
2	tablespoons margarine or butter
2	tablespoons all-purpose flour
1½	teaspoons dried basil, crushed
¼	teaspoon ground red pepper
1¾	cups milk
¾	cup shredded sharp cheddar cheese (3 ounces)
¾	cup shredded Gruyère cheese (3 ounces)
¾	cup shredded Gouda cheese (3 ounces)

[1] In a large saucepan cook macaroni in lightly salted boiling water for 10 minutes or until tender but firm. Add broccoli. Drain well. Meanwhile, snip dried tomatoes. Place in a small bowl; add enough warm water to cover. Let stand 10 minutes or until softened; drain well.

[2] In a medium saucepan cook onion in margarine until tender. Stir in flour, basil, ground red pepper, and ⅛ teaspoon salt. Stir in milk. Cook and stir until slightly thickened and bubbly. Add three cheeses, a little at a time, stirring constantly until melted after each addition. Stir in macaroni-broccoli mixture and softened tomatoes; transfer to a 1½-quart casserole.

[3] Bake, uncovered, in a 350° oven about 30 minutes or until hot and bubbly. Let stand 10 minutes before serving.

Nutrition Facts per serving: 445 cal., 23 g total fat (12 g sat. fat), 62 mg chol., 539 mg sodium, 37 g carbo., 3 g fiber, 23 g pro. Daily Values: 32% vit. A, 49% vit. C, 46% calcium, 14% iron

Cooking al Dente

Cook pasta as the Italians do—just to the al dente stage. Literally meaning "to the tooth," al dente describes the stage where the pasta offers just a slight resistance when bitten; cooking it to this stage also helps it soak up the sauces. To achieve this toothsome effect, taste the pasta often near the end of the cooking time.

Lasagna with Zucchini and Walnuts

[*The challenge of meatless lasagna is to make it as satisfying as the beef- or sausage-layered classic. Crunchy walnuts stand in for the meat, adding heartiness and texture. (Note that all brands of the no-boil lasagna noodles are not the same size, so use enough noodles to have three even, single layers.)*]

Prep: *35 minutes* **Bake:** *40 minutes* **Stand:** *15 minutes* **Servings:** *6* **Oven:** *375°*

2	medium zucchini
4	teaspoons olive oil
2	large carrots, finely chopped
2	cups finely chopped onions
4	cloves garlic, minced
2	cups purchased marinara sauce
1	tablespoon snipped fresh basil or 1 teaspoon dried basil, crushed
⅛	teaspoon pepper
1½	cups shredded mozzarella cheese (6 ounces)
½	cup grated Parmesan cheese
6	no-boil lasagna noodles
½	cups chopped walnuts

[1] Trim ends off zucchini. Thinly slice zucchini lengthwise. (You should have a total of 9 long slices, each about ⅛ inch thick.) Place in a single layer on a lightly greased baking sheet; brush lightly with 1 teaspoon of the oil. Broil 3 to 4 inches from heat about 5 minutes or until crisp-tender, turning once. Let cool before handling.

[2] In a large saucepan heat the remaining oil over medium-high heat. Add carrots, onions, and garlic; cook and stir about 5 minutes or until tender. Add marinara sauce, basil, and pepper. Bring to boiling; reduce heat. Cover and simmer 10 minutes, stirring occasionally. In a small bowl toss together the mozzarella and Parmesan cheeses; set aside.

[3] Grease a 2-quart square baking dish; arrange two noodles in the dish. Spread with a third of the sauce. Sprinkle with a third of the nuts. Top with a third of the zucchini; sprinkle with a third of the cheese mixture. Repeat layering, alternating direction of the zucchini in each layer and finishing with the zucchini; set remaining cheese aside.

[4] Bake, covered, in a 375° oven for 20 minutes. Uncover and sprinkle with remaining cheese mixture. Bake, uncovered, about 20 minutes more or until heated through. Let stand for 15 minutes before serving. If desired, sprinkle with a few chopped walnuts.

[230]
Vegetarian

Nutrition Facts per serving: 358 cal., 19 g total fat (6 g sat. fat), 23 mg chol., 839 mg sodium, 33 g carbo., 3 g fiber, 17 g pro. Daily Values: 100% vit. A, 28% vit. C, 29% calcium, 12% iron

Portobello Mushroom Stroganoff

[*Rather than making the mushrooms a supporting ingredient, we've made them the star. You won't miss the meat one bit, thanks to the meaty texture and rich flavor of portobellos. Because their stems are tough, discard before slicing the mushroom caps.*]

Start to Finish: *35 minutes*   **Servings:** *4*

8	ounces dried fettuccine
1	8-ounce carton light dairy sour cream
2	tablespoons all-purpose flour
¾	cup water
1	teaspoon instant vegetable bouillon granules
¼	teaspoon pepper
12	ounces portobello mushrooms
	Nonstick cooking spray
1	tablespoon margarine or butter
2	medium onions, cut into thin wedges
1	clove garlic, minced
	Snipped fresh parsley

[1] Cook fettuccine according to package directions, except omit any oil or salt. Drain and keep warm. In a small mixing bowl stir together the sour cream and flour. Stir in the water, bouillon granules, and pepper. Set aside. Remove stems from mushrooms; quarter and thinly slice mushroom tops and set aside.

[2] Coat an unheated large skillet with nonstick spray. Add margarine and heat over medium-high heat until melted. Add the mushrooms, onions, and garlic. Cook and stir until the vegetables are tender. Stir the sour cream mixture into skillet. Cook and stir until thickened and bubbly. Cook and stir for 1 minute more. Pour the mushroom mixture over the hot cooked fettuccine, tossing gently to coat. Sprinkle with parsley.

Nutrition Facts per serving: 376 cal., 8 g total fat (3 g sat. fat), 0 mg chol., 320 mg sodium, 63 g carbo., 2 g fiber, 14 g pro. Daily Values: 9% vit. A, 10% vit. C, 7% calcium, 26% iron

Feta and Tomato Pizza

[*This pizza is based on a classic Italian specialty called Pizza Margherita, which is usually topped with mozzarella cheese and fresh, ripe tomatoes. Our version may add a few twists, but they're certainly in keeping with the dish's distinctive Mediterranean feel: feta, ripe olives, and fresh basil.*]

Prep: *20 minutes*   **Bake:** *10 minutes*   **Servings:** *6*   **Oven:** *425°*

- 1   16-ounce Italian bread shell (Boboli)
- 1   cup shredded mozzarella cheese (4 ounces)
- 5   Roma tomatoes
- 1   cup crumbled feta cheese (4 ounces)
- ½   cup sliced pitted ripe olives
- ⅓   cup finely chopped green sweet pepper or thinly sliced green onions
- ⅛   teaspoon garlic pepper seasoning
- ½   cup shredded mozzarella cheese (2 ounces)
- 2   tablespoons snipped fresh basil

[1] Place bread shell on a baking sheet or pizza pan. Sprinkle the 1 cup mozzarella over bread shell. Halve tomatoes lengthwise; remove seeds and discard. Thinly slice tomatoes and arrange on top of mozzarella cheese. Sprinkle with feta cheese, olives, green pepper, and garlic pepper seasoning. Sprinkle with remaining ½ cup mozzarella cheese.

[2] Bake in a 425° oven for 10 to 12 minutes or until heated through. Sprinkle fresh basil over top before serving.

Nutrition Facts per serving: 349 cal., 15 g total fat (6 g sat. fat), 36 mg chol., 811 mg sodium, 38 g carbo., 2 g fiber, 19 g pro. Daily Values: 11% vit. A, 33% vit. C, 30% calcium, 13% iron

To Roma with Love

Robust Roma tomatoes are also good for making sauces. These meaty beauties, sometimes referred to as "plum tomatoes" or "Italian tomatoes," have firmer flesh than ordinary tomatoes, fewer seeds, less juice, and the Romas cook down to a thick, full-flavored sauce.

Index

Index

How We Analyze Recipes
Our Test Kitchen uses a computer analysis of each recipe to determine the nutritional value of a single serving. Here's how:
■ The analysis does not include optional ingredients.
■ We use the first serving size listed when a range is given. For example: Makes 4 to 6 servings.
■ When ingredient choices appear in a recipe (such as margarine or butter), we use the first one mentioned for analysis. The ingredient order does not mean we prefer one ingredient over another.
■ When milk is an ingredient in a recipe, the analysis is calculated using 2-percent milk unless fat-free milk is specified in the recipe.

Metric Cooking Hints

By making a few conversions, cooks in Australia, Canada, and the United Kingdom can use the recipes in this book with confidence. The charts on this page provide a guide for converting measurements from the U.S. customary system, which is used throughout this book, to the imperial and metric systems. There also is a conversion table for oven temperatures to accommodate the differences in oven calibrations.

Product Differences: Most of the ingredients called for in the recipes in this book are available in English-speaking countries. However, some are known by different names. Here are some common U.S. American ingredients and their possible counterparts:
- Sugar is granulated or castor sugar.
- Powdered sugar is icing sugar.
- All-purpose flour is plain household flour or white four. When self-rising flour is used in place of all-purpose flour in a recipe that calls for leavening, omit the leavening agent (baking soda or baking powder) and salt.
- Light-colored corn syrup is golden syrup.
- Cornstarch is cornflour.
- Baking soda is bicarbonate of soda.
- Vanilla is vanilla essence.
- Green, red, or yellow sweet peppers are capsicums.
- Golden raisins are sultanas.

Volume and Weight: U.S. Americans traditionally use cup measures for liquid and solid ingredients. The chart, below, shows the approximate imperial and metric equivalents. If you are accustomed to weighing solid ingredients, the following approximate equivalents will help.
- 1 cup butter, castor sugar, or rice = 8 ounces = about 230 grams.
- 1 cup flour = 4 ounces = about 115 grams.
- 1 cup icing sugar = 5 ounces = about 140 grams

Spoon measures are used for smaller amounts of ingredients. Although the size of the tablespoon varies slightly in different countries, for practical purposes and for recipes in this book, a straight substitution is all that's necessary. Measurements made using cups or spoons always should be level unless stated otherwise.

Metric

Equivalents: U.S. = Australia/U.K.

⅕ teaspoon = 1 ml
¼ teaspoon = 1.25 ml
½ teaspoon = 2.5 ml
1 teaspoon = 5 ml
1 tablespoon = 15 ml
1 fluid ounce = 30 ml
¼ cup = 60 ml
⅓ cup = 80 ml
½ cup = 120 ml
⅔ cup = 160 ml
¾ cup = 180 ml
1 cup = 240 ml
2 cups = 475 ml
1 quart = 1 liter
½ inch = 1.25 cm
1 inch = 2.5 cm

Baking Pan Sizes

U.S. American	Metric
8×1½-inch round baking pan	20×4-cm cake tin
9×1½-inch round baking pan	23×4-cm cake tin
11×7×1½-inch baking pan	28×18×4-cm baking tin
13×9×2-inch baking pan	32×23×5-cm baking tin
2-quart rectangular baking dish	28×18×4-cm baking tin
15×10×1-inch baking pan	38×25.5×2.5-cm baking tin (Swiss roll tin)
9-inch pie plate	22×4- or 23×4-cm pie plate
7- or 8-inch springform pan	18- or 20-cm springform or loose-bottom cake tin
9×5×3-inch loaf pan	23×13×8-cm or 2-pound narrow loaf tin or pâté tin
1½-quart casserole	1.5-liter casserole
2-quart casserole	2-liter casserole

Oven Temperature Equivalents

Fahrenheit Setting	Celsius Setting*	Gas Setting
300°F	150°C	Gas mark 2 (very low)
325°F	170°C	Gas mark 3 (low)
350°F	180°C	Gas mark 4 (moderate)
375°F	190°C	Gas mark 5 (moderately hot)
400°F	200°C	Gas mark 6 (hot)
425°F	220°C	Gas mark 7 (hot)
450°F	230°C	Gas mark 8 (very hot)
475°F	240°C	Gas mark 9 (very hot)
Broil		Grill

*Electric and gas ovens may be calibrated using Celsius. However, for an electric oven, increase the Celsius setting 10 to 20 degrees when cooking above 160°C. For convection or forced-air ovens (gas or electric), lower the temperature setting 10°C when cooking at all heat levels.